Crisis in Freedom

THE ALIEN AND
SEDITION ACTS

BOOKS BY JOHN C. MILLER

SAM ADAMS
Pioneer in Propaganda

ORIGINS OF THE AMERICAN REVOLUTION

TRIUMPH OF FREEDOM
1775–1783

CRISIS IN FREEDOM
The Alien and Sedition Acts

Crisis in Freedom

THE ALIEN AND
SEDITION ACTS

by

JOHN C. MILLER

An Atlantic Monthly Press Book
Little, Brown and Company · Boston
1952

ATLANTIC—LITTLE, BROWN BOOKS
ARE PUBLISHED BY
LITTLE, BROWN AND COMPANY
IN ASSOCIATION WITH
THE ATLANTIC MONTHLY PRESS

Published simultaneously
in Canada by McClelland and Stewart Limited

PRINTED IN THE UNITED STATES OF AMERICA

 30

TO

SAMUEL ELIOT MORISON

IN WHOSE HANDS

HISTORY BECOMES ENDURING LITERATURE

Acts of Congress Discussed in This Book

Naturalization Act: June 18, 1798.

Act Concerning Aliens (Alien Act): June 25, 1798.

Act Respecting Alien Enemies: July 6, 1798.

Act for the Punishment of Certain Crimes (Sedition Act):
July 14, 1798.

CHAPTER I

FOR the first ten years of its existence under the Federal Constitution of 1787, the government of the United States was in the hands of the Federalist party. It was this party that carried through Hamilton's financial measures, suppressed the Whisky Rebellion, inflicted severe defeat upon the hostile Indians, fought an undeclared war with France and, at the height of its success, fell victim to its political mistakes and to internal dissension. Vanquished in the election of 1800, the party lingered on in some states but never again became an important factor in national politics. The party of American nationalism, which had set as its goal the creation of a more perfect union, became in the last stages of its dissolution the party of unyielding conservatism, of states' rights, and, finally, of disunion.

The decline and fall of the Federalist party, one of the most striking events of our early political history, by no means signified the end of the ideals it had proclaimed in its prime. Even its conquerors, the Jeffersonian Republicans, carried on many of its policies — the very policies Jefferson had inveighed against while in opposition. Nevertheless, the achievements of the Federalists have sometimes been obscured by their errors, particularly by their efforts to destroy freedom of speech and of the press. When war with France threatened in 1798, the Federalists not only sought to put the country in a state of military preparedness but they attempted, under the guise of patriotism, of concern for the national welfare, and of "saving the country" from internal enemies, to break up the Republican party. At a time when unity was essential to the survival of the Republic, the party in power divided the people and almost precipitated civil war.

To the French Directory the Federalists owed the accession of popularity and power granted them in 1798. Affronted by the ratification of Jay's Treaty with Great Britain by the United States Senate in 1795, the French government, although in alliance with the United States, retaliated by withdrawing its minister from Philadelphia, refusing to receive the newly appointed United States minister, C. C. Pinckney, and seizing our shipping on the high seas. When President Adams sent John Marshall, Elbridge Gerry and Pinckney to Paris to settle our differences with the French Republic, they were treated with contumely: denied access to the Directory, they were approached by agents (designated in the American ministers' dispatches as X, Y and Z) of Talleyrand, the Minister of Foreign Affairs, who demanded a bribe for the Directory and a loan to France as prerequisites to negotiations. Not that this treatment was out of the ordinary: Talleyrand had made bribery and corruption adjuncts of statecraft and had extorted money from most of the powers with which France maintained diplomatic relations.

The Directory acted upon the apparently well-founded assumption that the United States had neither sufficient union nor courage to resist the demands of the French Republic, one of the greatest conquering powers Europe had seen. For France it was a fatal miscalculation: the X Y Z Correspondence was published by the United States government; the country was swept by an unexampled wave of patriotic feeling; and with the slogan "Millions for Defense but Not One Cent for Tribute" Americans prepared to fight, if necessary, to uphold their independence. The purpose of French policy was to divide the American people from their government; instead, for the moment at least, it united them and brought the Republican party — the friend of France — to the verge of ruin.

Americans might well close ranks: never since the darkest days of the War of Independence had the international situation been more alarming. The United States was seemingly being pushed into war by France at the very time that fortune abandoned Great Britain. Defeated upon the European Continent, its navy crippled by mutiny, and in the throes of a financial panic, Great Britain faced invasion by the French army poised on the channel. Under these circumstances, the United States could depend neither upon England nor upon the Atlantic Ocean for its security. England might soon be fighting for its very survival — in which case, said Hamilton, "we may have to contend at our very doors for our independence and liberty. When the wonders achieved by the arms of France are duly considered, the possibility of the overthrow of Great Britain seems not to be chimerical." Eighteen months previously, no one, he pointed out, dreamed that the British Isles would stand in danger of invasion; by the same token, eighteen months hence, the United States might be fighting against a French army. But even if the invasion of Great Britain failed, Hamilton contended that it was the part of wisdom to act as if it were likely to succeed. "What," he asked, "were the inconveniences of preparation compared with the infinite magnitude of the evil if it shall surprise us unprepared?"[1]

Next to the defeat of Great Britain was to be dreaded a negotiated peace between Britain and France which would leave the Directory a free hand in the Western Hemisphere. In that event, most Americans believed that for their temerity

[1] *The Works of Alexander Hamilton*, edited by Henry Cabot Lodge, VI, 302–304. New York, 1904.

in defying France, war would be forced upon them: the Directors were not likely to forgive a second-rate military and naval power for exposing their extortionate practices. Furthermore, it was well known that the French were seeking to secure the retrocession of Louisiana from Spain; and if they succeeded, there could be little doubt that the United States would have to fight. The release of hundreds of thousands of veteran troops, together with the armed Negroes of St. Domingo, for action in North America was a prospect before which even Fisher Ames of Massachusetts, who swore that the "Marblehead boys shall thrash them at the rate of two to three," might have quailed. In their imaginations, Americans beheld their dearest possessions endangered: "Your houses and farms with fire, plunder and pillage! and your wives and sweethearts with ravishment and assassination, by horrid outlandish sans-culotte Frenchmen!!" Every man must arm himself or "be torn limb from gut, and devoured alive by bloodthirsty cannibals." So menacing did this danger appear that, if Americans chose appeasement rather than war, they were advised by a Federalist newspaper to "remove your wives far from the Infernal Fraternal embrace, or you may prove witnesses of their violation and expiring agonies, or if reserved for future infamy, may increase your families not only with a spurious, but with a colored breed." "Remove your daughters," this hair-raising counsel continued, "unless you would be silent spectators of their being deflowered by the lusty Othellos. Remove your infants! unless you shall deem it more merciful and humane to shorten their agonies, by plunging your paternal daggers into their innocent bosoms."[2] Was it any wonder that many Americans resolved to fight to the last gasp and looked with dark doubt upon anyone who spoke with a foreign accent?

[2] *Albany Centinel*, October 12, 1798. *Porcupine's Gazette*, July 27, 1798. The *Pennsylvania Herald* and *York General Advertiser*, August 1, 1798.

By treachery or force, France had by 1798 overthrown almost every other republic in the world — only the United States and a few others had escaped the embrace of the "terrible Republic." Holland, Switzerland and Venice had all been conquered; and in the fate of these European republics, said Harrison Gray Otis, "we might read our own, unless all the prudence and energies of our country were summoned to avert it." As Rufus King, the United States Minister to Great Britain, said in 1798: "the poor Dutch after passing thro' Purgatory, are condemned to weeping, wailing and gnashing of teeth, Spain and Portugal are soon to meet their fate, and God only knows the number of days that remain to those who are last to be destroyed."[3] Presumably, the United States was on the French Directory's list; perhaps orders had already gone out from Paris for the work of destruction to begin; "the eyes of the devouring monster are upon us, it watches with fiend-like vigilance our every movement." If any doubted their country's danger, King urged them to study the fate of Switzerland "as a dreadful lesson."[4]

But Americans did not give way to their fears: the country began to get under arms and the spirit and unity of the people had never been higher. Ships were built by popular subscription to take the sea against French corsairs; volunteers by the thousands joined the colors; the Navy Department was created and, for the first time since the Revolution, American men of war went into action. The Fourth of July, 1798, was celebrated with military parades and the drinking of patriotic toasts: "The American Eagle: May it take the

[3] *Abridgment of the Debates of Congress*, II, 257. New York, 1857. *The Life and Correspondence of Rufus King*, edited by Charles R. King, II, 283. New York, 1894–1900.

[4] *Columbian Centinel*, October 27, 1798. *Philadelphia Gazette*, July 6, 1799. *Rufus King*, II, 445. *What Is Our Situation? by an American* [Joseph Hopkinson], 8. Philadelphia, 1798. Timothy Pickering to James Hendricks, July 27, 1798 (the National Archives).

Gallic Cock by the Gills"; "The Fair Sex: the only human beings to whom we will bend the knee"; "THE POINT BLANK to interior enemies, and the angle of 45 to invading foes."[5]

Excitement ran so high that Jefferson declared that "one who keeps himself cool and clear of the contagion, is so far below the point of ordinary conversation, that he finds himself insulated in every society." A French sympathizer who called for the *"Ca Ira"* or other Republican tunes in preference to "Hail Columbia" (written by Francis Hopkinson during the crisis) was fortunate if he were "not thrown out of the windows, or from the gallery into the pit, and that too by the *friends of order* and *good government*."[6] Crowds of young patriots wearing the black cockade — the emblem of the "true Americans" — roamed the streets looking for anyone brazen enough to flaunt the tricolor.

For the first time in his life, John Adams found himself genuinely popular. Hundreds of loyal "addresses" from American citizens (on the British model of addresses to the King) poured into Philadelphia until it was said that the President snuffed "incense from every gale that blows."[7] His conduct of foreign affairs was acclaimed as proof that he was "eminently calculated by his fortitude and genius to conduct the nation through the impending storm." He was hailed as the "SECOND FOUNDER OF THE REPUBLIC" — unaccustomed but welcome praise to a man who had always felt himself overshadowed in the public eye by Washington, Franklin and Hamilton. But now he had attained, if not surpassed, the popularity of his rivals in fame, and so, wrote

[5] *New Hampshire Gazette,* June 5, 1798. *Albany Centinel,* April 2, 1799.

[6] *Greenleaf's New Daily Advertiser,* May 19, 1798.

[7] Robert Liston to Lord Grenville, May 2, May 21, 1798 (British State Papers, Robert Liston Correspondence, Henry Adams Transcripts, LC). *Gazette of the United States,* November 19, November 20, 1798. *The Writings of Thomas Jefferson,* edited by Paul Leicester Ford, VII, 250. New York, 1896.

General Schuyler, it was "not surprising that the old Cock should be elated and crow audibly."[8] "The President," wrote an admirer, "seems to have all the ardor of youth and all the energies and firmness of meridian life. If he survive the struggle . . . no man that has figured on our theatre, will go down to posterity with greater lustre than *John Adams*. I will not even except *George Washington*."[9]

The slogan of the day was "Adams and Liberty" — soon to be given an ironic meaning by the passage of the Alien and Sedition Acts. Whenever Adams appeared in public, bands struck up "The President's March." At the "Federal Summer Circus" held in Philadelphia in May, 1798, the approach of the President and his family was heralded "by the sound of the trumpet, and his entrance welcomed with three huzzas from the spectators, followed by the band playing 'The President's March.' " When General Sumter of South Carolina refused to join in the ovation, he was hooted as a Jacobin. "The emperors of Rome," complained the Republicans, "in the height of their power, received from their humble subjects not more servile marks of submission than were paid to President Adams by the federal faction."[10] This may serve to reveal what celebrity Adams sacrificed in 1799, at least among a large part of his party, by courageously standing forth as a man of peace.

Early in June, 1798, Hamilton predicted that the spirit of patriotism was making such progress that "there will shortly be national unanimity as far as that idea can ever exist."[11] "Thanks be to God and our good Ally," said the Reverend John Murray of Boston in June, 1798, "I find converts (to

[8] Allan McLane Hamilton, *The Intimate Life of Alexander Hamilton*, 322. New York, 1910. *Gazette of the United States*, November 20, 1798.
[9] *Rufus King*, II, 362–363. Stewart Mitchell, *New Letters of Abigail Adams*, 167. Boston, 1947.
[10] *Albany Centinel*, May 23, 1798. Mitchell, *Abigail Adams*, 171–172.
[11] Hamilton, *Works* (Lodge), X, 291.

Federalism and religion) multiplying every day — it is the Lord's doings and it is marvellous in our eyes." It seemed probable that the Republican leaders, if they persisted in their opposition to preparedness and in their support of France, would become as unpopular as had the Loyalists during the American Revolution. Already, exulted a Federalist, the Republicans appeared confounded "and the trimmers dropt off from the party like windfalls from an apple-tree in September."[12] Whereas this sudden change in the international situation brought discredit upon Madison and Jefferson, the party of Adams and Hamilton stood higher in popular estimation than ever before.

And yet, this new-found union — certainly far stronger than had existed during the American Revolution — was in a large measure shattered by the Federalists themselves. By yielding to the temptation to proscribe, under cover of a war emergency, their political opponents as enemies of the country, the Federalist party in effect confessed its unworthiness to lead the nation at a time of tension and peril.

That the Federalists should have thus defeated their own purposes and betrayed their own ideals was owing primarily to the nature of the ideas with which they approached the problems of American politics. Nationalism alone was not enough to save them: ill-equipped to be the leaders of a people that aspired to move toward democracy, the Federalists in 1798 acted out of the fear of the people which was never far from the surface of their minds and which underlay many of their measures.

If the framers of the Federal Constitution had not foreseen the rise of parties, they both foresaw and dreaded the existence of faction. As Livy had said, "Factions have been and ever will be with all Nations more fatal in their consequences than Foreign Wars, than Famine, or Pestilence, or any other

[12] *The Works of Fisher Ames*, edited by Seth Ames, 263–264. Boston, 1854.

Public Evils inflicted upon Mankind by the Wrath of Heaven."
A faction stood for no principles; it was held together by the
pre-eminence of a leader and the hope of plunder and rapine.
It was a union of the vicious, the base and the ignorant under
the leadership of the unprincipled. And, as Hamilton said,
faction was "the natural disease of popular governments"
and accounted for the shortness of their life-expectancy.[13]

Therefore, when the Federalists saw resistance to their policies rising in the United States, they called it "faction" and
"enmity to the Constitution." Opposition to the administration thus became opposition to the Constitution; there could
be no organized political effort that was not hostile to peace,
good government and the national welfare. The party of
Jefferson and Madison was never recognized as a lawfully
begotten party: even after Jefferson became President, to the
Federalists he was still the leader of a "faction" whose objective was the subversion of the Constitution. As Gallatin said,
the Federalists "altogether confounded evidences of dissatisfaction at certain measures of Administration with a decided
hatred against a Government of their own choice."[14]

It remained only to brand this "faction" led by Jefferson
as disloyal to the United States and sold, body and soul, to
France. This the Federalists did gladly: there was, they said,
a "French faction" at work in the United States; and the
program, personnel, and political allegiance of the Republican party and this French faction were identical. They gave
their political opponents the benefit of no doubts; it had
become almost impossible for the Federalists to regard the
Republicans as other than traitors: from Jefferson down, they
were "*Frenchmen* in all their feelings and wishes."[15]

[13] Hamilton, *Works* (Lodge), IX, 30.
[14] *Albany Centinel*, April 2, 1799. *Annals of Congress*, X, 357.
[15] Hamilton, *Works* (Lodge), VI, 328, X, 285. *Newark Gazette*, May 21,
1799. *Albany Centinel*, October 30, 1798. *Salem Gazette*, November 30, 1798.

It is true that, despite all the unkindness dealt out to the United States by France, many Republicans persisted in regarding the Republic of France as the friend and ally of this country and in celebrating its military victories by roasting oxen, drinking toasts to French generals, and addressing each other as "citizen." More significantly, they talked as though their own country were sorely deficient in liberty, equality and fraternity. "Many of our countrymen," a Federalist complained, "like lovers, are still so enamored of French fraternity and French practices, that they are blind to every crime of which the object, so tenderly beloved, can ever be guilty." Another compared this hankering after France to the conduct of "a weak dupe, who finds himself compelled to turn an unfaithful wench out of doors, stopping her at the threshold to whine over their former loves, and to remind her of past Joys."[16] Yet this was no time for lovesick protestations; no time for sentimental blubberings; in fact, said Hamilton, it was no time even for gratitude to France — "it is at this shrine," he exclaimed, "that we are continually invited to sacrifice the true interests of the country; as if 'all for love, and the world well lost' were a fundamental maxim in politics."[17]

On the other hand, some vigilant patriots detected even among the Federalists themselves a dangerous foreign influence. Those, for example, who employed French tutors for their children were unwittingly inviting secret agents of the Directory into their homes. At best, these petits-maîtres indoctrinated the scions of the best families with a taste for frivolities and instilled "modern principles of morality, or the high science of universal citizenship" into their tender minds.[18] Was it not known that Jacobins were everywhere and that

[16] Gazette of the United States, March 15, 1799. George Gibbs, Memoirs of the Administrations of Washington and John Adams, II, 118. New York, 1846.
[17] Hamilton, Works (Lodge), IV, 462–463.
[18] Gazette of the United States, March 15, 1799.

"even the nursery is not exempt from the unremitting efforts of these disturbers of the human race?" Even children's books must be scanned: by planting seditious principles in the primers, Jacobins were seeking to corrupt the younger generation and "to make them imbibe, with their very milk, as it were, the poison of atheism and disaffection."[19]

Certainly it was shrewd propaganda to picture American Republicans as "thorough-paced" Frenchmen who took orders directly from the Directory. At one stroke, the entire party was placed under suspicion of treason, and Jeffersonian ideals were stamped with the dread trademark MADE IN FRANCE. The purpose of the opposition party was made to appear to be the advancement not of American interests but of those of France; it became axiomatic that no Republican could be a true American.

The fear and detestation in which American "Jacobins" were held were no less powerful than the abhorrence felt for the French revolutionists themselves. "Medusa's Snakes are not more venomous," declared a Federalist, "than the wretches who are seeking to bend us to the views of France."[20] "The open enemies of our country," declared the *Albany Centinel*, "have never taken half the pains to render our Government and our rulers infamous & contemptible in the eyes of the world, than these wretches who *call themselves* Americans, Patriots and Republicans." This "Gallic faction" was believed to be in close communication with Paris, "the immense reservoir, and native spring of all immorality, corruption, wickedness and methodized duplicity."[21] From this source they drew the inspiration, together with the financial aid, for the attain-

[19] *Gazette of the United States*, March 15, 1799; June 4, 1800.
[20] Loring Andrews to Peter Van Schaack, April 6, 1798 (Peter Van Schaack MSS., LC).
[21] *Gazette of the United States*, July 3, 1798. *Albany Centinel*, October 30, 1798.

ment of their presumed objectives: the destruction of the Constitution, a perpetual alliance, offensive and defensive, with France, and the liquidation of the wise, the good, and the rich. Federalist heads would roll in the sand and the United States would be given over to the crimes and horrors perpetrated in the name of liberty.[22]

Federalists professed to believe that many Republicans, being more French than American at heart, would join a French army of invasion should it land on these shores. Hamilton declared that they were "ready in the gratification of ambition, vanity, or revenge, or in compliance with the wages of corruption, to immolate the independence and welfare of their country at the shrine of France." If Bonaparte planted "his blood stained standard in the center of the hall of Congress," there would be found Americans hailing him as a deliverer.[23] Secretary of State Pickering was informed by his military advisers that in the West, the French had "a party of mad Americans ready to join them at a given Signal" in making this region a separate republic allied with France.[24] If disaffection had gone this length — and few Federalists doubted that it had — Republicans could not be trusted to defend the country; accordingly, the political opinions of prospective officers in the new United States Army were carefully examined by Washington, Hamilton and Pinckney. It was rarely that a Republican passed this scrutiny.

Thus the Federalists became in their own eyes the only truly American party; they alone could be trusted to guard the independence and welfare of the republic. The sole reason they were regarded by Republicans as a British party, said Hamilton, was that "every true *American* — every really inde-

[22] *What Is Our Situation?* 8.
[23] Hamilton, *Works* (Lodge), VI, 302. *What Is Our Situation?* 35.
[24] Major Rivandi to Pickering, November 29, 1797 (Pickering MSS., M.H.S.).

pendent man, becomes, in their eyes, a British agent — a British emissary."[25] In contrast to the Republicans, who supposedly wished to drag the United States into the vortex of European politics, the Federalist party dedicated itself to carrying out the principles of Washington's Farewell Address — no involvement in European wars; above all, no involvement on the side of revolutionary France.

* * *

To save the United States from the evils of unlimited democracy was to most Federalists one of the historic missions of their party. Democracy, said Fisher Ames, was the "worst of all governments, or if there be a worse . . . the certain forerunner of that. . . . Like death," he continued, "it [democracy] is only the dismal passport to a more dismal hereafter."[26] By the Federalist scheme of things, democracy always destroyed itself — consumed in the fires of vice and ignorance it generated. Like a volcano, said Ames, it contained the fiery materials of its own destruction: it ran its predestined course from disorder and licentiousness to chaos and from thence to dictatorship — a harrowing transition that left society bleeding and exhausted.

That democracy was incompatible with order and security was owing, the Federalists supposed, to the depravity of human nature. The special pride of the Federalists was that they took a realistic view of human nature; and, seeing men as they were, they had no illusions that the millennium was at hand or that democracy would work. Men were disposed to covet their neighbor's property, particularly if the neighbor was more successful than they in accumulating worldly goods. So powerful was this appetite that order and justice could not stand against it; and in a democracy, where restraints upon

[25] Hamilton, *Works* (Lodge), VI, 328.
[26] Fisher Ames, *Works*, II, 324, 353, 364.

the passions of men were weak and unavailing, the people were under constant temptation to invade the rights of others. For this reason, Chancellor Kent declared, "the tendency of universal suffrage is to jeopardize the rights of property and the principles of liberty."[27] Democracy, in short, was government by the passions of the multitude — a system which gave free rein to "the often fatal propensities of liberty."

Although the Federalists admitted the necessity of a measure of democracy in every well-ordered society, they insisted that government be endowed with sufficient power to hold in check the passions and prejudices of the people. Such restraint was in the peoples' best interest; a government that accommodated itself to the "ever-varying and often inordinate desires of the people" ended in anarchy.[28] Liberty could be preserved only by keeping under control the evil propensities of human nature; "To make a nation free," said Fisher Ames, "the crafty must be kept in awe, and the violent in restraint."[29] To a generation prone to regard government as an evil, the Federalists preached the beneficence of government as a protection against "the follies and vices of men." The evils of society, said John Jay, were like weeds — "and a good Government is as necessary to subdue the one, as an attentive gardener or husbandman is to destroy the other."[30] "Government should be a terror to evil doers," said the Federalists — an excellent maxim until they began to include their political opponents among the evildoers.[31]

[27] Sait's *American Parties and Elections*, edited by Howard R. Penniman, 22. New York, 1948.

[28] John Wynkoop to Peter Van Schaack, September 17, 1795 (Van Schaack MSS., LC).

[29] Fisher Ames, *Works*, II, 80, 393, 394. *Annals of Congress*, XI, 38.

[30] John Jay, *An Address to the People of the State of New York*, 1787, 6.

[31] *Porcupine's Gazette*, July 19, 1798.

And by whom were these salutary restraints to be imposed upon the people to save them from themselves? By the good, the wise and the rich, the Federalists answered; in their guidance lay the best hope of order and temperate liberty. That this meant government by the gentlemen of the country, the Federalist leaders did not deny; it was to them entirely fitting that those who owned the country ought to guide its destinies. They, the large property owners, had the greatest stake in its prosperity and well-being; and they knew none so well qualified as themselves to manage its concerns. Jefferson believed that they intended to make the United States a monarchy; but it is doubtful if these high-spirited, self-confident gentlemen could ever have brooked a monarch, or, indeed, any superior. Had they been given a free hand, they would have established an aristocratic republic; and from their conduct of affairs it would appear that they supposed that this was the kind of government the United States already possessed.

But, they acknowledged, the rule of gentlemen by gentlemen and for gentlemen encountered serious obstacles in the United States where the people wished to be sovereign in fact as well as in name and where there was a multitude of popular leaders — for in a democracy, said the Federalists, nothing succeeds like demagoguery.

One of the cardinal faults of democracy was that it tended to place power in the hands of the worst men — "the fiercest and most turbulent spirits in the society"; always, in free society "the most desperate and audacious men are the most likely to govern." Fisher Ames defined democracy as "a government by the passions of the multitude, or . . . according to the vices and ambition of their leaders." It was these leaders that the Federalists specially feared. "What caused the ruin of the Republic of Greece and Rome?" asked Gouverneur

Morris. "Demagogues, who, by flattery, gained the aid of the populace to establish despotism."[32] There was a natural alliance between demagogues and the evil-disposed members of every community: "The first," said Fisher Ames, "want to govern the state; and the others, that the state shall not govern them. A sense of common interest will soon incline these two original factions of every free state to coalesce into one."[33] And when this dreaded amalgamation had been consummated, good men might well tremble.

The Federalists thanked God that they had not stooped to the low arts of procuring popularity; if they had not won the applause of the multitude, it was because they would rather be right than be popular.[34] "Those who court the People have a very capricious Mistress," said Gouverneur Morris — "a Mistress which may be gained by Sacrifices, but she cannot be so held for she is insatiable."[35] Gouverneur Morris, not, perhaps, an expert on democracy, had long and varied experience with mistresses.

Among Federalists it was an accepted principle that "the delusions of democracy, like other delusions of the human mind, cannot be resisted by reason and truth alone."[36] Men were swayed more by their feeling than by their reason; creatures of emotion, they seldom allowed reason to prevail

[32] Fisher Ames, *Works*, II, 356, 359, 386, 392.

[33] Robert Troup to Rufus King, September 14, 1800 (King MSS., New York Historical Society). Emily Ford and Emily Skeel, *Notes on the Life of Noah Webster*, 479. New York, 1912. Noah Webster, *A Collection of Papers*, 218. New York, 1843.

[34] John Marshall toasted "Those few patriots who love the people well enough to tell them the truth."

James Cheetham, *Reply to Aristides*, 87. New York, 1804. *Annals of Congress, XI*, 41.

[35] Gouverneur Morris, *Diary and Letters*, edited by Anne Cary Morris, I, 338. New York, 1888.

[36] Samuel Eliot Morison, *The Life and Letters of Harrison Gray Otis*, I, 280. Boston, 1913.

until it was too late. And in a contest for control of the feelings of mankind, the Federalists lamented that they were at a disadvantage: their political opponents were far more adept as propagandists, and, moreover, they appealed to the very passions that the Federalists deplored. "The devil of sedition is immortal," said Fisher Ames, "and we, the saints, have an endless struggle to maintain with him." He was not convinced that it was not a losing struggle.[37]

Tossed on "the tempestuous sea of liberty," the Federalists craved security from the threat of Bonaparte's army, revolutions and subversive ideas. They wished quietly to enjoy their property, go about their business of accumulating more worldly goods and to have done with all innovations and projects of reform. If this were not the best of all possible worlds, they suspected that any change would be for the worse. "Experience," said Noah Webster, "is a safe *pilot*, but *experiment* is a dangerous ocean, full of rocks and shoals."[38] With rare devotion they clung to the world they knew so well and that had rewarded them so handsomely; with horror they recoiled from the world ushered in by the French Revolution. "We do not lust after the worship of naked strumpets," they declared; "we do not wish to divide our property with idlers, nor daily to tremble at the guillotine."[39] This they did not want — but they greatly feared that this was what they would get.

Despite the strides they had made since 1787 toward security, the Federalists were painfully aware that they had not yet attained this never-never land. Often the complaint was heard among them that the national government was not

---

[37] Fisher Ames, *Works*, I, 240. *Annals of Congress*, III, 924, 926. Robert Troup to Rufus King, September 14, 1800 (Rufus King MSS.).

[38] Harry Warfel, *Noah Webster*, 264. New York, 1936. Ford and Skeel, *Webster*, I, 432.

[39] *Porcupine's Gazette*, August 22, 1799.

sufficiently strong to resist the impulses of the people, the arts of demagogues and the subversive designs of the Jeffersonian "faction." "Our Constitution and administration," remarked one, "are marked with mildness, and evil doers are encouraged to think coercion is not a characteristic of either."[40] They found little evidence of general acceptance of their views of democracy; it was as the exponents of nationalism and vindicators of national honor against France rather than as the "enlightened few" who knew what was good for the people better than did the people themselves, that they enjoyed popular support. Increasingly they tended to regard themselves as a small band of gentlemen, scholars and statesmen beleaguered by hostile forces. "The chief duty and care of all governments," they said, "is to protect the rights of property, and the tranquillity of society"; but, they unhappily acknowledged, freedom and tranquillity were seldom found together.[41]

With these ideas the Federalists encountered the new world of the French Revolution; in an age of revolutionary ferment and war, they held fast to an ideal of liberty that, said Fisher Ames, "calms and restrains the licentious passions, like an angel, that says to the winds and troubled seas, be still."[42] But the winds blew and the seas rolled high until, in 1798, the United States was swept into the maelstrom and came face to face with the power of revolutionary France.

[40] Uriah Tracy to Jonathan Trumbull, January 2, 1799 (Trumbull MSS., Connecticut Historical Society).
[41] Fisher Ames, *Works*, II, 81.
[42] *Ibid.*, 82.

CHAPTER II

To the Federalists, their struggle with the Republicans was a conflict between good and evil on a scale almost without precedent since Biblical times. In this spirit, Fisher Ames, one of the most eloquent of the Federalist orators, compared the fall of the Republicans with the descent of Lucifer. Having been cast out as a result of the X Y Z affair, the Republicans, said Ames, "looked round, like Milton's devils when first recovering from the stunning force of their fall from Heaven, to see what new ground they could take."[1] Thanks to the Federalists, their fall was cushioned by the Alien and Sedition Acts; the Republicans landed on their feet, ready to fight on the issue provided them by the administration party: whether fundamental liberties should be surrendered and an entire political party interdicted out of panic. As a Republican journalist said, "the Aristocrats could not for their soul fight the battles of liberty better."[2]

By no means all or even the majority of Federalists were aristocrats. Yet the plain people who composed the bulk of the party were quite as apprehensive of Jacobinism as were the leaders; during this period, the mobs in both England and the United States were composed of conservatives; among the most zealous were those who had most to gain from revolu-

[1] Fisher Ames, *Works*, I, 246. Alexander Hamilton, *Works* (Lodge), VII, 370–371.
[2] *Time Piece*, July 25, 1798.

tion. It is true, however, that the panic began at the top and spread downward among the people: there was hardly a word to allay the alarm, a warning against too hasty action, or a plea that civil liberties be preserved, from the Federalist spokesmen in Congress. Instead, the party elders seem to have acted upon the assumption that their duty was to whip up the frenzy by screaming "Jacobins, Hell, and all the devils" at every street corner. They induced hysteria and then turned it to party purposes.

The state of mind of the Federalist leaders was that of a beleaguered garrison, surrounded by enemies and distrustful of the loyalty of half the population within the fortress itself. Such a frame of mind did not fit the facts as they existed in the United States in 1798. The Federalists exaggerated the amount of disaffection within the country and displayed a notable lack of trust in the good sense and patriotism of the American people. The leaders of this party, who prided themselves upon being the wisest of men — the "aristocracy of virtue" — were not, as they imagined, proper company for the angels, but all too human, passionate, panic-stricken and vengeful men, guilty of all the faults they supposed to be the exclusive property of the "swinish multitude."[3] Their conduct in office affords some convincing arguments against government by a few; yet it must stand to their credit that at a time of grave crisis, they took prompt and energetic measures of defense that helped spare the United States involvement in full-scale war.

Few Federalists ever made the mistake of supposing that all was well in the world or that they walked upon anything but quicksand. Confirmed pessimists (and, indeed, they had only to look to Europe to find their worst fears realized), their minds moved to such themes as "The Burning of Boston,"

[3] George Cabot to Pickering, March 23, 1798. (Pickering MSS., Massachusetts Historical Society.)

"The Pillaging of Philadelphia," "The Execution by Guillotine of President Adams and his Cabinet." Courage rather than political acumen was their most conspicuous trait; in an age of revolutions — doomed, as they supposed, to be the next victims of the sans-culottes — they resolved to fight gamely to the end. Lacking confidence in ultimate victory, they proposed to show that at least the gentlemen of the United States knew how to die.

But, as can easily be seen, they acted out of calculation as well as out of fear. That they were frightened is true; nevertheless, they were not so badly frightened as to be unable to see how their political opponents could best be injured and to lay their plans accordingly. If they seemed to be blinded by their fears, it must be admitted that their blindness was in part the consequence of their determination to stamp out, at all costs, opposition to their policies. Weakened and disorganized by the sudden turn of events in Europe, the Republicans seemed to be delivered into their enemies' hands; and the Federalists intended to give no quarter.

Nor were the people of the United States so lost to wisdom and patriotism as the Alien and Sedition Acts assumed. In June, 1798, Gallatin declared that "at no time were exhibited stronger symptoms of approbation of the measures of Administration than at the present." Even if the opposition leaders had wished to lead the country into the arms of France and overthrow the Constitution, such an attempt would have cost them the support of the people.[4] As a French observer reported to his government at this time, there was a French party and an English party in the United States — but there was also a middle party "composed of the most estimable men of the two other parties. This party, whose existence we have not even suspected, is the American party which loves its country above

[4] Robert Liston to Grenville, June 25, 1798. (Henry Adams Transcripts, Library of Congress.)

all and for whom preferences either for France or England are only accessory and passing affections."[5]

The Alien and Sedition Acts were enacted in the face of strong evidence that the Republican party was not a "French faction" bent upon subverting the Constitution. Not a single responsible Republican advocated overthrowing the government by force; although it is true that in denouncing the administration they used violent language, they intended to win their victories at the polls, not on the barricades. As Gallatin said, in 1798, "no change in the Constitution was desired by any set of men, no symptoms of disaffection had appeared anywhere"; the Republicans wished only "to preserve a constitutional and economical administration of Government."[6]

With conservatism thus strongly entrenched, many Federalists themselves acknowledged that the "Gallic faction" had received a stunning blow in the publication of the X Y Z Correspondence. On July 27, 1798, two weeks after the passage of the Sedition Act, Timothy Pickering thanked God "that the monstrous injustice, the unprecedented insults and the boundless ambition and rapacity of the French have at length opened the eyes of our countrymen; and that they are generally ready to arm to repel the aggressions of these enemies to the peace and repose of the civilized world."[7] Robert Troup, a close friend of Hamilton, said at about this same time that he did not believe that "a more rooted detestation of France exists in England, than prevails with a great mass of our fellow citizens. All the old prejudices instilled into our minds by our ancestors . . . seem to be revived."[8] On June 29, 1798,

[5] *American Historical Review*, XLVIII, 520.

[6] *New Jersey Journal*, March 26, 1799.

[7] Pickering to James Hendricks, July 27, 1798. (National Archives). Pickering to Andrew Ellicott, October 4, 1798. (National Archives).

[8] *Rufus King*, II, 403, 466. Pickering to Rufus King, June 27, 1798. (Pickering MSS., M.H.S.).

President Adams acknowledged that "the opposition to the federal government . . . is too small to merit the name of division; it is a difference of sentiment on public measures, not an alienation of affection to their country."[9]

Moreover, to ensure that the people remained sound in morals and political principles, the Federalists enjoyed the powerful support of the clergy. The "black regiment" that had done notable service in preaching up rebellion during the American Revolution was now engaged in inculcating love of order, orthodox religious doctrines and conservative political opinions. Many pulpits rang with imprecations against "the vices of atheism, and the tyranny of democracy," with illuminating asides upon the irreligion of Thomas Jefferson. It had been found that "Infidels in religion are apt to be democrats in politics" and that one of the most effective ways of running down a democrat was to call him an atheist.[10] For example, Jefferson "was indiscreet enough to accept the honor of a public entertainment in Virginia on a *Sunday*. This fact," remarked a Federalist, "has been trumpeted from one end of the continent to the other as an irrefragable proof of his contempt for the Christian religion and his devotion to the new religion of France. It has made an impression much to his prejudice in the Middle and Eastern States."[11]

Despite their complaints about the "licentiousness" of the press, it is doubtful if the press had ever been more favorably disposed to the Federalists than it was in 1798. As they themselves conceded, only a handful of newspapers were "prostituted to the designs of intriguing foreigners" and their in-

[9] *New Hampshire Gazette*, July 17, 1798.
[10] David M. Ludlum, *Social Ferment in Vermont, 1791–1800*, 30. New York, 1939.
[11] *Russell's Gazette*, June 7, 1798. Morison, *Otis*, I, 84 footnote. *Rufus King*, II, 432.

fluence was steadily declining.[12] Gallatin estimated that nine out of ten journals published in the United States supported the policies of the administration. His estimate was probably too high, but it is certainly true that the Federalists did not need the Sedition Act to ensure a loyal press; generally speaking, they already had it.

To this rule there were, however, some notable exceptions; and, although few in number, they seemed to the Federalists a host. Chief among them was the *Aurora*, edited by Benjamin Bache of Philadelphia. Sometimes called "Lightning Rod, Junior," Bache was the grandson of Benjamin Franklin; but, unlike his cool, circumspect, mild-mannered grandfather, young Bache was fiery, impetuous, and surcharged with passion which found outlet in the political quarrels of the day. Narrow and intolerant, Bache seemed always in a fret, always viewing with alarm, and always taking the extreme point of view — characteristics which admirably fitted him for his chosen role, that of gadfly to the Federalist party.

The fact that Bache was descended from Benjamin Franklin gave him no celebrity among Federalists. Franklin was no hero to them: they recoiled equally from his lax morals and from his political and social opinions. It was well known that the old philosopher had not practised, particularly where women were concerned, the high moral standard he preached; but even this would have been forgiven — as it was forgiven in the case of Alexander Hamilton — by the straitest-laced Federalists, had not Franklin challenged their most cherished political beliefs. Poor Richard did not admire the rich: the greatest rogues he had ever met, he once remarked, were the richest. Nor did he believe that gentlemen alone were qualified to rule

[12] Americans were said to be unanimous except for a few "incorrigible *gallic devotees* who kiss, with mean submission, the hand that smites them." (*Albany Centinel*, June 8, 1798.)

the country — a position which to most Federalists seemed dangerously subversive. No wonder that they traced Benjamin Bache's aberrations to his original misfortune of having a philosopher for a grandfather, "for that idea was the food of much of his extravagance of mind, and placed him in a state of pretence where he was obliged to act a part for which he had not talents."[13]

As a journalist, Bache displayed a degree of virulence, vindictiveness and scurrility that distinguished him even among the journalists of his generation. With Republicans, this passed for patriotism and public spirit; to the Federalists, it indicated that Bache was possessed of a devil — probably of French origin. Indeed, in Federalist circles, Bache figured as the typical American Jacobin: consumed by jealous hatred of his betters, eager to apply the torch to American cities and to set up the guillotine in every public square for the speedy liquidation of the best members of society — by which the Federalists (who never took a dim view of their own consequence) meant themselves.

In his brief career, Bache succeeded in cruelly galling every prominent Federalist from President Washington down. Unlike most Republican editors, Bache did not regard the Father of His Country as above party and therefore exempt from political attack; instead, Bache won his journalistic spurs by traducing Washington, and did his work so thoroughly that it was partly because of the abuse he had received in the *Aurora* that the first President decided to reject a third term. Making short shrift of Washington's military reputation, Bache declared that the commander in chief of the American army had displayed utter incompetence, redeemed only by "the small microscopic exploits of Trenton and Princeton" that were more owing to good fortune than to skill of execution.

[13] *Report of the American Historical Association for* . . . *1912*, 439. Washington, 1912.

Absurdly cautious, he "suffered the war to linger in his hands for seven whole years, notwithstanding he had to contend with some of the most inefficient generals in Europe." Had he been a reasonably competent commander, he would have procured supplies even though neglected by Congress and the people. Compared with any of the generals of the French revolutionary armies, the American Hero was hardly fit to command "a sergeant's guard."[14]

Even at his most scurrilous, Bache always professed to be acting from the purest motives: if he dragged a man's name in the mud it was because the good of the country required it. This, he believed, was particularly necessary in the case of President Washington because, adored as "the Grand Lama" of his country, the exemplar of all the virtues, he had become a menace to the liberties of the Republic. Ambitious and easily led by unscrupulous advisers, Washington might yet make that "bold push for the American throne" which Patrick Henry had predicted would be one of the first acts of an American President. To save free government, therefore, the people had to be taught that no man, however great and renowned, was indispensable; the greater his fame, the more he ought to be suspected of harboring designs against popular liberty. By Bache's way of thinking, one of the principal functions of journalism was to exhibit the feet of clay of so-called great men.

Bache fell to this work with such enthusiasm that he left Washington not a shred of respectability. In the *Aurora*, Washington found himself accused of drawing from the Treasury for his private use more than the salary allowed the President, and of having advanced his own pecuniary interest during the revolutionary war at the expense of his starving

[14] Benjamin Bache, *Remarks Occasioned by the Late Conduct of Mr. Washington*, 6–8. Philadelphia, 1797.

soldiers.[15] For these and other crimes, Bache predicted, history would damn Washington; the best that he could hope for was that it would consign him to oblivion. By way of anticipating this verdict, when Washington retired from the Presidency Bache delivered a valedictory compounded of acid, gall and wormwood. The first President, he declared, was "the scourge of all the misfortunes of our country," the man whose name had given "a currency to political iniquity, and to legalized corruption." Bache proclaimed a day of jubilee that the country was at last rid of this incubus — "if ever there was a period for rejoicing, this is the moment."[16]

That President John Adams fared better at the hands of the editor of the *Aurora*, at least until 1798, was owing more to Adams's comparative lack of popularity with the masses than to any sweetening of Bache's disposition. Even so, the catalogue of crimes of which Adams stood accused was formidable: nepotism, squandering public money, monarchical ambitions and warmongering. But, in general, Bache seems to have concluded that "the blind, bald, crippled, toothless, querulous ADAMS" was hardly worthy of backbiting; and, until Adams unexpectedly emerged as the leader of the American people in the X Y Z crisis, he could be thankful that he had been no more than scratched by Old Ben's cub.

Besides Bache's *Aurora*, Greenleaf's *Argus*, and Adams's *Independent Chronicle*, there were few Republican newspapers of more than local influence. Virtually every state had, however, at least one newspaper of the Jeffersonian persuasion; but without state printing contracts, official favor and large paid-up subscriptions, it was not easy for them to survive,

[15] Washington accepted no salary as President, asking only that Congress pay his household expenses. Bache, "Remarks," 62. Hamilton to Oliver Wolcott, October 26, 1795 (Wolcott MSS., Connecticut Historical Society).

[16] Quoted in *Gazette of the United States*, March 19, 1801.

particularly those published in Federalist states. Even the *Aurora* lost money over a long period of time; only a comparatively wealthy man like Benjamin Bache could afford the luxury of running it.[17] The *Albany Register*, which maintained in New York the Jeffersonian creed "in defiance of the frowns of power, and in the teeth of the landed aristocracy of this state," claimed that it consistently underbid all other printers on contracts for official printing, yet the jobs were always awarded to Loring Andrews, editor of the *Albany Centinel*, a Federalist newspaper of unimpeachable orthodoxy.[18]

Chief among the Federalist newspapers was the *Gazette of the United States*, published by John Fenno and, after his death, by his son John Fenno, Junior. The Fennos were subsidized by prominent members of the Federalist party — Alexander Hamilton among them — awarded printing contracts by the administration and aided by the pens of the best Federalist writers. The tone of the *Gazette of the United States* was quite as strident and dogmatic as that of any Republican newspaper. The younger Fenno, for example, declared that its purpose was to oppose the designs of "aspiring and restless demagogues; to fortify the existing ramparts of the constitution and laws; and to raise new bulwarks in those quarters where . . . the raging madness of Jacobinism, may have effected breeches in the barrier round the public weal."[19] Thus the *Gazette of the United States* waged a daily battle with "the monster of Jacobinism," and in name-calling, scurrility and harshness of tone was an equal match for the *Aurora*.

Of almost equal importance with their domination of the

[17] Bache lost over $14,000 during his eight years of newspaper ownership. (F. L. Mott, *American Journalism*, 128. N. Y., 1941.) William Duane to Gallatin, December 13, 1801 (Gallatin MSS., New York Historical Society). *Proceedings of the Massachusetts Historical Society*, Boston, XX, 263. *Philadelphia Gazette*, January 17, 1799.

[18] *Telegraphe and Daily Advertiser*, September 29, 1800.

[19] *Gazette of the United States*, May 14, 1800.

press was the Federalists' control of the mails. There were at this time about eight hundred deputy postmasters in the United States, each of whom enjoyed the privilege of franking letters and newspapers and of receiving them postage free. Since most of these postmasters were Federalists, opposition newspapers were either obliged to pay postage (Federalist newspapers invariably went free) or, as sometimes happened, they were deliberately suppressed in the post office.[20]

Moreover, a recent law of the United States had made it possible for the administration to influence the political allegiance of newspapers. By this statute, authorized newspapers were paid for publishing the laws of the United States adopted at each session of Congress; and for this authorization, as for all government printing, it was made plain that only administration newspapers need apply. Pickering carefully scrutinized the political opinions of newspaper editors; the decisive question was always "the politics to which he is inclined."[21] The Republicans complained that as long as Pickering was Secretary of State only those newspapers were favored which used "all the arts & retrick Hell can invent to blackguard the Republican printers & all they print."[22]

Yet, despite these handicaps, the few Republican newspapers held their ground. If the Republicans could do so much against such odds, what would happen, the Federalists anxiously asked themselves, should the Republicans, as a result of an overturn in the Federal government, take over the control of the post office? Then, most certainly, the country would be deluged with seditious newspapers, franked by

---

[20] *Massachusetts Mercury*, August 22, 1800. *Aurora*, July 14, 1800.

[21] *Democratic Republican* and *Commercial Daily Advertiser*, May 31, 1802. *Aurora*, July 3, 1800. *Gazette of the United States*, April 8, 1801. Hamilton to the Attorney General, August 13, 1793 (Hamilton MSS., LC.). Jacob Wagner to Richard Brown, June 29, 1799 (Pickering MSS., M.H.S.).

[22] *The Key to Liberty*, edited by Samuel Eliot Morison, 37. Billerica, Mass., 1922.

every deputy postmaster in the United States. With "the sluices of vice" thus thrown open, "we must prepare," exclaimed a Federalist, "to part with our religion, our property, and lives."[23] At all costs, therefore, the post office must be kept in the hands of the upholders of the established order.

Even though the people were not at the moment seditious, the Federalists felt no assurance that they would remain loyal if long exposed to Republican newspapers. "A few men of sense from base views, and some ignorant and wicked men," it was observed, "by falling in with all the popular clamors and flattering the popular passions can lead the people as they please."[24] And where would these "vile, despicable Printers," these "high-priests of Jacobinism," these "vile organs of a foreign democracy" who would "servilely caress and flatter even the fiends of hell itself, did they declare themselves inimical to our virtuous rulers and admirable constitution" — where would they lead the American people?[25]

*   *   *

It was all very well, said the Federalists, to speak of truth prevailing against falsehood, virtue triumphing over vice by the sheer weight of rectitude — but it was another thing to confide one's life and property to the uncertain operation of this principle.[26] "This was a fine moral sentiment," said

[23] *Massachusetts Mercury*, August 22, 1800.

[24] Alexander Addison to Pickering, November 22, 1798 (Pickering MSS., M.H.S.).

[25] *Pennsylvania Gazette*, October 18, 1797.

[26] "The proper weapon to combat error was truth," said Gallatin. "The best way to prevent libels," another Republican remarked, "is not to deserve them, and to despise them, and then they always lose their force. . . . Is there no intelligence among the American people that can enable them to distinguish truth from falsehood and right from wrong?" *Aurora*, May 10, 1798. *New Jersey Journal*, March 26, 1799.

Bayard, "but our limited knowledge of events did not verify it. There was scarcely a period in the world, at which the empire of falsehood was not as extensive as that of truth. The labor of truth was eternal, as fast as it vanquished one enemy another arose." Truth, viewed in this light, was a feeble sprout, requiring the fostering care of government; to leave it unprotected was to invite Jacobins to tear it up by the roots. Even though truth might prevail in the end, there seemed no good reason why it could not be helped along by such salutary legislation as the Sedition Act.[27]

True, the United States had no sans-culottes, no degraded and oppressed mobs; but the Federalists did not permit themselves for this reason to be lulled into security. As a Federalist observed: "the poor we have always with us, and . . . these, with many of the ignorant, are easily formed into a revolutionary corps in every country."[28] The poor, being incurably jealous of the rich, were peculiarly susceptible to the harangues of demagogues and offered a fertile field for the spread of subversive ideas, of which there were already altogether too many in the United States. "What anarchical notions we find prevailing!" exclaimed Fisher Ames. "What other government finds the elements of discord and dissolution so powerful within its very bosom!"[29]

It was the population of the cities that they particularly distrusted: "Cities," said a Connecticut Federalist, "are subject to sudden passions, and the dupes of design" — they were "the seats of vanity, ignorance and vice." In Boston, Stephen Higginson declared, dwelt "all the seditious and desperate" — in sharp contrast to the country districts, inhabited by a virtuous, conservative — and largely Federal-

[27] *Richmond Examiner*, June 21, 1798. *Porcupine's Gazette*, July 19, 1798. *Greenleaf's New Daily Advertiser*, February 21, 1799.
[28] Henry Cabot Lodge, *Life and Letters of George Cabot*, 231. Boston, 1877.
[29] Fisher Ames, *Works*, I, 223.

ist — yeomanry.[30] Jefferson was by no means alone in his love of the American farmer.

Admitting that there were only a handful of Jacobins of the true Parisian breed in the United States, the Federalists were still unable to relax. It was one of their firmly held convictions that a few Jacobins were more than a match for a host of good men. The wealth, virtues and talents of the country could not stand against men who "merely by perseverance in their endless arts of lying and intrigue" were able to accomplish their dire ends.[31] While honest men trusted to the superiority of their cause and took "Shelter under the Idea, that the *better Principles* must prevail," Jacobins worked night and day to undermine the pillars of Church and State; those who labored to destroy were always much more zealous and active than those whose purpose was merely to preserve.[32] "What our enemies want in numbers," said a conservative, "they make up in the most active intrigue; and what they want in manly spirit, they make up by the dark and underhanded conspiracy. They are Jeffersonians in cowardice as they are Catalines in villainy. But the coward has his weapon, and often strikes the surest and most fatal blows."[33] Indeed, some were prepared to believe that one Jacobin could set a nation aflame: "One frantic madman may bawl FIRE! at midnight, and disturb the peace and fears of a whole city — one furious Jacobin, alarm a whole country with ridiculous fears of the government. The alarm is caught by the weak, and spread by the foolish. . . . Consternation is a contagious

[30] George Gibbs, *Memoirs of the Administrations of Washington and John Adams*, 124–128. New York, 1846. *The Works of Alexander Hamilton*, edited by John C. Hamilton, V, 571. New York, 1851.

[31] Fisher Ames, *Works*, II, 110–111, 228. Lodge, *Cabot*, 160, 173.

[32] *Gazette of the United States*, November 12, 1798. Jonathan Trumbull to James Hillhouse, March 3, 1800 (Trumbull MSS., Connecticut Historical Society).

[33] *Gazette of the United States*, November 12, 1798.

disease, and none escape but the few, the very few who are wise enough to think for themselves."[34]

Although the "French faction" had been disconcerted by the X Y Z episode, the Federalists did not doubt that it would soon be back in force, sapping the foundations of religion and government. For the moment, the "Jacobins" were merely resting in their hiding places, said Fisher Ames, "like serpents in winter, the better to concoct their venom."[35] Washington did not expect any alteration in their sentiments; at most, they would merely change their tactics. "The cursed foul contagion of French principles has infected us," a Federalist exclaimed. ". . . The spirit of French democracy is as active as it is wicked, and thus becomes more than a match for every other sort of spirit."[36] If disaster were to be averted, no time could be lost: "Shall we not be aroused," Americans were asked, "till our Dwellings conflagrate, and till our public places mark in blood the progress of a deadly and more than hellish foe in our country?"[37]

Moreover, party alignments in Congress did not permit the Federalists to take a complacent view of the state of the union. Compared with the undergraduates at Harvard — "young men whose hearts are warm and without one drop of French blood in them" — Congress, from the Federalist point of view, left much to be desired. Measures providing for national security were pushed through by narrow majorities against the opposition of "railing, snarling, thickskulled Democrats."[38] "There is yet a wicked and a vile Spirit, visible in

[34] *What Is Our Situation?*, 29. *Philadelphia Gazette*, May 22, 1799. James McHenry to William L. Smith, October 20, 1798 (William L. Smith MSS., LC.).

[35] Fisher Ames, *Works*, II, 113.

[36] Lodge, *Cabot*, 160, 173.

[37] Loring Andrews to Peter Van Schaack, April 6, 1798 (Peter Van Schaack MSS.).

[38] *Gazette of the United States*, July 14, August 16, 1798.

Congress," said Stephen Higginson of Massachusetts, "which opposes everything energetic and dignified, but it must be subdued or expelled."[39] In particular, the Virginia members were held responsible for this state of affairs: they sent their constituents copies of Bache's *Aurora* together with "a flood of Jacobinic filth from their own pens."[40] No wonder, therefore, said the Federalists, that the country was afflicted with "a twaddling, whiffling Congress" incapable of acting until France had kicked some spirit into it.[41]

It was impossible for the Federalists to overlook the fact that the Republicans in Congress opposed every measure designed to put the country in a posture of defense.[42] A navy they dreaded as an offensive instrument of war certain to lead to outright war with France; the means of strengthening the North against the South, merchants against farmers, the Executive against Congress; and the favorite device of the Federalists for increasing the national debt. Any money voted for a navy, said Nicholas of North Carolina, would aggrandize the power of the President "by disbursing money into the hands of favorites, and by that means give to him the power of destroying a great part of the influence which it was intended the people should have in this Government."[43] As the Republicans interpreted British history, it was the navy which had destroyed the liberties of that country and beggared the people. So adamant were they on this matter, that Jefferson opposed even fortifying the harbors of the United States.

Just as privateers were the best defense by sea, so, in the Republicans' opinion, the militia was the most effective, and most truly democratic, defense by land. A large standing

[39] Stephen Higginson to Pickering, June 14, 1798 (Pickering MSS.); Rufus King to Theodore Sedgwick, July 1, 1798 (King MSS.).

[40] *Gazette of the United States*, July 14, 1798. Gibbs, *Memoirs*, II, 171.

[41] *Philadelphia Gazette*, May 6, 1799.

[42] *Lancaster Journal*, August 3, 1799.

[43] *Annals of Congress*, IX, 2854.

army they believed would ruin the finances, the morals and the industry of the country. Their method of meeting the perils of invasion was to wait for the enemy with a small regular army; then, upon his arrival, to call out the militia. Americans, said Matthew Lyon, ought to "raise in mass, and drive out the invaders, returning to their farms and their homes immediately."[44] Only by this means could it be guaranteed that the army would not destroy the liberties of the country.

As for the Federalist argument that blood was thicker than water, the Republicans would have rejoiced to see Great Britain humbled in the world. Nor did they agree with Secretary of State Pickering when he said that "the little finger of France in maritime depredations is thicker than the loins of Britain." Far from recognizing that the British navy was America's first line of defense, they protested every seizure of an American ship and every impressment of an American seaman by Great Britain.

The conquest of Great Britain by a "liberating" French army, so dreaded by the Federalists, would have been welcomed by the Republicans.[45] Jefferson did not conceal his enthusiasm for a French triumph; when that happy event occurred, he said that he would go to London and drink tea with the victorious generals. But it did not follow, as the Federalists supposed, that he would have invited the French generals to Philadelphia to drink tea with him.[46] In Jefferson's opinion, the continued existence of republicanism in the

[44] J. F. McLaughlin, *Matthew Lyon: The Hampden of Congress*, 332. N. Y., 1900.

[45] "Little more than for Buonaparte to cross the channel, and the cloud capp'd towers of feudal rights, the *gorgeous palaces* of monarchy, the *grand mausoleum* of despotism, the *great globe itself* of British naval tyranny, shall *vanish like a cloud*." Then France will "withdraw her legions and restore her sister realms as friends." (*Aurora*, February 9, 1798.)

[46] Jefferson, *Writings*, VII, 11–12. *New Jersey Journal*, March 22, 1799.

United States hinged upon the outcome of the struggle in Europe: "Never was any event so important to this country since its revolution, as the issue of the invasion of England," he declared. "With that we shall stand or fall."[47] If the United States had any interest in the European balance of power or stood in any danger of attack from a France victorious over Great Britain, Jefferson in 1798 failed to see it.[48]

[47] Jefferson, *Writings*, VII, 268.
[48] In March, 1798, Gallatin said that "he never believed there was anything like a real balance of power in Europe; it was a mere imaginary thing, and he thought there could not be a more ridiculous figure drawn than that of a President of the United States attempting to adjust the balance of power in Europe."

CHAPTER III

AT no time since the American Revolution had political feeling run as high as in 1798. When Dr. Reynolds, a Republican physician and friend of Benjamin Bache, was dismissed from his post at the Philadelphia Dispensary, a bitter controversy ensued, the Republicans raising the cry of political discrimination. To William Cobbett, publisher of *Porcupine's Gazette*, it was entirely proper that Dr. Reynolds's political opinions should be brought into the question. "A man's politics, at this time," Cobbett remarked, "are *every thing*. I would sooner have my wounds dressed by a dog than by a democrat." The relative merits of dogs and democrats were thereupon gravely discussed in the Federalist press. It was pointed out that the dog "is in reality a much more respectable character than the democrat; the dog will never take part with a stranger and an enemy against the family he was dwelt with, and fed among." If a dog was man's best friend, a democrat was his worst enemy — "a treacherous, malignant, hypocritical biped."[1]

When it was reported that a Philadelphia bank robber was "a noted Democrat," it occasioned no surprise among Federalists, to whom robber and democrat had become synonymous.[2] Moreover, when Cobbett warned the young women of America that it was "better to be married to a Felon or a

[1] *Russell's Gazette*, June 18, June 21, 1798.
[2] *Gazette of the United States*, November 20, 1798.

Hangman than to a *Democrat*," thousands of Federalist fathers fervently approved the sentiment; "No Bundling with Democrats" might well have been the motto hung in pious New England households.[3]

It was deemed significant, by some, that Jacobinism had first appeared in the United States at almost the same time the country suffered its worst outbreak of yellow fever — the great epidemic of 1793 that for several months made Philadelphia, then the capital of the United States, a mere ghost city. From this coincidence they drew the conclusion that "God had sent out one as a *corrective* of the other. Our cities have been punished in proportion to the extent of Jacobinism; and in general at least three out of four of the persons who have perished by pestilence have been over zealous partizans."[4] But apparently the Almighty could not destroy Jacobins as fast as His Great Adversary manufactured them, for since 1793 Jacobinism had grown mightily in the United States.

The Federalists firmly believed that the same conditions that had contributed to the downfall of European republics existed — in aggravated form — in the United States itself. A large French population together with a domestic "faction" eager to lay the country at the feet of France had already convinced the French that "we are a divided people, a degraded, insignificant, effeminate, dastardly race of beings, ready for the yoke."[5] Here were the familiar ingredients of French conquest: the Directory had merely to pull the strings of its puppets and set in motion its "liberating" armies and its bag of republics would be complete. It was this system, exclaimed Harrison Gray Otis in one of his loftiest oratorical flights, that had "watered the tomb of William Tell with the

[3] *Greenleaf's New Daily Advertiser*, November 13, 1798.
[4] *Gazette of the United States*, June 21, 1800.
[5] *Ibid.*, 1798.

blood of widows fighting over their slaughtered husbands, and with the tears of orphans who survive to swell the procession of the victors."[6] In enacting the Alien and Sedition laws, the Federalists professed to act upon this premise: that a dangerous French faction was at work in the United States and that the survival of the Republic required that it be stamped out.

In Federalist orations, the country was made to seem to swarm with "French apostles of Sedition" — enough "to BURN ALL OUR CITIES AND CUT THE THROATS OF ALL THE INHABITANTS."[7] Harrison Gray Otis, whose imagination was as lively as his rhetoric, declared that the existence of the United States was threatened by "that crowd of spies and inflammatory agents which overspread the country like the locusts of Egypt . . . fomenting hostilities against this country and alienating the affections of our own citizens."[8] These agents, among them General Jean Baptiste Collot, were reported to be trying to secure plans of American fortifications, laying the groundwork for rebellion in the West, and preparing to murder innocent Americans in their beds.[9]

Many Federalists shared Harrison Gray Otis's conviction that the root of all the evil in the United States was the large foreign-born population. Here was the chief source of opposition to government, the breeding place of faction, the recruiting ground of the democrats. Coming from "a quarter of the world so full of disorder and corruption" as Europe, it was to be feared that immigrants would "contaminate the purity and simplicity of the American character"; "their

[6] Morison, *Otis*, I, 111.

[7] *Albany Centinel*, August 7, 1798. *Porcupine's Gazette*, July 3, 1798. James McHenry to Pickering, September 10, 1798 (Pickering MSS., M.H.S.).

[8] *Abridgment of the Debates of Congress*, II, 257.

[9] *Country Porcupine*, November 10 and 12, 1798. James McHenry to Pickering, September 10, 1798 (Pickering MSS.).

principles spread like the leaven of unrighteousness; the weak, the ignorant and the needy are thrown into a ferment, and corruption threatens the whole mass."[10] True, some immigrants were industrious, peaceable, and voted the Federalist ticket — but for one such "good" European, lamented Noah Webster, "we receive three or four discontented, factious men" — "the convicts, fugitives of justice, hirelings of France, and disaffected offscourings of other nations."[11] "Generally speaking," said a Federalist, "none but the most vile and worthless, none but the idle and discontented, the disorderly and the wicked, have inundated upon us from Europe."[12] Clearly, the property and the virtue of the United States would not be secure until foreign immigration had been reduced to a mere trickle of hand-picked newcomers of approved political sympathies.

With about thirty thousand Frenchmen in the United States, it might seem that there was good reason for apprehension. But the great majority were either émigrés from France or fugitives from the uprising of the blacks in San Domingo. Gallatin estimated that ninety-nine out of a hundred of these French nationals were hostile to the principles of the Revolution and were far more eager to return to their own country and live in peace than to revolutionize the United States. In the eyes of the Federalists, however, every Frenchman was a potential enemy: whether royalists or revolutionists, they were eager to extend French influence over the United States, and, actuated by national pride, they might join a French army of invasion. Moreover, their notoriously

[10] *Annals of Congress*, III, 1028. *The Writings of George Washington*, edited by John C. Fitzpatrick, XXXIV, 23. Washington, 1942. *Albany Centinel*, August 7, 1798.

[11] Noah Webster to Pickering, July 7, 1797 (Pickering MSS.). Noah Webster, *Two Letters to Dr. Priestley*, 25. New Haven, 1800. *Gazette of the United States*, June 5, 1800. *What Is Our Situation?*, 21–22.

[12] The *Pennsylvania Herald* and *York General Advertiser*, August 1, 1798.

loose morals and irreligion threatened to infect Americans: "Evil communications," it was pointed out by the Federalists, "corrupt good morals." What, they asked, had pious, God-fearing Americans to do with a country which exhibited "a scene of more brutal sensuality, profligacy, and debauchery, than even Sodom and Gomorrah of ancient days." To perish in this "vile and loathsome embrace" would be a shocking end.[13]

Republicans, too, feared immigration — but from a different quarter. With "the approaching tumble of George the Third," it was predicted ". . . the friends of order will receive a numerous cargo of their dearly beloved Aristocratical Brethren" — dukes, lords and other titled gentry, to swell the forces of the Federalist party.[14] Thus most of the peerage of Great Britain might be transplanted to this hemisphere, with fatal consequences to American liberty if these aristocrats were freely admitted to the rights of citizens. A Republican congressman stoutly declared that he "did not want to see a Duke come here, and contest an election for Congress with a citizen": Americans might love a lord too well for their own good.[15] James Madison was reluctant to take this risk; although he admitted that loyalty oaths were of little real value, he contended that they ought to be used in the case of foreign aristocrats seeking citizenship.

Because most immigration by-passed New England, moving instead into the Middle States, New Englanders saw their influence in the national government seriously endangered. For this state of affairs, the Yankees themselves were in part to blame: since the original settlement, immigrants, particularly Irish and Germans, had been made unwelcome. Determined to preserve the purity of their race and creed,

[13] *Porcupine's Gazette*, July 3, 1798. *Albany Centinel*, September 25, 1798.
[14] *Aurora*, May 11, 1798.
[15] *Annals of Congress*, III, 1033.

the descendants of the Puritans had warded off foreign in-
truders; and they did not propose in the 1790's to let down the
bars. Indeed, the exclusion of foreigners had never seemed
more necessary than when a horde of wild Irish and English
revolutionists battered at the gates.[16] Rufus King, a Bostonian
who had settled in New York without losing any of his New
England prejudices, declared that the contrast between thrice-
blessed New England and those parts of the union that had
freely admitted foreigners was "a powerful admonition to us
to observe greater caution in the admission of Foreigners
among us." Pennsylvania, with its large population of Scotch-
Irish and Germans, was a horrible example of the results of
laxness in admitting foreigners — it was said that New England would have hanged the men who in Pennsylvania were
elected to Congress.[17] Harrison Gray Otis, spokesman of the
New England nativists, wanted no foreigners to help fill up
the continent: he "considered the native American germ to be
amply sufficient for the production of such scions as were
worth cultivation." Above all, he "did not wish to invite
hordes of wild Irishmen, nor the turbulent and disorderly of
all parts of the world, to come here with a view to disturb our
tranquillity, after having succeeded in the overthrow of their
own Governments."[18] At this time, abusing foreigners was the
road to political favor in Massachusetts; and it was a highroad
that many Federalists trod.

Of all this evil crew, none were more offensive to the Federalists than the Irish and English immigrants. Here they saw
the dregs of society, a great outpouring of the slums, the most
malignant of all the revolutionists of Europe descending upon
the United States. In relieving itself of this burden, Great

[16] Jonathan Trumbull to James Hillhouse, March 3, 1800 (Trumbull
MSS., Connecticut Historical Society).
[17] *Rufus King*, II, 371.
[18] *Country Porcupine*, November 8 and 9, 1798. Morison, *Otis*, I, 108.

Britain seemed bent upon making the United States a Botany Bay; as a result of its policy of deliberately dumping its undesirables upon this country, it was said, "many of the most active and bloody of their Jacobins and other convicts are embarking on special permission for the United States."[19]

England's experience with "Wild Irishmen" made them objects of terror to the Federalists. Irish leaders like Wolfe Tone had conspired with the French and prepared to welcome the invading armies of the Republic; the United Irishmen demanded universal suffrage and other reforms based upon social and political ideals inspired by the French Revolution. It was not doubted that this dreaded brotherhood had extended its operations to the United States: Wolfe Tone, Hamilton Rowan and Napper Tandy, the leaders of the United Irishmen driven from Ireland, had settled temporarily in the United States. All the Irish in the Republic were under suspicion of belonging to this revolutionary organization and engaged in plotting the overthrow of the government in the name of liberty, equality and fraternity. The Democratic Societies to whose influence the Federalists had ascribed the Whisky Rebellion were widely supposed to have been succeeded by the "dark and silent system of organized treason and massacre, imported by the UNITED IRISHMEN." These Irish, the Americans were told, were "so many serpents within your bosom. . . . They talk loudly of their attachment to this country, but believe them *not;* it is only a mask to cover designs formed against your rights and liberties."[20]

Their conduct on this side of the Atlantic, as the Federalists saw it, was of a piece with the treasonable activities that had

[19] *Gazette of the United States*, June 6, 1800. Noah Webster, *Ten Letters to Dr. Priestley*, 15.

[20] *Rufus King*, II, 426. *Salem Gazette*, November 29, 1798; January 1, 1799. *Country Porcupine*, September 6 and 7; November 8 and 9; November 10 and 12, 1798. *Gazette of the United States*, November 22, 1798. *Porcupine's Gazette*, November 10, 1798; February 12, 1799.

caused their motherland to cast them out. They seemed unaware that they had reached the land of the free; they continued their opposition to government quite as though they
were still combating Old World tyranny. They found fault
with everything: "These gentlemen are hardly landed in the
United States, before they begin to cavil against the Government, and to pant after a *more perfect state of society*." Federalists
ascribed this behavior to the persistence of habits contracted
in their mother country and to the heady effects of unaccustomed liberty: "Having been long confined within the limits
of an active and vigilant police, and under the restraints of
energetic government, they break loose with unbounded
license, and in shaking off the shackles of their former condition, they spurn at the most wholesome subordination. Any
government, and all laws are now too tyrannical for these
new-born sons of liberty. These free spirits can suffer no
restraint. They consider the bolts and bars that secure their
neighbor's property — the fence that encloses his land, and
the very walls that form his house, as encroachments upon
their *natural rights*, as a prostration of LIBERTY and EQUAL-
ITY." From their insight into the Irish character gained at
close range, the Federalists concluded that the rebellion in
Ireland was owing more "to the restless turbulence of the
united Irishmen, than to the oppression of government."[21]
"A terror and a torment to America," they were loaded in
this country as well as in Great Britain "with all the infamy
attached to traiterous and seditious Spirits."[22]

Principally, however — and this was their real offense —
the Irish expressed their dissatisfaction with things as they
were in the United States by joining the Republican party.

---

[21] *Country Porcupine*, September 6 and 7, 1798. *What Is Our Situation?*, 19.
Selections from *Cobbett's Political Works*, edited by John M. Cobbett and
James P. Cobbett, I, 32. London, 1835.
[22] *Rufus King*, II, 426.

For the Federalists, they had the same regard that they had for the English Tories: both were aristocrats and enemies of the rights of man. As a result, the Republicans seemed destined to control the country with the aid of this formidable auxiliary, the foreign-born vote. No wonder that the Federalists groaned that the United States was becoming "the vassal of foreign outlaws" and demanded that "the Legislation of the country be placed in the hands in which it belongs, the proprietors of the country."[23]

For this reason, the Federalists had long sought to make naturalization more difficult for foreigners. The law of 1790 permitted naturalization after two years' residence, but in 1795 the Federalists succeeded in raising the residence requirement to five years. Even this did not satisfy them: the imprudent liberality of the United States in granting citizenship, they said, had admitted hundreds of "treasonable ingrates into the bosom of our country."[24]

Dealing with such practised subverters of the established order, a residence requirement of fourteen years before naturalization did not seem to the Federalists excessive; it required at least this long to transform rebels and incendiaries into respectable, peace-loving American citizens. Accordingly, the Naturalization Act of 1798, passed by a Federalist Congress, raised the probationary period from five to fourteen years.

The purpose of this law was to make the Republican party wither on the vine by cutting off its supply of foreign-born voters. In fact, however, it had no such effect: the Federalists sacrificed their last shred of influence over the foreign vote without materially reducing the strength of the Republican party. As long as the states possessed the power of naturaliza-

[23] John Ward Fenno, *Desultory Reflections*, 53–54. N. Y., 1800.
[24] Frank George Franklin, *The Legislative History of Naturalization*, 70–71. Washington, 1901. *Porcupine's Gazette*, September 5, 1798.

tion, a Federal law was not likely to be of much utility. Pennsylvania, for example, permitted naturalization, including the right to vote in Federal as well as in state elections, after two years' residence; and Maryland required only one year. Thus the states were able to defeat the best-laid plans of the Federal government.[25]

Obviously, to accomplish the Federalists' objective, the Naturalization Act needed to be buttressed by other laws against foreign-born voters. Although no one favored going the length of the Athenian law, by which it was made a capital offense for foreigners to intermeddle in political affairs, the Federalists were certainly moving in that direction. Foreigners, whether naturalized or not, ought, it was said, to be forbidden to teach school or edit newspapers; and Harrison Gray Otis proposed in Congress to exclude all foreign born in the country, not at that time citizens, from all offices of honor, trust or profit in the government of the United States.[26] Thus, only birth would entitle a man to the full rights of citizenship; and, while this would injure some worthy foreign-born citizens, Otis declared it was essential to the security of the country. To permit foreigners to hold political office was, he said, to open the door to the intrigues of European powers: "America is growing into a nation of importance, and it would be an object with foreign nations to gain an influence in our councils."[27]

Otis's motion was defeated fifty-five to twenty-seven in the House of Representatives but the idea of restricting citizenship to the native born was by no means laid aside. Late in

[25] It was acknowledged that all persons who were citizens of a state were also citizens of the United States. The Naturalization Act was repealed by the Republicans in 1802.

[26] Franklin, *The Legislative History of Naturalization*, 70–71. Henry William Saussure to Pickering, September 6, 1799 (Pickering MSS.).

[27] *Abridgment of the Debates in Congress*, II, 255.

1798, the legislatures of Massachusetts and Connecticut proposed a constitutional amendment making foreigners naturalized since the Declaration of Independence ineligible to the office of Representative, Senator or President.[28] This proposal was tabled in Congress, but it was taken up by some of the state legislatures where it succeeded only in stirring up dissension among the Federalists themselves. In the New York legislature, "many decided federalists dissented from the Massachusetts proposition" and Aaron Burr, a Republican bidding for the Irish vote, made a speech in which he contended that the only instances of corruption in the history of the United States were furnished by natives: foreigners, he concluded, were always virtuous.[29]

This proposed constitutional amendment was directed primarily against one man — Albert Gallatin, who, although a resident of the United States, had been born in Switzerland. In 1794, Gallatin had been excluded from the United States Senate on the ground that he had not been a citizen for nine years as required by the Constitution; "heaven and earth were moved in order to gain that point" by the Federal party in order to preserve its majority in the Senate and to keep that body free of the presence of a man suspected of having abetted the Whisky rebels. But Gallatin was immediately elected to the House of Representatives, where, after Madison's retirement, he became the Republican floor leader and financial expert of the party, the only Republican who could challenge Hamilton in that field. The Federalists never forgave Gallatin for defying their mandate to stay out of politics. His foreign birth made him specially vulnerable: "the sly, the artfull, the insidious Gallatin," it was said,

[28] *Gazette of the United States*, April 29, 1799. Herman V. Ames, *The Proposed Amendments to the Constitution*, 30, 74. Washington, 1897.

[29] *Albany Centinel*, February 19, 1799. *Rufus King*, II, 524.

imported his ideas direct from Paris: "if the *French* had an *agent* in that house, it would have been impossible for him *to act his part better.*"[30]

*   *   *

The Naturalization Act and the projected amendment to the Constitution were long-range measures obviously designed to weaken the Republican party. However congenial this work was to many Federalists, they were obliged to turn their attention to what they regarded as the immediate need of the hour — stamping out the menace of alien enemies.

This power was given the Federal government by the Alien Enemies Act signed by the President on July 6, 1798. Alone of the four measures passed by this Federalist Congress dealing with aliens and seditious practices, this Act alone was truly a war measure. According to its provisions, in case of war or threatened invasion, the President was given authority to seize, secure or remove from the country all resident aliens, citizens of the enemy nation. There was, of course, only one such enemy in view; the certainty that it would be used against France, if it were used at all, accounts for the strenuous Republican opposition to this bill.

As a measure designed to safeguard the United States, the Alien Enemies Act suffered from a serious shortcoming: it went into effect only upon the declaration of war or imminence of invasion. If these events did not occur, aliens would be out of the reach of the government; and no one could be sure that France would declare war. Perhaps, as Harrison Gray Otis pointed out, the Directory might find it more convenient to pillage American commerce and to stir up rebellion in the United States than to embark upon

[30] *Albany Centinel*, May 25, 1798. Mitchell, *Abigail Adams*, 154. Henry Adams, *The Life of Gallatin*, 121. Philadelphia, 1879.

outright war. To provide against this contingency, Otis urged that Congress take precautionary measures "against the residence of alien enemies existing in the bosom of the country, as the root of all the evil which we are at present experiencing." In this hour of danger, Otis did not propose to "boggle about slight forms . . . but to seize these persons, wherever they could be found carrying on their vile purposes. Without this," he concluded, "everything else which had been done in the way of defence would amount to nothing." To give point to his warnings, he recalled the experience of European republics: Venice, Switzerland and Holland had lost their independence because they waited for a declaration of war before taking action against French agents.[31]

There were even more weighty objections to the Alien Enemies Act: it limited the powers of the government to alien *enemies* alone and, as a Republican congressman suggested, the Federalists were much more eager to move against alien *friends*, particularly the Irish, than against alien enemies. Whether or not actual war broke out with France, it would be relatively easy to round up French subjects, but the Irish and English radicals resident in the United States were not so easily disposed of. No one envisaged a war with Ireland by which Irish aliens in the United States would come within the purview of the Alien Enemies Act; and therefore it was held necessary to accompany the Alien Enemies Act with a law giving the Federal government power to deport, in time of peace, all aliens, whether French, Irish or English, suspected of being engaged in subversive activities.

As introduced into the Senate by Hillhouse of Connecticut, the original alien bill was a draconic measure conceived in the spirit of William Cobbett, who declared: "Were I president, I would hang them or they should murder me. I never would hold the sword of justice, and suffer such miscreants to escape

[31] *Abridgment of the Debates of Congress,* II, 257.

its edge."[32] By its provisions, the President was given authority
to deport all such aliens as he judged dangerous to the peace
and safety of the United States. If an alien ordered out of the
country was found at large, he was to be imprisoned for a term
not exceeding three years and forever debarred from becoming a citizen; if an alien sent out of the United States should
voluntarily return, he faced a sentence of imprisonment at
hard labor for life.

The Senate bill encountered in the House the determined
opposition of the Republicans; there was an "incessant combat" of three weeks' duration in which they sought to defeat it,
word by word, by means of amendments. Moreover, its provisions were so severe as to alienate the more moderate Federalists. As Gallatin pointed out, hard labor for life had never up
to this time been introduced into the code of the United
States: the punishment for a misprison of treason was seven
years' imprisonment, but not at hard labor. At the motion of
Robert G. Harper, one of the Federalist leaders of the House,
the hard-labor provision was stricken out and, in place of the
words "imprisonment during life," imprisonment "so long as
in the opinion of the President the public safety" required, was
substituted. And Harrison Gray Otis introduced a wholly new
section enabling an alien ordered out of the country to take his
property with him.[33]

Nevertheless, the House retained intact the provisions
in the original Senate bill giving the President virtually
unlimited power over all aliens in the United States. There
was no requirement that the government prove its case before
a judicial authority; no provision was made for use of the

[32] *Porcupine's Gazette*, July 19; August 22; September 13, 1799. *Aurora*,
August 2, 1800.

[33] *Albany Centinel*, June 29, 1798. *Independent Chronicle*, August 20, 1798.
Aurora, May 25, 1798. Pickering to President Adams, August 12, 1798 (the
National Archives).

writ of habeas corpus; there was no possibility of release
by judicial authority. Aliens imprisoned under this Act might
be removed from the country on the order of the President;
and if they returned without permission, they ran the risk
of being imprisoned for a term wholly at his discretion. Ship
captains were obliged to make a detailed report on all aliens
they brought into the country; and every alien resident in the
United States was required to register with the government.

*   *   *

On June 8, 1798, the alien bill passed the Senate, fifteen
votes to eight. It was a highly sectional vote: only two senators
from states south of the Potomac favored the bill. In the House
of Representatives, final action came on June twenty-first
when the measure passed, forty-six to forty. Here again, the
voting was along sectional lines, the Southern states giving
eight votes for and twenty-seven against the bill; eleven out
of the twelve Virginia representatives in attendance cast their
ballots in opposition. Clearly, it was the virtually solid vote of
New England, twenty-four to two, that ensured the passage
of the Alien Act.

If the sectional nature of the vote augured rough going
for the Alien Act in the country, the debate it touched off
inside Congress was hardly less ominous. In a speech in the
House of Representatives, Edward Livingston of New York
branded the bill as "a sacrifice of the first born offspring
of freedom" and warned the Federalists that if they took
advantage of "an honest noble warmth, produced by an indignant sense of injury" on the part of the people, to introduce
tyranny into the land, they would go down in infamy and contempt; "The people of America, sir," he exclaimed, "though
watchful against foreign aggression are not careless of domestic
encroachment; they are as jealous, sir, of their liberties at
home, as of the power and prosperity of their country abroad."

In the Alien Act, said Livingston, the Federalists had revealed their ulterior motives: to "excite a fervor against foreign aggression only to establish tyranny at home; that, like the arch traitor, we cry 'Hail Columbia' at the moment we are betraying her to destruction."[34]

[34] *Aurora*, July 2, 1798.

CHAPTER IV

THE Federalists, in all their raging against French agents and wild Irishmen, never supposed that mere nativity ensured loyalty. The existence of the Republican "faction" — and the necessity of destroying it — were considerations always uppermost in their minds. There were no greater enemies of order and good government than those native-born radicals, French sympathizers to a man, who compounded sedition with treason — "unnatural children" who were ready to join the French army in subjugating the United States. As William Cobbett said, "Surely we need a sedition law to keep our own rogues from cutting our throats, and an alien law to prevent the invasion by a host of foreign rogues to assist them."[1]

On April 26, 1798, Jefferson recorded that "one of the war party, in a fit of unguarded passion, declared some time ago they would pass a citizen bill, an alien bill, & a sedition bill."[2] Long contemplated by the Federalists, the sedition bill was the last of the crisis measures to be enacted by Congress, but there were many portents of its coming. It was observed, for example, that President John Adams in his speeches against France did not confine himself solely to the foreign menace: it was, said Jefferson, "his own fellow citizens, against whom

---

[1] *Country Porcupine,* November 8 and 9, 1798. *Gazette of the United States,* November 23, 1798.

[2] Jefferson, *Writings,* VII, 244–245.

his threats are uttered."[3] In a public letter, the President ominously declared that "the delusions & misrepresentations which have misled so many citizens, must be discountenanced by authority as well as by the citizens at large." In short, the government must be given power over the press in order to strike at one of the chief sources of disaffection and sedition.[4]

The Federalists, far from holding public opinion in contempt, regarded it as the mainspring of government: "Of such force is public opinion," said Judge Alexander Addison, "that, with it on its side, the worst government will support itself, and, against it, the best government will fall." In a republic such as the United States, public opinion was of incalculable importance: "poison the fountain of its being," said a Federalist congressman, "and the whole frame is palsied, and must sink into lethargy or die in convulsions."[5]

If public opinion formed the basis of government, the press in turn formed public opinion. The press had vast powers of good or evil: in its hands lay the destiny of monarchies and republics alike; war or peace, revolution or order, licentiousness or liberty, were within its province. "Give to any set of men the command of the press, and you give them the command of the country," said Judge Addison, "for you give them the command of public opinion, which commands every thing."[6]

Blind, indeed, would the Federalists have been had they failed to give due weight to public opinion and to the influence of the press in molding it — the French Revolution was a signal demonstration of its powers. For centuries, they pointed out, the French monarchy had been maintained by a firmly entrenched and widespread belief in the Divine Right of Kings; when this support was withdrawn, the entire fabric

[3] Jefferson, *Writings*, VII, 247.
[4] *Russell's Gazette*, June 7, 1798. *Columbian Centinel*, January 1, 1799.
[5] *Annals of Congress*, X, 409, 946.
[6] *Columbian Centinel*, January 1, 1799.

collapsed. And in bringing about the downfall of the Ancient Regime, "the undaunted licentiousness of the Press" seemed to have been a prime cause. "Calumny and abuse upon the Fairest Characters and the best Men in France," said Mrs. John Adams, sapped the peoples' confidence in their government and prepared the way for revolution.[7]

Moreover, revolutionary France itself had made spectacular use of the press to aid in its European conquests. By means of her sympathizers and propaganda — "corrupt partisans and hired presses," the Federalists called them — the people had been prepared to receive liberty, equality and fraternity at the hands of the French army. Their loyalty to Church and State had been undermined, their discontents magnified and the established order brought into contempt — such was the power of propaganda.

That there was urgent need in the United States for preventive measures against revolution was not doubted by the Federalists. Just as the French monarchy had been overthrown by calumny and abuse, so, said Mrs. John Adams, "have their emissaries adopted the same weapons in this Country and the liberty of the press is become licentious beyond any former period."[8] Washington deplored the "cowardly, illiberal and assassin like" efforts on the part of newspapers to "destroy all confidence in those who are entrusted with the Administration" — the prelude, as the experience of European republics had revealed — to revolution.[9] "Jacobinism" worked upon the principle, said Hamilton, that "the influence of men of upright principles, disposed and able to resist its enterprises, shall be at all events destroyed"; and thus a great "conspiracy of vice against virtue" had begun —

[7] *Warren-Adams Letters*, II, 338. Boston, 1917. *Columbian Centinel*, January 1, 1799. *Greenleaf's New Daily Advertiser*, July 17, 1798.

[8] *Warren-Adams Letters*, II, 338.

[9] Washington, *Writings* (Fitzpatrick), XXXVI. Feb. 6, 1798.

a conspiracy in which the reputation of every honest public servant was blackened, traduced and misrepresented. Political defamation had reached the point, lamented a Federalist, where "to give a man an office is to set him up as a mark for every blackguard to spit at."[10]

The favorite device of these assassins of character, said Hamilton, was the Big Lie: "it is maxim deeply engrafted in that dark system, that no character, however upright, is a match for constantly reiterated attacks, however false. . . . Every calumny makes some proselytes, and even retains some; since justification seldom circulates as rapidly or as widely as slander. . . . The public mind, fatigued at length with resistance to the calumnies which eternally assail it . . . is apt at the end to sit down with the opinion that a person so often accused cannot be entirely innocent."[11] Against this weapon there seemed to be no defense — unless it was cutting off defamation at the source.

The Alien Act was expected to do much toward working a reformation in the press. Upon arriving in the United States, Irish and English radicals seemed to be smitten with an irresistible desire to establish a newspaper and give vent to their cherished political convictions. A whiff of printers' ink and they became journalists; and almost without exception their newspapers supported the Republican party against the administration. It was this strong journalistic bent that gave color to the Federalists' crusade against aliens. "The people of America," it was said, "have long been abused by a detestable banditti of foreign invaders . . . defaming with vile slanders the purest and most virtuous characters."[12] By what

[10] Hamilton, *Works*, VII, 370–372. *What Is Our Situation?*, 28. *Albany Centinel*, July 20, 1798.

[11] Hamilton, *Works* (Lodge), VII, 377.

[12] *Gazette of the United States*, November 20, 1798. *Porcupine's Gazette*, January 9, 1799.

right, asked the Federalists, did these low-born outcasts and renegades — "fugitive felons . . . men without a name and without a home, who have nothing to lose, and every thing to gain by the public ruin" — presume to criticize the government of the United States and to vilify the gentlemen who administered it?[13]

But it was hardly to be hoped that the Alien Act alone could lay "the devil of sedition": the press itself must be brought under control. The press, said Fisher Ames, "has left the understanding of the mass of men just where it found it, but by supplying an endless stimulus to their imagination and passions, it has rendered their temper and habits infinitely worse. It has inspired ignorance with presumption, so that those who cannot be governed by reason are no longer to be awed by authority." It had taught the people grievances they never knew existed and had raised in them the hope — always fatal to good order — that the world could be made better.[14]

And so the Federalists were driven to the conclusion that every government that depended upon the support of public opinion must take measures to ensure that it enjoyed a favorable press. This could be done only by suppressing criticism and slander directed against the government and its officers. It was "of the highest importance," they reasoned, "that none but pure sentiments and good principles, should be disseminated" by the newspapers.[15] "The Government," said a Federalist Congressman, "is bound not to deceive the people, and it is equally bound not to suffer them to be deceived. Delusion leads to insurrection and rebellion, which it is the duty of the Government to prevent. This they cannot prevent unless they have a power to punish those who with wicked designs attempt to mislead the people. . . . For Gov-

[13] *Albany Centinel,* August 7, 1798.
[14] Fisher Ames, *Works,* II, 357.
[15] *Russell's Gazette,* June 7, 1798.

ernment willingly or weakly to suffer the people to be misled, is to commit treason against them. It is our duty to defend them against deception, and when they are rightly informed, there is no doubt but, in their turn, they will defend the Government."[16] In short, the press must be enlisted in defense of the government and the established order; and public opinion must be made to flow only in those channels prescribed by the government.

It is true that there was little cause for alarm in the state of public opinion in 1798, but in the newspapers, and in the speeches of Republican leaders, the Federalists found enough scurrility, defamation and disaffection to furnish convincing arguments for the necessity of passing a law to restrain the freedom of the press.

*   *   *

By April, 1798, Bache's *Aurora* had gained the distinction of being the leading Republican newspaper in the United States. To a great degree, it set the tone of the opposition press; Bache's caustic comments upon Federalist policies and his broadsides against Federalist leaders were reprinted throughout the country. As the Federalists unhappily admitted, Bache had devised "the most noted engine for spreading filth; and spreads it over the continent, like a blasting mildew, in the pestilential pages of the Aurora." No other Republican journalist could match his record: disseminating "the atheistical principles of Paine"; publishing forged letters of Washington; accusing the Secretary of State of taking a bribe; disclosing state secrets by publishing (with the aid of Senator Mason of Virginia) the text of Jay's treaty, before it had been ratified.[17] Had he deliberately set out to destroy the

---

[16] *Annals of Congress*, X, 409.

[17] *Massachusetts Mercury*, August 22, 1800. *Albany Centinel*, May 18, 1798. William Cobbett described Bache — the loudest "yelper of the Democratic

peace and happiness of the country, lamented the Federalists, he would not have acted differently. How one so young could be so bad puzzled them: "He has sounded the lowest depths of human depravity," it was said, "and now exhibits to the world an example of wickedness that no man of his years ever arrived at before."[18] Perhaps such precocity in the ways of iniquity came from early exposure to French revolutionary principles and from having in childhood sat on Old Ben's knee — an experience likely to warp the strongest morals. In any event, for the Federalists, Bache had come to epitomize "everything that is monstrous in human nature."

Bache's calumnies and falsehoods did not, Harrison Gray Otis lamented, lose their force upon the desert air. On the contrary, they affected even intelligent people — and so, asked the Federalist orator, "What can you expect from the gaping and promiscuous crowd who delight to swallow calumny? What from the sons of riot, and intemperance, and idleness, who cluster in the villages and dram-shops of your cities. What from the more innocent but equally deluded yeomanry, among whose sequestered retreats these poisons are scattered by officious missionaries who prowl through the country, disturbing the silence of the woods and tranquillity of the cottage."[19] In a word, what could be expected but revolution, rapine, murder and terror, in all the horrendous forms they had taken in Paris?

Bache's journalistic activities were played out against a background of rumors of Jacobin plots to burn American

kennel" — as "an ill-looking devil. His eyes never get above your knees"; in fact, to Cobbett, he looked like "a fellow who has been about a week or ten days on a gibbet."

[18] *Gazette of the United States*, June 5, 6, 1798. *Albany Centinel*, May 18, 1798. *American Annual Register*, 110. Philadelphia, 1797. Jonathan Trumbull to Jeremiah Wadsworth, December 8, 1795, June 6, 1796 (Trumbull MSS., Connecticut Historical Society).

[19] *Annals of Congress*, X, 956.

cities and cut the throats of all honest citizens. The day set for the massacre was thought to be the Fast Day proclaimed by President Adams in May, 1798. On this occasion, when the people were seeking divine guidance and praying for peace, about forty young men wearing French cockades were observed loitering about the President's house. When ordered to disperse, they answered that "it was a land of liberty, and they should go where they pleased." A fight immediately broke out between the wearers of the French cockade and the President's supporters. From a window in the President's house, Adams watched the melee; "Market street was as full as men could stand by one another, and even before my doors," he later wrote; "when some of my domestics, in frenzy, determined to sacrifice their lives in my defence." Adams himself was resolved to go down fighting; preparing for a last-ditch stand in the President's house he ordered chests of arms from the War Office to be brought down by lanes and alleys. Such desperate measures were not necessary: "the citizens flew to arms, and the villains were dispersed." Thousands of Philadelphians massed themselves about the President's house; a large troop of horses paraded in the vicinity; and squads of volunteers patrolled the streets all night. The metropolis remained quiet and the wearers of the French cockade took cover.[20]

This incident demonstrated to the Federalists that the citizens possessed "a noble solicitude for the safety of the President, and the support of the government." It also strengthened their fears that there was some foundation to these rumors of insurrection and massacre and that a serious effort probably would soon be made to overthrow the government by force. To the Federalists, the Fast Day fighting in Philadelphia was an attempt "by persons out of sight, to see what could be

[20] *New Hampshire Gazette*, May 22, 1798. *The Works of John Adams*, edited by Charles Francis Adams, X, 47–48. Boston, 1853.

done, how great a force they could raise, and how vigorously the friends of government would meet and oppose them." The Jacobins would be back — and next time in overwhelming force.[21]

At the very moment that the debate in Congress over the sedition bill was reaching its climax, Bache virtually ensured its passage by publishing in the *Aurora* Talleyrand's conciliatory letter to the American envoys. This was not the first time Bache had embarrassed the administration by printing a secret state paper; but the offense was particularly heinous in the case of Talleyrand's letter because when Bache broke the story the letter from the French minister had been received by the Secretary of State only the day previous and it had not yet been laid before the President. Moreover, Bache justified his publication of Talleyrand's letter by charging that the administration was deliberately withholding it in order to force the country into an unnecessary war with France.

Republicans insisted that by making public Talleyrand's letter, Bache had scored a journalistic scoop of inestimable service to the cause of peace.[22] "What miserable shifts are the aristocratic Journals reduced to," they asked, "when they accuse the Editor of the *Aurora* of treason, because he had address, industry, and interest enough, to procure an important State Paper before them? . . . Is it treason to tell our fellow citizens that the French will settle our differences with Mr. Gerry, without war — horrid, bloody war, useful to a few placemen and pensioners."[23] Blessed are the peacemakers, said the Republicans; and Bache, in their eyes, was among that goodly company — hence he was persecuted by the warmongers.

[21] *New Hampshire Gazette*, May 22, 1798.
[22] Benjamin Bache, *Truth Will Out*, 1–3. Philadelphia, 1798.
[23] *Time Piece*, June 22, 1798.

The most important question raised by Bache's action was: How did a journalist, certainly not in the confidence of the administration, procure a copy of Talleyrand's letter before even the President knew of its existence? Philadelphia was soon buzzing with this query, and the Federalists quickly came up with an answer; Talleyrand wished to give publicity to his letter before the answer of the United States envoys could counteract its effect, and Bache, in direct communication with Talleyrand, was playing the Directory's game of stirring up the people against their government. Bache's explanation that he had received the letter from a traveler recently arrived from France carried no conviction among Federalists: Bache was a French agent, and Talleyrand had "received his cue from the more abandoned traitors in our own country."[24] Indeed, it is doubtful whether the Federalists were more angry with Bache or with Talleyrand or which they regarded as the greater enemy of the country.

From the debates in Congress, it appeared that Benjamin Bache's *Aurora* was the most telling Federalist argument for the passage of a sedition law. Federalist members denounced him as a renegade American hired by the Directory to infect the minds of Americans with "the infernal French disease" preparatory to a French armed invasion of the United States. "Monsieur" or "Talleyrand" Bache was sounding the tocsin of insurrection and calling it freedom of the press.[25] Americans would be inviting disaster if they permitted Bache to continue his treasonable activities. "No Nation, no Government was ever so insulted" as Bache had insulted the United States; he was a menace to the national security, a challenge to the existence of stable government at a time when the very exist-

[24] *New Hampshire Gazette*, June 26, 1798. *Russell's Gazette*, June 28, 1798.
[25] *Aurora*, June 25, 1798. *Time Piece*, June 22, 1798. *Gazette of the United States*, July 19, 1798. *Truth Will Out*, 1–3. *Albany Centinel*, June 29, July 13, 1798.

ence of the Republic was in jeopardy.[26] In any other country than the United States, it was said, Bache would not be permitted to run around loose, much less edit a newspaper: he would long since have been behind bars, either of a prison or madhouse.[27]

Yet Bache was in truth no sans-culotte; he probably would have been properly horrified had he encountered a French Jacobin of the true Parisian breed. Although Bache fought the Federalists in the same spirit that French revolutionists exhibited toward adherents of the Ancient Regime and seemed to put them in the same category as the French nobility, he was actually a Jeffersonian Republican with a decided flair for billingsgate and defamation.

Nevertheless, so eager was the administration to bring Bache to justice that it did not wait for the passage of the Sedition Act before taking action. "The people can bear it no longer," it was said in justification of this haste, "and call loudly for something to be done."[28] On June 27, 1798, two weeks before the sedition bill was signed by the President, Bache was arrested on a warrant issued by Justice Richard Peters of the United States Supreme Court, charging him with having libeled the President and the government in a manner tending to excite sedition and opposition to the laws.

This indictment was made at common law without benefit of statutory authority. According to the generally accepted Federalist theory, this was entirely legal because the government of the United States enjoyed jurisdiction over all crimes and misdemeanors punishable at common law. Since seditious libels were offenses at common law, the government was

[26] *Albany Centinel*, June 29, 1798. *Gazette of the United States*, June 16, 20, 22, 1798.
[27] *Albany Centinel*, June 29, 1798. *Columbian Centinel*, July 7, 1798.
[28] *Columbian Centinel*, July 4, 1798.

within its powers in instigating action under its common law authority against Bache.

And yet Bache had no serious apprehension that the government's case would stand in court. Justice Samuel Chase of the United States Supreme Court had a few months before declared his opinion that, in the absence of express statute, the Federal government could not support such prosecutions. Although Justice Peters obviously did not agree with his colleague, Bache relied upon this difference of opinion in the Federal Bench to spare him from fine and imprisonment.[29]

The Federalists, too, were aware that in view of Justice Chase's opinion, Bache and other "Jacobins" might escape punishment if the Federal government trusted to its presumed authority under the common law. This prospect spurred efforts to secure the speedy passage of the Sedition Act. Since the powers of the Federal government to act in cases of libel and sedition were questioned, its authority must be affirmed by the enactment of a law expressly giving it such powers.[30]

The treason and sedition bill, introduced into the Senate by General James Lloyd of Maryland against considerable opposition, was intended to achieve this purpose.[31] More impor-

[29] Bache, *Truth Will Out*, Preface. *Bee*, July 4, 1798. The prosecution of Bache was not the first time that the Federal government had taken action against libel. In 1797, the Spanish minister to the United States complained that he and his King had been libeled in *Porcupine's Gazette*, published by William Cobbett. The Spanish minister was called "a fop, half don and half sans-culotte" and the King of Spain "a poor degraded creature" who had entered into an alliance with the murderers of the head of his family. Accordingly, the Federal government ordered prosecution against Cobbett begun in the Federal courts; and the State of Pennsylvania began a separate prosecution in its own courts. But the grand juries refused to return a true bill, and the case against Cobbett collapsed.

[30] The bill included a provision against seditious acts. This section was incorporated into the Sedition Act of July 14, without protest by the Republicans.

[31] The House of Representatives was working on a similar bill. Early in June, 1798, Jonathan Sewall of the House Committee for the Protection of

tantly, it was a virtual declaration of war against France: the people and government of France were branded as enemies of the United States; and any American citizen convicted of giving the enemy aid and comfort incurred the penalty of death. This section was struck out by the Senate; but it dealt more tenderly with the third and fourth sections of the bill, which declared any persons, aliens or citizens, who combined or conspired with intent to oppose or defeat the operation of any law of the United States or to discourage or prevent any person holding office under the United States "or shall threaten his person with any damage to his character, person or property, or attempt to procure any insurrection, plot or unlawful assembly or unlawful combination" should be fined not more than five thousand dollars and imprisoned for not more than five years. A like fine and imprisonment was to be imposed upon those found guilty of seditious printing, writing or speaking. Seditious libel, by General Lloyd's bill, was defined as an attempt to defame or weaken the government and laws of the United States by inflammatory declarations or expressions tending to induce a belief in the citizens that the government, in enacting a law, was induced to do so by motives hostile to the Constitution, or the liberties and happiness of the people; or tending to justify the hostile conduct of the French government toward the United States or attempts to defame the President and other Federal officials "by declarations directly or indirectly tending to criminate their motives in any official transaction."[32]

In this form, the measure passed the Senate on July 5, 1798, by a vote of eighteen to six.

It is apparent that, in writing his sedition bill, General

Commerce and the Defense of the Country, reported a bill "for the prevention and restraint of dangerous and seditious practices." *Russell's Gazette*, June 11, 1798. *Annals of Congress*, VIII, June 4, 1798.

[32] *Independent Advertiser*, July 5, 1798. *New Hampshire Gazette*, July 24, 1798.

Lloyd was deeply indebted to William Pitt, the British Prime Minister. Fighting for its life against revolutionary France, the British government had taken strong action against French sympathizers and radicals of all description. In 1794, Pitt declared that there were Englishmen so lost to patriotism and virtue that they were ready to "congregate into an enormous torrent of insurrection, which would seep away all the barriers of government, law and religion."[33] To crush this "dangerous domestic faction" were enacted the Law against Treasonable Practices, the Law against Seditious Meetings, and other statutes by which it became possible to speak and write as well as to act treason; and inciting hatred of the government became a high misdemeanor. Thanks to the English common law, the government was already armed against sedition; for that reason, Parliament passed no Sedition Act. But a system of registration effectively placed the press under censorship; foreign news of dangerous tendency could not appear in English newspapers. Democratic societies were broken up, newspaper editors imprisoned or sent to Botany Bay, and remarks dropped in conversation were made the basis of indictments. Muir, a Scottish lawyer, found guilty of recommending Tom Paine's *Rights of Man*, was sentenced to Botany Bay for fourteen years. A man who shouted "No George, no war," was imprisoned for five years at hard labor. Even agitation for extension of the franchise was held to be sedition; anything, in fact, that smacked of reform was under the ban.[34] The Habeas Corpus Act, suspended in 1794, was not restored until 1801. Thus the traditional liberties of Englishmen became casualties of the Great War with France; but, harsh

[33] Erich Eyck, *Pitt Versus Fox*, 317–318. London, 1950. Philip Anthony Brown, *The French Revolution in English History*, 123–125, 136. London, 1918.
[34] William Hunt, *The History of England from the Accession of George III to the Close of Pitt's First Administration*, 367; London, 1905. *The Parliamentary History of England*, edited by T. C. Hansard; XXX, 612. London, 1812.

as these measures were, they were not resented by the great
majority of the people to whom this was truly a war for survival.

It was this system that the Federalists proposed to copy,
although the United States was still technically at peace with
France. But in giving their votes to the sedition bill, many
Federalists had other objectives in mind than their ostensible
purpose of protecting the country from the machinations of
French agents: like the Naturalization Act, it was intended to
injure the Republican party by striking at freedom of the
press. If the Federalists seemed to be putting the cart before
the horse in enacting the Sedition Act before war with France
had been declared, it was perhaps because they were more
interested in whipping the horse than in making the cart go.

Gallatin warned his fellow Republicans that the Federalists
were following "step by step, all the measures adopted by the
British Government" and that they might not stop short of
outright war with France. The Federalists themselves, far
from denying their indebtedness to British example, cited it as
proof that the leaders in both countries had "vigor and sense
enough to discover the danger, and courage to resist it."
Because both nations were threatened by the same danger —
the "Terrible Republic" and a disloyal domestic faction —
the Federalists argued that methods which worked in Great
Britain would be equally effective in this country.[35]

But the sedition bill, as it came from the Senate, was too
strong for the taste of the moderate Federalists. In order to
secure its passage it was, therefore, found necessary to subject
it to considerable amendment. Harrison Gray Otis, Robert

---

[35] The Republicans denied that the British example could serve as a
proper guide for the United States: "A dictatorial power over the press, in
time of war, as in Great Britain, is a very different thing from the attempt
in the United States to restrain the freedom of publishing our opinions on
the conduct of our public agents." *Mirror of the Times*, August 9, 1800.

G. Harper and James A. Bayard, the Federalist floor leaders, took General Lloyd's sedition bill in hand and virtually rewrote the entire bill. In its revised form, the sedition bill required that malice and intent be proved; a clause was inserted permitting evidence of the truth of the alleged libel to be given as a justification; and the jury was accorded the right to determine the law as well as the fact. Harper proposed to amend by inserting a new section providing that "nothing shall be construed, or extended to abridge the freedom of speech, or of the press; or the right of the people peaceably to assemble, and to petition the government for a redress of grievances, as secured by the constitution of the United States" but he was persuaded to withdraw this motion. In the bill as passed by the House it was provided, however, that its duration should be limited to March 3, 1801.[36]

*　　*　　*

On the Fourth of July, 1798, James Madison toasted the Freedom of the Press — "The Scourge of the guilty and the support of virtuous Government"[37] — but it could hardly be doubted that time was running out for this particular freedom. Passed by the House of Representatives on July 11, the Sedition Act became law with the signature of President Adams on July 14, 1798.

The vote in the House of Representatives was forty-four to forty-one — a narrow margin of victory, made even less convincing by the highly sectional nature of the vote. Only two members from states south of the Potomac cast their votes in favor. Most of the support for the Sedition Act came

[36] The Alien Act was to expire on June 25, 1800. *Albany Centinel*, July 17, 1798. Henry Adams, *Gallatin*, 207–208.
[37] *Washington-Madison Papers*, edited by Stan V. Henkels, 153. Philadelphia, 1892.

from New England congressmen eager to smite down "the troublers of our Israel." Of all the measures of national defense proposed by the Federalists in this session of Congress, the Sedition Act was resisted on the floor of the House with the most bitterness, and it gave promise of encountering equally bitter resistance in the country as a whole.

Although the Republicans frequently asserted that Congress was under the control of the "Hamiltonian phalanx," this control was not evident at the time of the passage of the Alien and Sedition Acts. As unofficial adviser to Adams's cabinet — serving in the capacity of an elder statesman although hardly forty years old — Hamilton was the guiding spirit in the defensive measures undertaken against France in 1798. But at no time did he suggest legislation resembling the Alien and Sedition Acts. Hamilton wanted a nation of warriors, not a nation of witch-hunters. Long the advocate of "energetic" government, he reminded his Federalist friends in 1798 that there was a difference between energy and violence. Moreover, he had sought to create a united nation, but, as he warned, the Sedition Act carried the threat of civil war. "I hope sincerely the thing will not be hurried through," he wrote. "Let us not establish a tyranny." Although no Federalist had suffered more from the attacks of journalists, Hamilton had a much deeper regard for the freedom of the press than had many of his fellow conservatives.[38]

Nor were the Alien and Sedition Acts administration measures in the sense that they were recommended by the President — a circumstance which in later years enabled

[38] But when accused in *New York Argus* of having accepted money from the British minister to the United States for the purpose of buying the *Aurora* — thereby ridding the Federalists of this thorn in their flesh — he took action in the New York state courts. Frothingham, the foreman of the *Argus* printing shop, was accused by the State of New York with having libeled Hamilton. Frothingham was convicted and sentenced to fine and imprisonment. Hamilton, *Works* (Lodge), X, 295.

Adams to disclaim all responsibility.[39] For over ten years, Adams had been pilloried in the Republican press as a monarchist because of the opinions he had advanced in his *Defence of the Constitutions of the United States*. From this experience he had learned a lesson which, unfortunately, he seems to have forgotten when the Sedition Act came to him for signature. "The more they write and the more they lie about those volumes," he wrote in January, 1797, "the more good they do. They have caused them to be read in the last six months by more persons than would have read them in an hundred years. It is very difficult to stimulate people to read such writings, but faction has accomplished what curiosity would never have effected. I have been three times tried for those Books by the people of America and as often acquitted." His experience thus seemed to confirm the truth of the principle he had laid down at an earlier time: "A free press maintains the Majesty of the People."[40]

But, oppressed by growing fears of the power of "faction" in the United States and the "licentiousness" of the Republican press, Adams was in no temporizing mood in 1798. The X Y Z affair removed his last doubt that the United States must fight for its existence against revolutionary France: and by his speeches he helped whip the country into a state of excitement which prepared the way not only for the measures taken by Congress to strengthen the army and navy but for the Alien and Sedition Acts as well. It is significant that the President and Mrs. Adams were charmed by Secretary of State Pickering's defense of the Sedition Act.[41]

These laws were the work of the Federalist party, acting

[39] John Adams, *Works*, IX, 291. Henry Adams, *Gallatin*, 203–204.

[40] *Aurora*, July 3, 1800. C. A. Duniway, *The Development of Freedom of the Press in Massachusetts*, 143–144; New York, 1906.

[41] O. Pickering and C. W. Upham, *The Life of Timothy Pickering*, III, 479; Boston, 1867–73. Mrs. Adams, in April, 1798, in complaining that "Not a paper from Bache's press issues nor from Adams's Chronicle, but what might have been prosecuted as libels upon the President and Congress,"

out of fear of "Jacobinism," admiration of the stern repressive measures taken by the British government — and under the fervent conviction that the good of the country required the rooting out of all French sympathizers. They were passed by Congress against the advice of Alexander Hamilton, but with the approval of President Adams and with the warm benediction of Secretary of State Timothy Pickering. Of all the highly placed members of the administration, Pickering found the Alien and Sedition Acts most congenial to his temper and most suited to his purposes. In his hands, quite properly, was placed the chief responsibility for their enforcement.

Madison and other Republicans took comfort in the hope that the hot-headed proceedings in Philadelphia were "not well relished in the cool climate of Mount Vernon."[42] But actually, Washington approved all the Federalist measures, including the Alien and Sedition Acts, and broke his retirement to take command of the enlarged United States Army. His own experiences with newspaper "licentiousness" had seriously weakened his devotion to the ideal of liberty of the press. Moreover, with France, aided by its "Gallic faction" threatening war upon the United States, Washington was under no illusion that these were tolerating times; "all secret enemies to the peace and happiness of this Country should be unmasked," he said, "for it is better to meet *two* enemies in the *open* field of contest than *one* coward behind the scenes." As for Republican opposition to the Acts, he observed that "any thing else would have done; and something there will always be, for them to torture, and to disturb the public mind with their unfounded and ill favored forebodings."[43]

declared that "nothing will have an Effect until Congress pass a Sedition Bill, which I presume they will do before they rise." (Mitchell, *Abigail Adams*, 165.)

[42] *The Writings of James Madison*, edited by Gaillard Hunt, VI, 323. New York, 1901.

[43] Washington, *Writings*, XXXVI, 352; XXXVII, 32.

CHAPTER V

In the Sedition Act, the United States government was in effect declaring war upon the ideas of the French Revolution. To protect the American way — as interpreted by the Federalists — the people were to be safeguarded against the dangerous opinions spreading over the world. As the Federalists admitted, it was not only against sans-culottes that defenses must be erected; philosophers were an even greater menace to the established order. "Philosophers," said Robert G. Harper, "are the pioneers of revolution. They advance always in front, and prepare the way, by preaching infidelity, and weakening the respect of the people for ancient institutions. . . . They talk of the perfectibility of man, of the dignity of his nature; and entirely forgetting what he is, declaim perpetually about what he should be. Thus they allure and seduce the visionary, the superficial, and the unthinking part of mankind."[1] According to this theory, the only way to preserve the health of the body politic was to impose a quarantine upon ideas.

Moreover, the Sedition Act was an implied acknowledgment by the Federalists that force and coercion rather than reason and argument were to be the ultimate arbiters of political controversy in the United States. Differences of opinion were to be erased and the American mind was to be forced

[1] *Annals of Congress*, VIII, March 29, 1798 (Speech of R. G. Harper).

into an intellectual strait jacket fashioned by Harrison Gray
Otis and company.

Obviously, this necessitated an unprecedented extension
of the authority of the Federal government into the lives of
American citizens. Only the prospect of impending war with
France and the fear of a stab in the back by a domestic
"French faction" could have persuaded the American people
to consent to such an encroachment upon their liberties.
Finding fault with men in office was already an old American
custom; indeed, it had become an essential part of the pursuit
of happiness. "The independent citizens of the United States,"
it was said at this time, "will never be deterred from a manly
censure on their servants, when their measures are considered
as leading to an annihilation of their Liberties and a violation
of the Constitution."[2] Americans expected their public men
to stand up under a barrage of name-calling; public servants
must submit to the beratings of their masters and not talk back
to the sovereign people. These men, after all, were merely
hired by the people to administer the government, and it
was deemed an effective way of keeping them honest and
attentive to remind them frequently of their inferior status.

Under the Sedition Act, by expanding the definition of
seditious libel, an end might be put to all organized political
opposition, and the Republican party driven underground.
"What," asked Gallatin," is a false, scandalous, and malicious
libel?" — and the Federalists did not stay to answer but went
off in search of Jacobins. Presumably, therefore, the definition
would be left to the Federal judges, and from them the Republicans expected an extension of libel to include virtually all
expressions of opinion. There would be no room for political
dissent: men would be punished, Gallatin predicted, "for
avowing opinions, not criminal, but perhaps erroneous."

[2] Gibbs, *Memoirs*, II, 83. *Aurora*, August 2, 1799. *Independent Chronicle*,
July 5, 1798.

Even respectful remonstrances and humble petitions and, indeed, "any argument in defense of an opinion uttered on the subject, might be tortured into a seditious speech." Those who were so ill-advised as to write or say that Jefferson would make a better president than John Adams and who did not "on all occasions declare the most holy reverence for the *sacred person* of the chief magistrate" were likely to experience the full rigors of the law. Thus the Sedition Act seemed "calculated to put a stop to the people saying anything whatever about their government, or the men who execute the measures of it."[3]

By this means, the Federalists could ensure the perpetuation of their party's control of the national government. The Sedition Act might be used to procure congressional majorities for measures favored by the administration; in this political inquisition, no critic of the administration could hope to escape. Although Robert G. Harper declared that "it was not intended to restrict the freedom of speech on that floor, but the consequences of it out of doors," Southern Congressmen made a practice of writing public letters to their constituents regarding the proceedings of Congress — and such letters might very well serve as the basis of an indictment under the Sedition Act. "What an excellent harmonizer of parties the sedition bill will be," ironically remarked a Republican; "they must all sing to the same tune."[4]

In this new order, there were no real safeguards — other than the discretion of the judges and the President — to protect the democratic right of dissent. The Federalists had fashioned a weapon that could be used to strike at the very heart of American freedom. After this law had done its work, Americans might have no liberties worth speaking or writing about.

Thus a tempting prospect opened before the Federalists:

[3] *Aurora*, November 7, 1798. *Richmond Examiner*, December 24, 1798.
[4] *Time Piece*, July 13, 1798.

to enjoy indefinitely the sweets of office without the inconvenience of a vigilant, faultfinding opposition. No doubt this was for politicians the highest felicity, but, as the Republicans pointed out, it was not republicanism: "to do public mischief without hearing of it, is only the prerogative and felicity of tyrants."[5]

Instead of proscribing a whole political party, the Federalists ought to have labored to unite Americans in defense of the country, for, if France attempted a military invasion of the United States (as many Federalists predicted it would), the Republic would need every ounce of its strength to survive. Instead of enacting the Alien and Sedition Acts and employing them for political purposes, the administration ought to have proclaimed the principle that "We are all Federalists; we are all Republicans." "If they had the art to attempt a reconciliation," said a Republican journalist, "perhaps republican generosity had pardoned their follies and their crimes."[6] Instead, they declared in effect that there were only two parties in the United States, Federalists and Jacobins: the one the party of Americanism and constitutionalism, the other pledged to make the Republic a French province and to destroy the Constitution. Edmund Burke said that one could not indict a whole people; the Federalists implicitly indicted half a people — and thereby brought about their own downfall.

In contrast to the prevailing Federalist view, Jefferson believed that dissension, discord and parties were inevitable in a free society. The origin of parties he traced to the nature of man: "an association of men who will not quarrel with one another," he said, "is a thing which never yet existed, from

[5] *Abridgment of the Debates of Congress,* II, 307. *Greenleaf's New Daily Advertiser,* July 17, 1798. *Independent Chronicle,* July 5, 1798. Henry H. Simms, *Life of John Taylor,* 76. Richmond, 1932.

[6] *Time Piece,* July 25, 1798.

the greatest confederacy of nations, down to a town meeting or a vestry." Instead of deploring parties as an unmitigated evil, Jefferson held them to be an effective means of promoting the public interest: party division, he wrote in 1798, was perhaps necessary "to induce each to watch and relate to the people the proceedings of the other."[7] Certainly, this is what he and Madison sought to do in the Virginia and Kentucky Resolves of 1798–1799 in which the unconstitutionality of the Alien and Sedition Acts was affirmed. It is true, however, that after the triumph of the Republicans in 1800, parties began to seem much less desirable to Jefferson.

* * *

The American Revolution furnished the Federalists with numerous precedents for suppressing the freedom of the press. The test Acts — the Acts punishing crimes against the public safety, the Acts for apprehending internal enemies — had punished dissent, whether expressed in speech or writing, and had effectively silenced the Loyalist minority. If such measures had been found necessary in the struggle for American freedom, said Chief Justice Dana of Massachusetts, how much more cause did the Federalists have in 1798 to take action against the "foreign faction" which threatened the existence of the United States! The American Jacobins, he declared, were more venomous than the Loyalists: at least, the Loyalists were guilty only of adhering to a government to which they owed allegiance, whereas the Jacobins of '98 were "opposing a Government of their own legislative choice, and arraying themselves under the banner of a foreign nation to whom they had never owed allegiance."[8]

Moreover, the Federalists saw no injury to American lib-

[7] Collections of the Massachusetts Historical Society, Boston, Seventh Series, I, 62–63.

[8] *Columbian Centinel*, December 15, 1798.

erty in laying under restraint Republican newspapers — all they contained was misrepresentation, slander and falsehood, and they propagated "lies and liars, as a hot day breeds maggots or musketoes." Keeping such reading matter out of the hands of the people was held to be meritorious because it destroyed "the instruments of revolution, which shall exalt atheism and Anarchy on the ruins of public peace and established laws." That there were two sides to the questions that divided the Federalists and Republicans was not admitted: as Judge Addison said, "truth has but one side, and listening to error and falsehood is indeed a strange way to discover truth."[9]

By Federalist theory — although this had been denied by Justice Samuel Chase — the courts of the United States, by virtue of the common law, held jurisdiction over cases of libel and seditious writings.[10] The advantage of justifying the Sedition Act by reference to the common law was that it automatically resulted in a vast extension of Federal power. If offenses were cognizable by the Federal courts merely because they were offenses at common law, the Federal judiciary might confidently expect to supersede the state courts in almost every particular. Moreover, by this theory, the Sedition Act became a mere affirmation of a prior authority in the Federal government; it made no innovation upon "the immemorial laws and customs of the country" but, as Robert G. Harper said, was "introduced as a declaratory act — an act to render

[9] *Albany Centinel*, November 2, 1798. *Newark Gazette*, June 18, 1799. *Philadelphia Gazette*, April 7, 1799.

[10] Justice Chase's opinion was sustained by the Supreme Court in February, 1812, when it denied that the Federal government had common-law jurisdiction over seditious libel. This does not mean, however, that the Federal government has no constitutional power to enact a sedition law. This power can be inferred from the "necessary and proper" clause; moreover, attempts to interfere with the conduct of a war are not protected by the Bill of Rights. (Alfred H. Kelly and Winfred A. Harbison, *The American Constitution*, 198–199. New York, 1948.)

a preexisting fact notorious and so express, that 'he that runs may read it.' "[11]

At common law, in questions of seditious libel, the liberty of the press consisted solely in the government's "laying no *previous* restraints upon publications." This was not held to mean, however, that "the most groundless and malignant lies, striking at the safety and existence of the nation, should be countenanced. It never was intended that the right to side with the enemies of one's country in slandering and vilifying the government, and dividing the people should be protected under the name of the Liberty of the Press."[12] On the contrary, anyone who published seditious and libelous matter must take the consequences of his temerity — a heavy fine and a long term of imprisonment. Every man had an inalienable right to lay his sentiments before the public, but the government had the right to punish him if his writings were deemed improper, mischievous or illegal. Everyone, in short, was answerable to the public for the expression of his views; no one enjoyed without any consequences to himself freedom to publish what he pleased; all were under restraint — a restraint deemed essential to the existence of peaceful, orderly society.

Many of the states had enacted statutes affirming the common-law doctrine of seditious and malicious libels — and this in spite of the strict injunction written into their constitutions providing for the freedom of the press. Thus it is clear that the press was not left wholly beyond the reach of government; the states had never acted under the assumption that they were at the mercy of seditious and slanderous writing and speaking.[13] The Federal government, in the Sedition Act,

[11] *Aurora*, February 28, 1800. *Annals of Congress*, X, 417. *Columbian Centinel*, December 15, 1798.

[12] *Columbian Centinel*, July 7, 1798. Leon Whipple, *The Story of Civil Liberty in the United States*, 18–19. New York, 1927.

[13] *Columbian Centinel*, January 1, 1799.

did not propose to do more than the states had already done; nor did it alter in any way the time-honored common-law definition of sedition. Thus, said Harrison Gray Otis, if the Sedition Act "were a violation of the Constitution, each State had infringed upon its own constitution."[14]

If this premise were granted, the Federalists contended, it followed that the Sedition Act did not interfere with the true freedom of the press — it merely restrained its licentiousness, and, as Blackstone said, "to censure the licentiousness is to maintain the liberty of the press."[15] Negating the right to utter slander and to publish libel and sedition was not abridging freedom of speech and of the press, because this right had never belonged to them. And so, the Federalists asserted, nothing had been changed by the Sedition Law; there had been no diminution of liberty; and the authority of the Federal government had not been extended. Moreover, they assured the people that no honest man need fear this law: it was aimed solely at "those pests of society and disturbers of order and tranquillity," and was intended to impress on "turbulent and unprincipled men some respect for the government of our country"; "to keep in awe desperate and abandoned characters" who waged "eternal war against the sober minded part of the community."[16]

*　　*　　*

As proof of their tender concern for civil liberties, the Federalists invited comparison of the Sedition Act with the common law governing seditious libels. By common law,

[14] *Abridgment of the Debates of Congress*, II, 308. *Greenleaf's New Daily Advertiser*, August 8, 1798.

[15] *Albany Centinel*, January 1, 1799. *The Proceedings of the House of Representatives*, 6–7. Philadelphia, 1799.

[16] *Albany Centinel*, November 14, 1800. *New York Evening Post*, November 17, 1801. *Massachusetts Mercury*, June 15, 1798. Pickering and Upham, *Life of Pickering*, III, 475.

it was not necessary to prove intent to produce disaffection or insurrection: the mere fact of publication was sufficient to incriminate. The Sedition Act, on the other hand, required that wicked intention be proved; unless it were made evident to court and jury that the writing was done with malicious design, the action would not stand. Common law and the statute law of most of the states did not admit evidence of the truth of the alleged libel; as Blackstone said, "It is immaterial, with respect to evidence of a libel whether the matter of it be true or false; since the provocation, and the falsity, is the thing to be punished criminally."[17] In such a prosecution, the tendency of libels to create animosities and to disturb the public peace was all that the law considered. The Sedition Act, on the contrary, admitted truth as a defense. "It was no matter," said James A. Bayard, "how wicked the motive of an author might be, provided his publication was true, nor was it material how groundless the publication was provided the motive was honest. It was the combination of wickedness and falsehood alone that was punished." Common law held that the judge was to determine the law; the Sedition Act incorporated the principle contended for at the trial of John Peter Zenger (1734) — that the jury was to be judge of the law as well as of facts. Finally, common law left punishment to the discretion of the court; the Sedition Act set limits to the fine and imprisonment that could be imposed.[18]

Thus the Sedition Act was made to appear as "a wholesome and ameliorating interpreter of the common law," a triumph of justice, benignity and good will to man.[19] If it were admitted that the Federal courts enjoyed jurisdiction over offenses at common law, these courts had less power under the Sedition

[17] *Annals of Congress*, X, 917.
[18] *Ibid.*, 407. *Albany Centinel*, February 26, 1799.
[19] *Annals of Congress*, X, 917. *The Proceedings of the House of Representatives*, 6–7.

Act than they had hitherto possessed. As Oliver Ellsworth, Chief Justice of the United States Supreme Court, said, this act of Congress, by permitting "the truth of a libel to be given in justification, causes that, in some cases, not to be an offense which was one before." If this act should ever be repealed, Ellsworth remarked, the preamble of that repeal should read: "*Whereas* the increasing danger and depravity of the present time require that the law against seditious practices should be *restored to its former vigor.* . . ."[20]

*　*　*

Even granting that the Federal government had always possessed the right to punish seditious libels, the Sedition Act was nevertheless a new and unprecedented exercise of that right. Except in the case of Benjamin Bache, it had not hitherto claimed jurisdiction in this field. As a result, it was generally believed that in the United States the freedom of the press was virtually unlimited. James T. Callender, one of the victims of the Sedition Act, said in 1797 that it was "the happy privilege of an American, that he may prattle and print, in what way he pleases, and *without any one to make him afraid.*"[21] An English traveler observed at this time that "The grand bulwark of liberty in America is the freedom of the press — its latitude is infinite — it cannot be restrained — whether for or against the government, there is no power that can prevent the voice of truth from being heard. Conscious of that greatest of blessings, the American dares to bring every deliberation of his mind before the eye of his fellow citizens, without fear or dread. He can only be censured by the public opinion." It was commonly supposed that any harm that might arise from this extensive freedom of the press was incomparably

[20] Oliver Ellsworth to Pickering, December 12, 1798 (Pickering MSS., M.H.S.).

[21] James T. Callender, *The History of the United States for 1796*, 39. Philadelphia, 1797.

less than that which would be produced by restrictions. "If, therefore," concluded this English observer, "you wish to find out a country where you can write or speak whatever you please . . . you must come to America."[22]

Moreover, no people owed more to the freedom of the press than did Americans: to it in a large measure they might ascribe their freedom and independence. As Madison said, had the Sedition Act been in force during the American Revolution, the United States might have remained "miserable colonies, groaning under a foreign yoke."[23]

As might be expected, the Republicans stubbornly refused to acclaim the Sedition Act as a model of benevolence; they, after all, were to be its victims, and for that reason, perhaps, failed to see the patriotism, humanity and mercy that so profoundly impressed the Federalists. On the contrary, the Jeffersonians expected to contend with packed juries, biased judges and predetermined verdicts. The President directed the prosecution; the process was issued in his name; the Federal marshal who summoned the grand and petit juries was appointed by the President, as was the district attorney who conducted the prosecution. From this it could reasonably be supposed, said the Republicans, that the juries would be packed with "high toned Federalists" and that the culprit would be haled before "some toad-eating judge, some reptile who is gaping for a seat on the Federal bench, or an embassy to England." Judge and jury would combine to turn the screws remorselessly upon the hapless victim.[24]

As for the modification made in the common law of seditious libel by the Sedition Act, in permitting truth to be admitted

[22] *Emigration to America Candidly Considered*, 4–5. London, 1798.

[23] Madison, *Writings*, VI, 386–389.

[24] *Report of the Trial of Justice Chase*, Appendix, 59; Baltimore, 1805. *Greenleaf's New Daily Advertiser*, July 11, 1798. James T. Callender, *The Prospect Before Us*, I, 34; Philadelphia, 1800. St. George Tucker, *A Letter to a Member of Congress*, 31. Virginia, 1799.

as a defense, this occasioned no rejoicing among Republicans. It was observed that the charges brought against the President or Congress were seldom founded on a single fact capable of being proved by testimony as, for example, an accusation of stealing a horse might be proved. "All political writings," said George Nicholas of North Carolina, "contain not only facts, but also reasoning and deductions drawn from those facts." And so, a man might be convicted because he failed to prove the truth of that which was incapable of being proved.[25] This fear was borne out: in none of the Sedition trials of 1798–1800 was truth successfully presented as a defense.[26]

The requirement that malicious intent be proved was likewise no guarantee to Republicans of justice under the Sedition Act. As Madison said, "It is manifestly impossible to punish the intent to bring those who administer the Government into disrepute or contempt, without striking at the right of freely discussing public characters and measures."[27] And, as the trials under the Sedition Act revealed, intent was inferred from the alleged tendency of the libels to stir up sedition; the publication alone was usually sufficient to secure a conviction.

[25] St. George Nicholas, *A Letter to a Member of Congress*, 16.

[26] Of the provisions of the Sedition Act entrusting criminality to the jury and admitting truth as a defense, Professor Zechariah Chafee has said that "freedom of speech might exist without these two technical safeguards. The essential question is not, who is judge of the criminality of an utterance, but what is the test of its criminality. The common law and the Sedition Act of 1798 made the test blame of the government and its officials, because to bring them into disrepute tended to overthrow the state." (Zechariah Chafee, *Freedom of Speech*, 25. New York, 1920.)

[27] Madison, *Writings*, VI, 396.

CHAPTER VI

The Sedition Act was chiefly known by its victims: had it succeeded in apprehending dangerous revolutionaries, thereby averting the overthrow of the government of the United States, it no doubt would have earned the gratitude of the country and the admiration of historians. On the other hand, if the law merely terrorized a few journalists and other critics of the administration, it is apparent that it would deserve neither gratitude nor admiration. The Federalists had said that the country was full of Jacobins and other "disorganizers"; it now remained for them to prove it, and, with the aid of Sedition Act, to save the Republic from the dangers by which it was supposedly beset.

Whenever Republicans criticized the President or the policies of the administration party, the Federalists had visions of guillotines, massacres and rapine with themselves as the victims. That finding fault with the Chief Executive and the party in power was a manifestation of political feeling inevitable — and sometimes desirable — in a free society seems not to have been dreamed of in their philosophy. Rather than expose the President and other Federal officials to the seamy side of politics, the Federalists seemed bent upon making them sacrosanct. To them, Justice Chase's dictum carried the force of an eternal law: "If a man attempts to destroy the confidence of the people in their officers, their supreme magistrate, and their legislature, he effectually saps the foundation of the government."

In this struggle against Jacobinism, Timothy Pickering, the Secretary of State, emerged as the knight-errant of Federalism, the foremost champion of the forces of "law and order." At one time, Pickering, a native of Massachusetts, had been sympathetic toward the French Revolution and unfriendly to Great Britain; consequently, he brought to Federalism the zeal of a convert eager to atone for past errors by a whole-hearted espousal of the new faith. To his ardor in upholding the principles of Federalism and harrying radicals of every hue, Pickering joined an industry and perseverance that made him one of the hardest-working of our Secretaries of State. He spent long hours at his desk, like an attorney's clerk — toiling, without benefit of secretaries, over his correspondence.[1]

Yet, despite his diligence, patriotism and devotion to his ideals, Pickering was one of those austere, deadly serious, humorless individuals who are impenetrably armored in rectitude. Always he conceived of himself as standing by the dyke ready to save the country from being overwhelmed by the rising floodwaters. Never for a moment did he relax his vigilance nor doubt that the dangers he saw on every side actually existed. Grim and forbidding, irascible and unyielding, he nevertheless seemed to many of his contemporaries the man of the hour, eminently fitted for the work of saving the country from the peril of Jacobinism. There was good reason why he should be a hero to conservatives: of all the Federalist leaders, Pickering was the best equipped to play the role of a counterrevolutionary: he fought fanaticism with fanaticism and matched the revolutionists' single-minded devotion to the attainment of their objectives with a similar devotion to the preservation of the established order. As harsh

---

[1] *Annual Report of the American Historical Association . . . 1912*, 453. Washington, 1912.

and intolerant as the Jacobins themselves, Pickering had something of the personality and intellectual range of Robespierre. Certainly, he had no conception of a democracy which gained strength and respect by admitting the right of dissent.

Every morning Pickering methodically pored over the Republican newspapers in search of seditious material; although all this calumny and sedition to which he exposed himself did not have the slightest effect in weakening his principles, he did not trust his fellow Americans to behave so intelligently. From all parts of the country friends and admirers sent newspapers suspected of having violated the law. Of all United States District Attorneys, Pickering demanded close scrutiny of Republican newspapers published in their districts and prompt prosecution of offenses, even of seditious matter copied from another newspaper. In such cases, he asked that immediate notice be given the Department of State in order that prosecution might also be commenced against the original publisher. He also insisted upon prosecution of both author and publisher: except in extraordinary cases, "the publishers should not be encouraged to expect forgiveness on condition of rendering up the author."[2] The wonder is that amid all this activity, Pickering found time to conduct the foreign affairs of the United States.

Pickering set high store upon the activities of these amateur Jacobin-hunters; from the office of Secretary of State he halloed them on to more vigorous exertions in the chase. Had his wishes been fully carried out, every community would have had its watch and ward society to ferret out violations of the Sedition Act. In New England, indeed, he came close to achieving this state of affairs: a particularly careful scrutiny

---

[2] Pickering to William Rawle, July 5, July 24, 1799; to Thomas Nelson, August 14, 1799; to Richard Harison, August 17, 1799 (Pickering MSS., M.H.S.). Pickering to Richard Harison, June 22, 1798 (the National Archives).

was kept over the activities of Republicans and United Irish-men, but even schoolboys did not escape this omniscient vigilance. At Suffield, Connecticut, on the Fourth of July, "a couple of boys, having been trained for the purpose, delivered Orations fraught with sedition." Lest the public be thrown into a panic by this untoward event, it was announced that "measures are taking to bring these *speakers* to the bar of the courts." And, it was observed, "a few months' sober contem-plation in the solitude of a prison, will cure such young offenders."[3] Presumably they would emerge from prison con-firmed Federalists, singing hosannas to John Adams to whom their happy salvation from Republicanism was due.

This display of energy and zeal won for Pickering the title "the Scourge of Jacobinism." Republicans recognized him as their arch-enemy: more malignant, said the *Aurora*, than a beast of prey: "even the Tyger who crouches before he strikes his prey, will inscribe his [Pickering's] name . . . on some adamantine niche in his horrid den." Outdone in cunning and treachery, the "creatures of the night" were obliged to confess the superiority of Pickering's talents.[4] The Jeffersonians needed to look no further for a Federalist ogre.

By Pickering and his followers, it was held that since honest men who valued the national welfare would not cavil at the Sedition Act, it could be presumed that those who criticized it were no better than Jacobin fellow-travelers. It was laid down as a sound principle that "when a man is heard to inveigh against this law, set him down as a man who would submit to no restraint which is calculated for the peace of society. He deserves to be suspected." Thus, Jacobin sympa-thizers were to be known by their attitude toward the Sedi-tion Act; a critical or skeptical frame of mind was *prima facie* evidence of guilt. The Secretary of State looked darkly upon

---

[3] *Porcupine's Gazette*, July 31, 1799.
[4] *Aurora*, September 18, 1799.

such troublemakers: "Those who complain of legal provisions for punishing intentional defamation and lies, as bridling the liberty of speech and of the press," he said, "may, with equal propriety, complain against laws made for punishing assault and murder, as restraints upon the freedom of men's actions."[5]

In this murk of suspicion and distrust, every hue and shade of liberalism assumed a pinkish cast, and it became impossible for the Federalists to distinguish between a genuine, freedom-loving American democrat and a French Jacobin bent upon overturning religion, morality and the State. The Federalists seemed to be denying that there was a native liberal tradition in the United States; liberal ideas were exclusively of foreign importation. Every village Hampden in America became a potential Robespierre or Marat; conformity was the cardinal virtue and so many ideas were labeled subversive that it began to seem that there would be no ideas of any kind left.

* * *

Much to the gratification of the Federalist leaders, immediately after the passage of the Sedition Act several newspaper editors promised to conform to the law by excluding all seditious and libelous matter from their publications. The printer of the Portsmouth, New Hampshire, *Oracle*, who had been flirting with Jacobinism, now took his stand with the Federalists — an action which prompted the generous admission that "he deserves credit for his conversion, though late."[6] James Greenleaf, printer of the *Daily Advertiser*, declared that he would scrupulously regulate his conduct as a newspaperman by the Sedition Law until it was repealed. "We shall, however, continue to state facts," he remarked; and, under this saving clause he set about awakening the people to "the

[5] *Albany Centinel*, February 26, 1799. *Pennsylvania Gazette*, February 20, 1799. *Salem Gazette*, November 30, 1798. *Annals of Congress*, X, 932.

[6] *Porcupine's Gazette*, August 7, 1798.

awfulness of their situation."[7] The editors of the Savanna, Georgia, *Advertiser* asserted that "in future no word shall find a place in their paper which has a tendency to vilify the Government of the United States."[8] Charles Holt, editor of the New London, Connecticut, *Bee* — subsequently imprisoned as a violator of the Sedition Act — promised in 1798 to obey its provisions: "Our correspondents," he wrote, "are desired to observe that the Sedition Bill has passed, and temper their communications accordingly."[9]

The *Aurora*, it is true, made no pledges of future good behavior and continued to besmirch the reputations of prominent Federalists quite as though the Sedition Act had never been heard of; but even the *Aurora* seemed to be losing its ability to goad administration supporters into fury. Its most seditious and libelous flights were now said to "resemble merely the brayings of a cudgell'd Ass to the wind."[10] When Benjamin Bache asked if it would be construed as high treason to cure a Frenchman of the colic, the Federalists answered that this was a very pertinent question, "the party being at present violently convulsed with the *gripes*."[11]

Little evidence of this promised reformation appeared in the comments of Republican newspapers upon the Sedition Act and its maker, General Lloyd. On the contrary the editors, far from being cowed and repentant, were eager to outdo each other in denouncing all concerned in the Sedition Act. General Lloyd was castigated in terms calculated to remove from Federalists' minds any lingering doubts regarding the necessity of the act. Lloyd's name, said the New York *Time Piece*, "ought to possess that species of immortality by the ruffian who burnt the temple of Ephesian Diana. . . . Let the

---

[7] *Greenleaf's New Daily Advertiser*, July 13, 1798.
[8] *Albany Centinel*, October 2, 1798.   [9] *Bee*, July 18, 1798.
[10] *Gazette of the United States*, January 5, 1799. *Philadelphia Gazette*, July 6, 1799.
[11] *Albany Centinel*, July 6, 1798. *Philadelphia Gazette*, July 6, 1799.

name of this *Vandal*, this *Goth*, this *Ostrogoth*, this *Hun*, be a
bye word through the world; this sacriligist that attempts to
burst into the temple of liberty, and defile the altar of American independence." Good Republicans, said this newspaper,
ought to "hold him while living to the contempt and execra-
tion of mankind, and consign him, when dead, to the abhorrence of posterity."[12]

Yet the majority of American newspapers had nothing but
kind words for the Sedition Act and the restrictions it imposed
upon the freedom of the press. Blinded by their hatred of
Jacobins — "a set of parricidal miscreants who have been
preying on the vitals of the country" — they failed to see that
a blow was being struck at the roots of freedom and that they
might be its next victims. For the moment they rejoiced in
the discomfiture of Republican editors and obligingly pointed
out to the government violations of the Sedition Act committed by their fellow journalists. William Cobbett compiled
a list of Jacobin newspapers, singling out, among others, the
Baltimore *Intelligencer* — "a sink of abuse, scurrility and democracy," edited by "an imp of democracy, as wicked &
depraved as his master the Devil." The *Massachusetts Mercury*
denounced an article in the *Independent Chronicle* — a newspaper it described as "a nuisance more virulent than the
Yellow fever" — as a breach of the Sedition Act and urged
the United States District Attorney to take action. "The moderation of our rulers towards the French agents [the editors
of the *Independent Chronicle*]," said the *Massachusetts Mercury*,
"lurking in the bosom of our Country, has endangered the
safety of the Commonwealth. It is now time that the Dio-
clesian [*sic*] sword of justice, which has been long suspended
over the lives of these wretches, should extirpate them from
the society of their insulted fellow citizens."[13]

[12] *Independent Chronicle*, June 13, 1798.
[13] *Massachusetts Mercury*, September 25, 1798.

When they did not actually aid in enforcing the Alien and Sedition Acts, the Federalist newspapers saluted the laws as wise, just and necessary measures in no way inimical to the fundamental liberties of Americans. The Sedition Act, declared the *Albany Centinel*, "does not contain a single provision infractive of the principles of that liberty which renders a state of society enviable. . . . It only opposes a barrier to the introduction of that mad licentiousness which ever has proved, and ever will prove (if unchecked) as destructive of the just rights and highly prized privileges of the people as the weapons of a band of mercenaries under the controul of a tyrant." "There is no rigor at all," this same newspaper observed, "in punishing men who, in the teeth of a positive law will publish malicious and wilful lies, with design to injure and ruin the government of the people." In short, the Federalist press concluded, these were laws "on which at this critical moment the safety of our nation depends."[14]

By these newspapers, the arrest of Benjamin Bache was praised as a wise and statesmanlike act, essential to the peace and good order of the country. "Every friend to government and order," it was said, "every supporter of the genuine freedom of the press, and every advocate for decency, and respect for the laws, rejoice that government has at length interposed."[15] When Bache raised the question whether there was more liberty and safety in Constantinople or in Philadelphia, the Federalists answered that if the government of the United States was not strong enough to protect them against such incendiaries as Benjamin Bache, they would feel safer in Constantinople.[16]

When, following his indictment for seditious libel at com-

---

[14] *Albany Centinel*, July 20, 1798, February 26, 1799. *Salem Gazette*, December 25, 1798.

[15] *Columbian Centinel*, July 4, 1898. *Albany Centinel*, July 10, 1798.

[16] *Columbian Centinel*, July 7, 1798.

mon law, Benjamin Bache appeared before Judge Richard Peters of the United States Supreme Court, he brought with him, as counsels, Moses Levy and Alexander James Dallas, two radical Philadelphia lawyers. His bail was given by Thomas Leiper, a tobacconist, and Israel Israel, a Quaker merchant and tavernkeeper. Among the friends who attended Bache on this occasion were a hatter and a tailor; not one of them could pretend to the name of gentleman. "What a concatenation of characters!" exclaimed a Federalist newspaper. ". . . A farrago of pure, genuine jacobinical democratical spirits." Let Bache and his friends triumph and the dregs of society would rule over the rich, the wise and the good.[17]

Bache was bound over to appear before the Circuit Court, scheduled to meet in Philadelphia late in 1798. In the meantime, he was free to edit the *Aurora* — which meant, as Lightning Rod, Junior, construed the word, flaying the Federalists as monarchists who had sold themselves to the British, "parricides of American liberty" and monsters of corruption and depravity.

That the Federalists would wait for the slow and cumbersome machinery of the law to extinguish the lightning bolt that descended upon their heads every morning in the shape of the *Aurora* seemed improbable to Republicans. The assassination of its editor would be a much quicker method of freeing themselves from this incubus. Bache himself feared the worst at the hands of Federalist bravos: "It might," he said, "be a gratification to some, that I should have my throat cut, without the trouble of going through the tedious and uncertain forms of law."[18] Therefore, when Bache and John Fenno, Junior, son of the editor of the *Gazette of the United States*, became involved in a fight in Philadelphia, it was sup-

[17] *Massachusetts Mercury*, July 6, 1798.
[18] John Wood, *Administration of John Adams*, 126–127. Benjamin Bache, *Truth Will Out*, Preface. *Aurora*, May 4, 1798.

posed that young Fenno was acting under orders to put the
Republican editor out of the way. Actually, however, Fenno
was seeking to avenge his father, whom Bache had denounced
as a British agent. In the encounter, which took place in the
streets of the City of Brotherly Love, Fenno bit Bache's
knuckle; but Bache pinned his antagonist to the wall and
beat him over the head with a cane until spectators succeeded
in separating the two gladiators.[19]

As this incident indicates, there were more direct and expe-
ditious methods of vindicating one's reputation than resorting
to the Sedition Act or to the state courts. A duel — or even an
assault in the streets — often afforded balm for outraged
honor. Judge Livermore of New Hampshire was attacked
by one Lee, an offended political opponent: the Judge
"closed in with Lee, and seizing him by the throat, would
have strangled the Jacobin in a few minutes, had not the
spectators then interfered, and took him off." Shortly after,
the "Boxing Judge" beat Lee soundly with a stick until "some
meddlers disarmed the judge, after he had given ten or twelve
blows; but then he at Lee with his fist and gave him an *Irish
coat of arms.*" Finally Lee escaped in a hack with his coat half
torn off.[20] In New York, James Jones accused Brockholst
Livingston of slandering him in the newspapers. When the
two men met on the Battery, Livingston admitted having
written the newspaper article in question: "I suppose," said
Livingston, "I must give you such satisfaction as one gentleman expects from another." "That you shall," answered
Jones, "and I'll begin by taking it now." With which he
attempted to take Livingston by the nose. This unseemly
scuffling was broken up and a duel arranged between the two

[19] Fenno proved "by separate trials against the wall that Bache's skull
was even more impenetrable than could have been supposed." *Porcupine's
Gazette*, August 9, 1798. *Aurora*, August 10, 1798.
[20] *Porcupine's Gazette*, September 13, 1799.

men. Jones ought to have been content with pulling Livingston's nose, for in the duel that followed he was shot dead.[21]

*   *   *

Before Bache could be brought to trial or disposed of otherwise, he died of yellow fever in the great epidemic of 1798.
Federalists hardly tried to conceal their joy at Bache's abrupt
leave-taking; in Boston, they were said to have displayed
"indecent joy," one gentleman even wearing a "broad grin"
as he congratulated his friends upon the happy event.[22] It
seemed appropriate that Bache had been carried off by
yellow fever: "Bile is the basis of the yellow fever," it was
pointed out. "Is it surprising that it killed Bache?"[23] The
event was regarded by some pious Federalists as particularly
felicitous evidence that God was just and avenging. That He
had struck down one of the most troublesome Jacobins in the
country and had at the same time spared Alexander Hamilton
showed where His political sympathies lay. But when John
Fenno, Senior, died in the same epidemic that killed Bache,
there was some reason to fear that the Deity was taking a
neutral position between Federalists and Republicans.

The only result of the government's prosecution of Bache
was to increase the influence and the circulation of the *Aurora*
— which, over a course of years, had steadily lost money.
But after Bache had been stigmatized as an enemy of his
country, "Freemen indignant at the excesses of arbitrary
power, in an attempt to abridge a right solemnly guaranteed
by the Constitution, roused from their inactivity" even to the
extent of paying their back subscriptions to the *Aurora*.
Carried on by Bache's widow, aided by William Duane,

[21] *Greenleaf's New Daily Advertiser*, May 12, 1798. Matthew L. Davis to
Gallatin, May 9, 1798 (Gallatin MSS., New York Historical Society).
[22] *Independent Chronicle*, September 17, 1798.
[23] *Annual Report of the American Historical Association . . . 1912*, 489.

the *Aurora* continued to set the tone for the Republican press. Here, said the Federalists, "was the heart, the seat of life. From thence the blood has flowed to the extremities by a sure and rapid circulation, and the life and strength of the party have thus been supported and nourished."[24]

* * *

In the summer of 1798, Pickering exulted that at last an Irishman had been delivered into his hands. And what an Irishman! Americans would now have an opportunity of seeing a genuine wild Irishman in captivity — a spectacle which, Pickering supposed, would open the eyes of all citizens to the necessity of the Alien and Sedition Laws.

John Daly Burk had been born in Ireland; he had been expelled from Trinity College, Dublin, on charges of deism and republicanism; and he had fled Ireland as a fugitive from justice.[25] Pickering needed to know no more; any further probing into Burk's past would, he believed, merely add [cor-roborative detail to this picture of total depravity.

Being expelled from college was not yet a criminal offense in the United States; but Pickering looked with the lofty contempt of a Harvard A.B. upon those who had failed to make the grade. In the case of an Irishman, particularly, it was conclusive evidence of a turbulent disposition; for it was notorious that the Irish university spawned vast numbers of rebels and "French philosophers" — in unhappy contrast to Harvard and Yale, where order, sobriety and soundly conservative political opinions were the order of the day.[26]

[24] *Independent Chronicle*, September 13, September 17, 1798.

[25] In attempting to rescue a man being led by soldiers to execution, Burk precipitated a riot. When a warrant was issued for his arrest, he escaped aboard ship in woman's clothing given him by a friend, Miss Daly. In gratitude, Burk took her name, becoming John Daly Burk.

[26] John Quincy Adams, attending Harvard at the beginning of the Federal Period, regarded himself as the only true republican in the institution.

Burk first settled in Boston, where he established a newspaper, the *Polar Star*, and wrote a play, *Bunker Hill*, in which he gave free rein to his passion for liberty, his hatred of Great Britain (what brought the house down was the spectacle of "two or three Englishmen rolling down the hill") and his weakness for turgid rhetoric. With this box-office success behind him, Burk moved to New York and bought an interest in the *Time Piece*, a newspaper which became under his editorship one of the most uncompromising Republican sheets in the country.

It could not be expected that Burk would stand by idly while France and the United States prepared to engage in war — a war which he considered "the most *melancholy, ruinous and disastrous* to Liberty, and the *subject of demoniac satisfaction to Kings.*" John Adams he held responsible for this impending conflict; if France and the United States came to blows it was because the President had set his heart upon making himself king and his country an ally of Great Britain against the French Republic. "When the champion of the well born [John Adams], with his serene court, is seen pronouncing anathemas against France," exclaimed Burk, "it shall be my fault . . . if to tears and execrations be not added *derision* and *contempt*."[27]

Stronger emotions than derision and contempt were likely to be aroused against the President by Burk's charge that in order to prevent a reconciliation between the United States and France he had deliberately falsified Elbridge Gerry's letter to his home government. To the Federalists, this was the last straw. "How long, ye slumbering Americans, will you

---

After a brief flirtation with radicalism, Yale was restored to political and religious orthodoxy by President Dwight. So complete was this triumph that Yale men prayed for the regeneration of Harvard.

[27] *Salem Gazette*, July 17, 1798.

be thus insulted," exclaimed the *Salem Gazette*. "Awake from your deathlike stupor, and spurn from the society of free men this wretch, who is composed of that stuff of which the spy, the assassin and the sycophant are formed."[28] Secretary Pickering needed no prodding: he immediately instructed Richard Harison, the United States District Attorney for New York, to examine carefully the offensive article in the *Time Piece* and to comb the back numbers for writings of a similar "seditious tendency."[29]

At this critical moment, knowing that he was under the scrutiny of the government, Burk tossed discretion to the winds. Upon hearing a report that the French had landed in Ireland, he was alleged to have exclaimed that if the news proved true, "he would not give a damn for the federal villains in this country — that he believed the French would come here, and he wished to God they would, when every scoundrel in favor of this Government would be put to the guillotine — that it had been hinted that he would be sent away as an alien — but then he would let them know who was the stronger party." [30]

These words — together with the articles he had written in the *Time Piece* — gave the government its case against Burk. Although he indignantly denied having uttered the words imputed to him — he was, he said, being condemned on the testimony of a "contemptible informer" — no time was lost in putting the law into execution against him. In July, 1798, he was arrested by two United States marshals, on a warrant signed by President Adams, charging him with seditious libel. At the same time, his partner, James Smith, was also taken into custody, but the charge against him was

---

[28] *Salem Gazette*, July 19, 1798.
[29] Pickering to Richard Harison, July 7, 1798 (Pickering MSS.).
[30] Richard Harison to Pickering, July 13, 1798 (Pickering MSS.).

only for a libel. Each gave bail for two thousand dollars and trial was set for the next meeting of the Federal Circuit Court in October.[31]

For a time, Pickering was in doubt whether Burk ought to be arraigned under the Alien Act or the Sedition Act. "If Burk be an Alien," he wrote, "no man is a fitter object for the operation of the Alien Act"; on the other hand, if he had become a citizen, the Sedition Act was the indicated remedy. But even after it had been ascertained that Burk was an alien, Pickering's doubts persisted: deportation seemed slight punishment for a man guilty of treasonable speech and of editing "a vehicle of the most profuse & attrocious slander of the Government, & a ready instrument of sedition."[32] The Secretary finally decided to punish Burk under the Sedition Act, and then deport him as an undesirable alien.

Burk protested that it was hard that he, the author of a patriotic drama who had spent almost two years "in composing a Poem of the Epic kind, on the American Revolution, in which he has at least attempted to ennoble and immortalize that glorious event," should be prosecuted by the government of the United States.[33] But, thanks to the Sedition Act, patriotism had become a dangerous creed in the United States: if it deviated from the official brand it might easily be construed into sedition. It is ironical that those who proclaimed themselves patriots were among the first to come under suspicion of harboring subversive ideas.

Burk's bail was put up by Aaron Burr, who, said Burk, filled for him "the place of a friend and father." This friendship had been of some standing: Burk had dedicated *Bunker Hill*

[31] *Time Piece*, July 6, July 9, 1798. John Wood, *Administration of John Adams*, 162–163.
[32] Pickering to Richard Harison, July 7, 1798 (Pickering MSS.).
[33] *Time Piece*, July 30, 1798.

to Burr, and Burr had acted as his patron in New York.[34] If it is true, as Burr's enemies said, that he kept his eyes fixed on the political main chance, his support of Burk becomes a shrewd play for the Irish vote in New York — a vote which contributed materially to the Republican victory of 1800.

Before Burk's trial took place, Burr suggested to the administration that the editor be let off on condition that he leave the country immediately. To this the President and Secretary of State agreed, although Pickering insisted that precautions be taken to ensure that Burk actually left the United States and did not return. Indeed, the Secretary went so far as to declare that Burk's presence could not be tolerated upon the North American Continent: "such a turbulent mischievous person ought not remain on this side the Atlantic," Pickering warned; "if he does, he will find his way to Florida or Louisiana & finally perhaps to some part of the United States, where the arm of the Government may not easily reach him." District Attorney Richard Harison was instructed to keep the prosecution in readiness to be resumed at any moment if Burk violated the terms of amnesty.[35]

Burk's deportation could have been ensured had the United States government been willing to pay the cost of his outward passage, but here Pickering's New England parsimony stood in the way: the culprit, he declared, must pay his own way. Although eager to return to aid Ireland in achieving emancipation, Burk found good reasons for remaining in the United States: want of money, the prospect that the British would seize him on the high seas, and the haven offered by Virginia to fugitives from the Alien and Sedition Acts, persuaded him

[34] Edward Wyatt IV, "John Daly Burk," in *Southern Sketches* (No. 7), 9. Charlottesville, Va, 1936.
[35] Pickering to Richard Harison, January 1, 1799; to Winthrop Sargeant, May 22, 1799; to Edward Dunscomb, May 22, 1799 (Pickering MSS.).

to take his chances, however uncertain they might be, with Timothy Pickering.

And so, instead of returning to Europe, Burk went to Virginia, where he took an assumed name and disappeared in the obscurity of the academic profession. Apparently he could not have chosen a better way of hiding out: as "principal of a college" he was completely lost to sight by Pickering and his agents. It was Burk's extracurricular activities which again brought him into public view. An irate husband, suspecting that Burk was becoming intimate with his wife, threatened to kill the dashing Irishman. According to Burk, it was much ado about nothing; and the husband, finally seeing it in this light, publicly apologized to Burk for his unworthy suspicions. In a Virginia tavern a few years later, however, Burk affronted a Frenchman by damning the French as "a pack of rascals." Challenged to a duel, Burk fell at the first fire. Thus, in 1808, Burk stood on solid Federalist ground and died for expressing an opinion that in 1798 would have endeared him to those who then damned him as a Jacobin.

*　　*　　*

In the debate over the Sedition Act, one of the arguments advanced by the Federalists was that it would affect only Jacobins and other public enemies; no loyal American need fear its rigors. "People had been told," said Senator Mason of Virginia, "that the Sedition Bill was harmless, was only meant as a bug-bear, and would not be enforced."[36] No hint was dropped that members of Congress might come under its provisions, yet the first victim of the act was Matthew Lyon, a member of Congress from Vermont.

A few months before the passage of the Sedition Act, Lyon had won notoriety by spitting in the face of a fellow congressman, Roger Griswold of Connecticut. Because Griswold was

[36] *Greenleaf's New Daily Advertiser*, December 4, 1798.

one of the Federalist leaders of the House, Lyon brought upon himself the wrath of the entire Federalist party and thereby virtually ensured his indictment under the Sedition Act.

It is true that Lyon committed "the disgraceful, the nasty, the worse than brutal action of spitting in a brother member's face" under some provocation. Lyon was talking to a group of friends about the peculiar backwardness of the people of Connecticut that prevented them from seeing the light of Jeffersonianism. This he ascribed to the malign influence of the politicians of that state; "they were pursuing their own private views, without regarding the interests of the people; they were seeking offices, which they were willing to accept, whether yielding $9,000 or $1,000." Lyon boasted that "if he should go into Connecticut . . . although the people of that State were not fond of revolutionary principles, he could effect a revolution, and turn out the present Representatives." Griswold of Connecticut, standing nearby, heard as much as he could endure, then broke in with an uncomplimentary reference to Lyon's military record in the War of Independence.[37] Touched in an exceedingly sore spot, Lyon retaliated by spitting in Griswold's face.[38]

Shortly after, finding Lyon in his seat in Congress, Griswold attacked the Vermonter with a cane. Before Lyon could rise from his seat, he had received several severe blows; but, seizing a pair of fire tongs, he fought back valiantly. Finally, the two men grappled on the floor, Griswold uppermost. "The members in the House, who till now seemed to look on with amazement at the scene, without an attempt to put an end to it, got round the parties and separated them" but not before Lyon had aimed a final blow with his fire tongs at

[37] General Horatio Gates had "damned him for a coward." Tried by court martial for refusal to obey orders, he was sentenced to be cashiered. He was later exonerated and reinstated.

[38] *Abridgment of the Debates of Congress*, II, 209–210.

Griswold's head which the latter luckily succeeded in dodging. Both men were game to the end: Griswold had to be pulled off Lyon by the legs; and Lyon "expressed disapprobation at being parted, and said, as he was rising, I wish I had been left alone awhile." In fact, as soon as they were outside the House they made for each other "and but for the doorkeeper and some gentlemen present, would have renewed the combat."[39]

Priding themselves as they did upon their gentlemanly regard for the proprieties, the Federalists demanded that Griswold and "the Spitting Lyon" of Vermont be expelled from Congress. In their eyes, Lyon was not fit company for gentlemen: a "disgraceful," "nasty," "worse than brutal," "spitting animal," Lyon seemed to exhibit the most objectionable traits of a Jacobin.[40] And to his depravities could be added the fact that he was an Irishman. "I feel grieved," said a Bostonian, "that the saliva of an Irishman should be left upon the face of an American & He, a New England-man."[41]

In thus looking down their noses at Lyon, the Federalists did him an injustice. Although he had been born in Ireland and had come to America as a poverty-stricken young man, he had succeeded in accumulating a considerable amount of property and had married the daughter of Governor Chittenden of Vermont. Among his own people, Lyon was a man of parts; if his politics seemed a bit on the rough-and-tumble side, this merely endeared him the more to his constituents.

Congress spent fourteen days debating the motion that Lyon be expelled from Congress. The Vermonter was accused of having brought indelible disgrace upon Congress; already people in Philadelphia were saying to each other: "There is

[39] *Abridgment of the Debates of Congress,* II, 209–210.
[40] *Porcupine's Gazette,* January 10, 1799.
[41] Morison, *Otis,* I, 87.

nothing to do in Congress today — there's no fighting going on." Dana of Massachusetts declared that he did not envy "any gentleman the pleasure they would have in the company of the gentleman from Vermont; if they chose to associate with such a *kennel of filth*, let them do so. . . . He himself would put him away, as citizens removed *impurities* and *filth* from their docks and wharves."[42] Harrison Gray Otis confessed that Lyon's conduct had so deeply affected him that "he thought of it by day, and when upon his pillow he had not forgotten it." The conclusion at which Otis arrived after profound meditation was that even in the history of the Indian savages there was no "instance of outrage so monstrous and so abominable. It was conduct which could not be suffered in a brothel or in a den of robbers." Lyon, it was suggested, ought to be sent on a diplomatic mission to Kamchatka, where he would be at home "among the furred tribes."[43]

Despite their best oratorical efforts, the Federalists failed to rid themselves of Lyon. When the vote was taken, fifty-two were for expelling Lyon, with forty-four opposed; and, as a two-thirds majority was required for expulsion, Lyon retained his seat. The Federalists did not take this defeat lightly: one congressman who resigned in order to accept an appointment as United States district attorney rejoiced that he was no longer "a partaker of the dishonor which attached to the body of which Lyon is a member, and who could retain him, when a fair opportunity offered of getting rid of the animal."[44]

Although "the Spitting Lyon of Vermont" spat no more upon Federalist gentlemen, he was frequently on his feet in

[42] *Annals of Congress*, VII, February 23, 1798: Speech of Francis Dana.
[43] Morison, *Otis*, I, 78.
[44] Griswold likewise retained his seat. In the debate that raged over Lyon, Griswold had been almost forgotten. John H. Morison, *Jeremiah Smith*, 135.

Congress denouncing the Federalists as warmongers and opposing every measure of national defense. As a result, by the time Congress adjourned in the summer of 1798, Lyon was one of the most hated "Jacobins" in the United States. In the theater, the English comedian Villiers portrayed before an highly appreciative audience, "the beast of Vermont, in ragged Mat, the Democrat."[45] All the "friends of order" turned out to speed Lyon on his way to Vermont; at Trenton and Brunswick he was hissed and hooted and serenaded with the "Rogue's march." But this, the Federalists promised themselves, was nothing compared "to the honors which await him, on his return to his own district in Vermont."[46]

Actually, what awaited him was a martyr's crown. Many years before, Lyon had quarreled with Nathaniel Chipman: when Chipman in the Vermont legislature called Lyon "an ignorant Irish puppy," the hotheaded Irishman had seized his tormentor by the hair, whereupon Chipman's friends had intervened and carried Lyon across the room and dumped him in a corner, "laughing very merrily at the scene."[47] In the following years, Chipman became one of the most powerful Federalist politicians in Vermont. His vindictiveness towards his enemies became a byword; and he never forgot the hair-pulling he had received at Lyon's hands.

Probably at the instigation of Nathaniel Chipman, to whom the Sedition Act seemed an effective means of striking at his political enemies, Lyon was indicted under the Sedition Act soon after his return to Vermont. The first section of the indictment dealt with an article Lyon had published in the *Vermont Journal* containing much the same strictures upon the administration that he had already made in his speeches in Congress. Under President Adams, he declared, "every

[45] *Salem Gazette*, June 12, 1798.
[46] *Gazette of the United States*, July 23, 1798.
[47] *Annals of Congress*, VII, 999–1000.

consideration of the public welfare was swallowed up in a continual grasp for power, in an unbounded thirst for ridiculous pomp, foolish adulation, and selfish avarice." Honest men were turned out of office, religion was prostituted for party purposes and the people crushed beneath enormous taxes.[48] In the second place, Lyon was accused of having published a letter from Joel Barlow, a onetime Connecticut Wit turned revolutionist. Barlow, safe in France, urged Congress to commit President Adams to the madhouse; but instead of adopting this excellent advice, he lamented, the Senate treated Adams "with more servility than ever George III experienced from either House of Parliament."[49]

Lyon was so little frightened by this impending effort to throttle the freedom of the press that he established a magazine: *Lyon's Republican Magazine* — "The Scourge of Aristocracy and Repository of Important Political Truths." This semimonthly publication, which first appeared in October, 1798, was dedicated to preparing Americans to resist the Federalists' efforts to establish "a state of abject slavery and degrading subjection to a set of assuming High Mightinesses in our own country, and a close connection with a corrupt, tottering monarchy in Europe." Federalists found consolation in the story that as a stage driver was distributing Lyon's magazine "the horses disdaining to prostitute their services, set off at full speed, and left the precious cargo in the mud." But not all horses could be relied upon to shy at the sight of seditious literature, and *Lyon's Republican Magazine* seemed likely to reach at least a part of its subscribers.

In these publications, as well as in his speeches, Lyon believed that he was conducting a loyal opposition. On several occasions, he pledged his support to the President

---

[48] Lyon was also accused of having read this letter in public at Middletown, Vermont, thereby raising a tumult.

[49] *Greenleaf's New Daily Advertiser*, November 12, 1798.

once he was persuaded that Adams was sincerely seeking the happiness of the people.[50] Moreover, although the offending article in the *Vermont Journal* was published after July 15, it had been written before the passage of the Sedition Act.

At his trial at Rutland, Vermont — a strongly Federalist community — Lyon based his defense upon the unconstitutionality of the Sedition Act.[51] But this plea was given short shrift by the court, and the jury brought in a verdict of guilty as charged. In imposing sentence, Justice Paterson of the United States Supreme Court dwelt upon the leniency of the Sedition Act which did not permit judges to inflict as heavy punishment as did the common law. After this exordium, he sentenced Lyon to four months' imprisonment and imposed a fine of one thousand dollars. Lyon had not expected imprisonment; a small fine and a reprimand from the court was the most he had anticipated — for, as a member of Congress, he did not suppose he would be treated like a common criminal.[52] However, this was a day of surprises for Lyon: he was not permitted to go to his lodgings to procure his papers or given time to arrange his affairs; instead, he was hurried off to jail at Vergennes with an armed escort and thrown into a cell used for "horse-thieves, counterfeiters, runaway negroes and felons." His cell had "a necessary in one corner, which," it was said, "affords a stench about equal to the Philadelphia docks in the month of August."[53] Baited by his Federalist jailor and denied heat in his cell,

[50] *Greenleaf's New Daily Advertiser*, November 12, 1798.

[51] In the course of his trial, Lyon asked Justice Paterson whether he had not frequently "dined with the President, and observed his ridiculous pomp and parade." Justice Paterson answered that "he had never seen any pomp or parade; he had seen, on the contrary, a great deal of plainness and simplicity."

[52] *Greenleaf's New Daily Advertiser*, November 12, 1798.

[53] J. F. McLaughlin, *Matthew Lyon: The Hampden of Congress*, 352. New York, 1900. *Greenleaf's New Daily Advertiser*, February 21, 1799.

Lyon's plight was called to the attention of the entire country; if he should be frozen to death in prison, the Republicans swore that it would be a plain case of murder.[54]

With hardly an exception, the Federalists were jubilant over Lyon's conviction: with "the vile career of the beast of the mountain" apparently ended in disgrace, they could breathe easier. Lyon's downfall was hailed as a momentous victory over the licentiousness of the press — the triumph of law over "that unbridled spirit of opposition to government, which is at the present moment, the heaviest curse of America."[55]

That they had made a martyr to the freedom of the press seems not to have entered the minds of the champions of law and order. Perhaps for this reason, Lyon was permitted to write freely in jail and his letters and articles were published in most of the Republican newspapers in the country. Contrary to Federalist opinion, Lyon's most formidable weapon was not a pair of fire tongs but his pen.[56] Given a forum from which to appeal to the sense of justice of the American people and to berate his Federalist persecutors, Lyon ceased to appear as a barroom brawler but as a Republican hero suffering unmerited punishment for having upheld freedom against its enemies. As he wrote on this occasion: "Every one who is not in favor of this mad war is branded with the epithet of Opposers of Government, Disorganizers, Jacobins, &c. . . . It is quite a new kind of jargon to call a Representative of the People an Opposer of the Government, because he does not, as a Legislator, advocate and acquiesce in every proposition that comes from the Executive."[57]

---

[54] *Greenleaf's New Daily Advertiser,* November 13, 1798.

[55] *Salem Gazette,* October 23, 1798. *Gazette of the United States,* November 2, 1798.

[56] *Albany Centinel,* January 16, 1799.

[57] McLaughlin, *Lyon,* 334.

In imprisoning a member of Congress for speaking and writing against the policies of the administration, the Federalists seemed to have rung up the curtain on what might be called "The Tragedy of American Freedom." Although the Federalists professed to be following the example of Great Britain, nothing like this had yet occurred under William Pitt: Fox and Sheridan were still free to oppose the government. Moreover, it was all too evident that Lyon was punished not so much for his allegedly seditious writings as for having incurred the enmity of the political boss of Vermont, for the mortal affront he had given the Federalists by spitting in Griswold's face and for opposing administration policies.

When Lyon first returned to Vermont in June, 1798, his political prospects had been anything but bright; thanks, however, to the free publicity given him by the administration, he more than recovered his former popularity. In the election held in September, 1798, Lyon, as a candidate for re-election to Congress, came within twenty-six votes of winning a majority in a field of six contestants. At the election runoff held in December, 1798, although Lyon was serving sentence under a Federal offense, he was re-elected by a margin of two thousand votes over his nearest opponent.

Meanwhile, Lyon's friends were engaged in collecting money to pay his fine. By means of a lottery, the Vermont Republicans raised sufficient money for this purpose, and, at the same time, Senator Stevens T. Mason of Virginia succeeded in gathering a like sum from Lyon's admirers in the Old Dominion. As a result of these fund-raising activities, a race ensued between the Vermonters and the Virginians for the honor of releasing the Republican martyr from jail.

Carrying Lyon's "ransom" in his saddlebags, Senator Mason set out from Virginia, arriving at his destination just as the Vermonters were on the point of paying the fine. Rather than send Senator Mason back to Virginia with full saddlebags, the Vermonters magnanimously consented to permit him to pay half of Lyon's fine.[58]

Even after his release from prison, Lyon was not safe in Vermont: the local authorities were prepared to arrest him on charges of having violated the state laws on libel and seditious writings. Therefore, when Lyon stepped out of jail, he was careful to announce that he was a member of Congress on his way to take his seat; and under this immunity he set off for Philadelphia. Vermont had become too hot for Lyon: two other bills for sedition were "cut and dry" awaiting his return to that state; and it was for this reason that in 1799 he went to Kentucky — a proper abode, said a Federalist, for one of his stamp, for Kentucky promised to become "the rendezvous of the seditious." "It is to be wished," remarked a Federalist newspaper, "his abettors, supporters, and all who think and act like him, may soon follow."[59]

Lyon took his seat in Congress, where, it was observed, he looked "remarkably well for a gentleman just out of jail." To celebrate the event, the Philadelphia Republicans held a frolic where, a Federalist journalist reported, they got "as drunk as democrats generally do whenever they get a chance to swig."[60]

[58] The *Salem Gazette* suggested that Senator Mason be investigated as a suspicious person. The Reverend Mr. Ogden, who carried a petition from Vermont to President Adams requesting Lyon's release and who remained in Philadelphia to collect money for Lyon's fine, was arrested in Connecticut on his return trip to Vermont on the orders of Oliver Wolcott, Secretary of the Treasury. The Republicans declared that this was done to prevent the money reaching Lyon and thereby to keep him out of Congress, but Wolcott insisted that it was a private affair dating back to a loan he had made Ogden several years before and which had never been repaid. Ogden was a noted radical, author of a pamphlet, *Views of the New England Illuminati*. *Salem Gazette*, November 23, 1798. *Richmond Examiner*, June 21, 1798. *Aurora*, September 1, 1800.

[59] *Albany Centinel*, March 26, May 17, 1799. *Springer's Weekly Oracle*, April 29, 1799.

[60] *Porcupine's Gazette*, February 21, 1799.

CHAPTER VII

In executing the state and Federal laws against libels and seditious writings, the zeal of the Federalists sometimes outran their discretion. Perhaps a district attorney, itching to put himself in the public eye as an enemy of Jacobinism, or a politician, eager to brand his enemies as enemies of the Constitution, or some timid soul who saw "Jacobins" behind every bush — any of these might be the starting point for an attack upon an innocent individual. Whatever their motives, the Federalists gave too little attention to the danger that they would make themselves and the law ridiculous by prosecuting a harmless critic of the administration and thereby raising to consequence the obscure and unimportant followers of Thomas Jefferson.

Before 1798, Luther Baldwin was hardly known outside the New Jersey village where he lived; yet he became — not, however, through any efforts of his own — one of the best known victims of the "Reign of Terror." From tavern lounger to Republican hero was quite a leap, but Baldwin, aided by the Federalists, covered the distance nicely and landed on his feet.

In the newspapers, Baldwin was reported to have expressed the wish that President Adams were dead. Actually, although he no doubt would have heartily approved this sentiment, Baldwin did not put his thought in exactly those words. In June, 1798, on his way to New England, Adams had passed through New Jersey, where the citizens greeted him with cheers and the firing of cannon. Luther Baldwin, whose political opinions had made him obnoxious to Federalists, took this occasion to get drunk — a patriotic act, under the circumstances, it might be supposed. In this mellow mood, Baldwin was addressed by a drinking companion: "There goes the President, he exclaimed, — and they are firing at his ——. Luther, a little merry, replies that he did not care if they fired thro' his ——. Then exclaims the dram seller, that is sedition."[1]

Baldwin was certainly guilty of making a bad joke, but perhaps his condition might be regarded as an extenuating circumstance. Nevertheless, the Federalists saw nothing humorous in this incident; instead, Baldwin was charged with sedition. The indictment was drawn at common law and the prosecution was conducted by the State of New Jersey. Apparently it made little difference to the Federalist newspapers by whom Baldwin was prosecuted: the important thing was to put this Jacobin behind bars. To wish for the President's demise was sedition of the blackest dye: this was "the wish, the longing desire of the French faction. The PRESIDENT is almost the only bar in the way to general pillage."[2] Baldwin's case inspired a New Jersey Federalist editor to make the following observations upon the nature of sedition: "Sedition," he wrote, "by all the laws of God and man, is, and ever has been criminal; and when it is not, the laws will be crimes and magistrates will swing. Behold France! Government after government has been laid down, till the sword cut off the tip of Sedition's tongue."[3] The moral, apparently, was that Luther Baldwin might become another

---

[1] *Greenleaf's New Daily Advertiser*, October 15, 1709.

[2] *Newark Gazette* and *New Jersey Advertiser*, April 16, 1799. *Country Porcupine*, November 8 and 9, 1798.

[3] *Guardian: Or New Brunswick Advertiser*, November 13, 1798.

Robespierre or Marat unless his career was cut short by a heavy fine and long imprisonment.

These expectations were not wholly realized: Baldwin was sentenced to pay a fine of one hundred dollars but he was not imprisoned. The Republicans, moreover, had the last word: "Can the most enthusiastic Federalists or Tories," they asked, "suppose that those who are opposed to them would feel any gratification in firing at such a disgusting target as the —— of John Adams?"[4]

*   *   *

Nothing might seem more innocent than the raising of a maypole or liberty pole; but few sights more unnerved Federalists and set them screaming for the enforcement of the Sedition Act. Surmounted by a Liberty Cap or the tricolor, these liberty poles were regarded as "emblems of sedition" — the dread symbols of bloody revolution.[5] When it was reported that "a gang of insurgents" had erected a liberty pole and burned the Alien and Sedition Acts, the *Albany Centinel* declared that "the erection of these poles, and the burning of the laws, is an open insult to the government" that called for the execution of the Sedition Act.[6]

When, therefore, a liberty pole was raised in Dedham, Massachusetts, with a placard attached reading: "No stamp act, no sedition and no alien acts, no land tax. Downfall to the tyrants of America: peace and retirement to the President: long live the Vice President and the minority," the local Federalists marched in a body upon the pole, resolved to cut it down. But the Republicans massed to defend it, a fracas

[4] *Greenleaf's New Daily Advertiser*, October 15, 1798.
[5] *Newark Gazette*, September 4, 1798. *Porcupine's Gazette*, February 2, 1799. *Salem Gazette*, September 18, 1798. *Bee*, February 20, 1798. Charles Warren, *Jacobin and Junto*, 103–104. Cambridge, Massachusetts, 1931.
[6] *Albany Centinel*, December 14, 1798.

ensued, the Federalists were victorious and toppled the "emblem of sedition."

It was soon ascertained that this liberty pole, together with the placard, was the work of David Brown, a Connecticut Yankee who after serving in the Revolutionary army had shipped aboard a merchant ship to see the world. A tour of the European ports seems merely to have whetted his taste for travel: after his return to the United States, he knocked about the country, drifting from job to job, but always seeing new places. By 1798, he claimed to have been in "nineteen different states and kingdoms in Europe, and in nearly all the United States." In particular, he set himself up as an authority on the state of public opinion in Massachusetts, having, he said, visited over eighty towns and conversed with hundreds of people on public affairs.[7]

Brown's reading and observation of the ways of the world led him to the conclusion that all government was a conspiracy of the few against the many, a device to squeeze wealth out of farmers and artisans for the benefit of the rich and powerful. "The occupation of government is to plunder and steal," he declared; and the Federalist government of the United States seemed to him to be doing a superlative job. It imposed taxes in order to enrich speculators; the majority of Congress had been corrupted, and now sought to make the people tenants; it was, in short, "a tyrannic association of about five hundred out of five millions" to engross "all the benefits of public property and live upon the ruins of the rest of the community."[8]

Despite the fact that one of his manuscripts was entitled *A Dagger for Tyrants*, Brown confined his subversive [activities to cracker-barrel discussions of politics, harangues to village crowds assembled on militia training days and parlor readings

[7] *Salem Gazette*, March 29, 1799.
[8] *Massachusetts Mercury*, June 21, 1799. *Porcupine's Gazette*, June 21, 1799.

from his political pamphlets to small groups of followers. Wherever he went, he found admirers: some susceptible citizens would "caress him — carry him to their houses — give him meat and drink" — always exercising care, however, said the Federalists, to put the family valuables under lock and key.[9]

Brown might have lived and died a harmless radical: the crackerbox philosopher who delighted to scandalize the good folk with his unorthodox opinions. In the eyes of the good folk themselves, he was considered only "a vagabond ragged fellow," a ne'er-do-well who was against the government because he was a failure and an outcast. Better to have left him in this obscurity than to give him, as the Federalists did, the stature of a public menace, a "Priest of Sedition," and virtually a one-man revolution.

Dedham was the home of Fisher Ames, one of the stanchest pillars of the established order. It was also the home of Fisher's brother, Dr. Nathaniel Ames, as ardently Republican in his political convictions as his brother was Federalist. Raising a liberty pole in the vicinity of Fisher Ames was to invite disaster, for Ames had declared repeatedly that to lay the devil of sedition "government must appear *in terrorem*," and he was not likely to overlook a Jacobin lurking in his own back yard. Moreover, the Massachusetts Federalists hoped that Brown would prove to be a mere agent of high-placed Republicans; who could say that the trail would not lead to Vice President Jefferson himself? "Though Brown is not wanting in understanding," it was observed, "there is reason to believe many of the materials [of his pamphlets] were furnished by abler heads than his." Few Federalists doubted that Jefferson was capable of employing Brown as a "missionary of sedition."[10]

[9] *Massachusetts Mercury*, April 2, 1799.
[10] Fisher Ames, *Works*, I, 247. *Salem Gazette*, March 29, 1799. *Massachusetts Mercury*, June 21, 1799.

An attempt was made to arrest Brown in Dedham, but he had set out on his travels before a warrant could be procured. But the law soon caught up with him; he was arrested on a charge of sedition and held in the Salem jail for want of four thousand dollars' bail.[11]

Brown came up for trial in June, 1799, in the Circuit Court of the United States, Samuel Chase presiding. Brown could hardly regard as a stroke of good fortune the presence of Mr. Justice Chase on the bench; no culprit, and above all, no Jacobin, was ever known to rejoice when he looked upon that black-robed dispenser of Federal justice. Hardly second to Pickering himself, Chase was imbued with a high sense of mission against "Jacobinism" and all its works. Hated and feared by the Republicans, he was, by them, compared with Judge Jeffreys of "Bloody Assize" fame; if the United States had twenty such judges as Chase, said the *Aurora*, liberty would be totally destroyed. For once, perhaps, the *Aurora* was guilty of an understatement: single-handed Chase made himself a terror to those whose political opinions ran counter to his own.[12]

It was Chase's firmly held conviction that in a republic, above all other forms of government, the press must be restrained. "There is nothing we should more dread than the licentiousness of the press," he declared. "A republican government can only be destroyed by the introduction of luxury and the licentiousness of the press. The latter is the more slow, but more sure and certain means of bringing about the destruction of the government." In the United States, the learned judge had no doubt havoc seemed likely to be wrought by the press rather than by luxury: already it had gone far towards impairing the confidence of the people in their government. The next step, by his dismal prognosis,

[11] *Federal Galaxy*, April 9, 1799.
[12] *Aurora*, June 10, 1798; July 7, July 22, August 4, 1800.

was the advent of demagogues in whose hands the liberties of the people perished.[13]

Although a justice of the Supreme Court, Chase's reputation was in some respects not greatly superior to that of some of the culprits he condemned. As a member of Congress during the War of Independence, he had profiteered by taking advantage of secret information concerning the commercial policies of Congress. As a result, he had been dropped from the Maryland delegation, but he made his political comeback as an uncompromising Federalist.

When first arraigned, Brown had pleaded not guilty, but, confronted by Mr. Justice Chase, he changed his plea to guilty. By this unexpected move, he seemed to have deprived Chase of his opportunity to expose in all its horrible detail the iniquity of the so-called "missionary of Sedition." But the judge adroitly got round this difficulty: the court, it was said, "thought proper to examine the witnesses present, that the degree of his guilt might be duly ascertained."[14]

After the testimony of the prosecution witnesses had been put on the record and Brown's own writings had been held up for the abhorrence of the spectators, Brown was brought to the bar for sentencing. He seemed to be in a repentant frame of mind: he expressed regret for having uttered his political sentiments, "more especially," he added, "in the way and the manner I did utter them." Seeing that the prisoner was beginning to weaken, Chase attempted to press home his advantage: Would Brown give the court the names of those who had aided him in any way, together with a list of subscribers to his writings? But Brown refused to name any of his associates, saying simply: "I shall lose all my friends." This contumacy angered Chase and perhaps accounts for the extraordinarily severe sentence he imposed.[15]

[13] *Columbian Centinel*, May 3, 1800.   [14] *Aurora*, September 20, 1800.
[15] *Porcupine's Gazette*, June 21, 1799.

The punishment meted out to Brown was the heaviest inflicted on any offender under the Sedition Act. He was fined four hundred and fifty dollars and sentenced to eighteen months in jail. Such was the effect upon Mr. Justice Chase of a plea of guilty, a public confession of wrongdoing and repentance and a promise of future good behavior.[16]

But the Federalists had not done with the pole-raising at Dedham; a crime of such enormity, it is said, called for the punishment of all involved. Fortunately for the Dedham Republicans, a wholesale proscription was found impracticable; all that could be done was to make an example of some prominent member of that party whose part in the affair could be established beyond any doubt.

The Federalists found their man in the person of Benjamin Fairbanks, a wealthy farmer and Dedham selectman, a good patriot in the Revolution but now a Jeffersonian. Fairbanks was indicted with Brown as an accessory in erecting the liberty pole, and his bail, like that of Brown, was set for four thousand dollars. Finding himself in a tight spot, Fairbanks tried to enlist legal aid from the administration party; no less a Federalist big-wig than Fisher Ames was invited to become his counsel. Ames, of course, firmly declined the honor; it would be most unbecoming, he said, for him to come forward as the advocate of a Jacobin. However, he did consent to appear as *amicus curiae* in order to mitigate Fairbanks's punishment. The accused, he said, being "a man of rather a warm and irritable temperament, too credulous and too sudden in his impressions," was easily misled; and apparently this weakness had caused him to become involved within the Jacobin net.

Like Brown, Fairbanks pleaded guilty and threw himself upon the mercy of the court. Admitting that he was present

[16] Brown actually remained in prison for two years because he could not pay his fine. He was not released until pardoned by President Jefferson, John Adams having refused his plea for clemency.

at the raising of the Dedham liberty pole, he said that he was then unaware "how hainous an offence it was." Now, fully sensible of its enormity, he pledged his future good behavior: "I am in heart a friend to my country, its liberty and independence," he exclaimed, "and will try to conduct so in the future, as to show my sincerity and duty as a good citizen, in support of the laws and government of the United States." Mr. Justice Chase was impressed by Fairbanks's sincerity: it was evident, he declared, that reformation had already been accomplished, and since the government of the United States was "mild, dispassionate, and considerate, and exercised its authority with humane and liberal views," Fairbanks was let off with a sentence of imprisonment for six hours and a fine of five dollars, together with costs.[17]

* * *

Even in Boston, the very citadel of "high toned" Federalism, there was a Republican newspaper, the *Independent Chronicle*, edited by Thomas Adams. This sheet — called "a libel on government, on truth and decency" — was a stench to the Federalists: "the lenient laws of our country," they said, "have too long withheld the lash of Justice from its conductor." Yet the *Independent Chronicle* showed no signs of collapsing of its own accord; Thomas Adams was not intimidated by threats — "Take care, citizen Adams, should you escape the halter of government" — or by social ostracism. On the grounds that "A JACOBIN, at this day, should not be admitted into the company of honest men," he was expelled from the New Relief Fire Society in Cambridge, the members voting not to have intercourse "with any man whose time and opportunities have universally been exerted to disgrace the American character."[18] But what could be done with a man who did

[17] *Massachusetts Mercury*, June 11, 21, 1799.
[18] *Russell's Gazette*, July 16, 1798.

not take hints — what, indeed, but call upon the law to take this incorrigible "Jacobin" in hand?

Action was begun in 1798 against Adams under the Sedition Act; and, while this indictment was pending, he was indicted by the State of Massachusetts for libeling the members of the Massachusetts General Court. In the *Independent Chronicle*, Adams charged that the members of the Massachusetts legislature who had rejected the Virginia and Kentucky Resolves on the ground that the state legislatures did not have the right of deciding upon the constitutionality of Acts of the Federal government were guilty of violating their oaths of office. Action on this alleged libel was brought under the common law; but this did not make matters easier for Adams: the common law as enforced in the courts of Massachusetts left nothing to be desired by the most zealous Federalists.

With two indictments — one in the Federal, the other in the state courts — hanging over his head, Thomas Adams's chances of escaping punishment seemed very slim indeed. Yet some Federalists, given to taking a gloomy view, doubted if Adams would ever be brought to justice: "a Jacobin," they said, "had rather hang himself to defraud honest Jack Ketch of his fee, than not cheat at all." And, as they predicted, Adams succeeded in cheating the hangman: before he could be brought to trial he died of a lingering illness. The deathbed scene, as reported in the Republican newspapers, befitted a martyr: to his last breath "he ever expressed his warm attachment to the liberties of his country."[19]

The death of Thomas Adams did not wholly balk the course of justice: his brother, Abijah, had also been indicted in the prosecution begun by the State of Massachusetts and upon him the full force of the law was turned. True, Abijah Adams had served only as bookkeeper; but as he sometimes sorted out the papers, he was legally held to be a principal.

[19] *Independent Chronicle*, March 7, May 16, 1799.

The trial of Abijah Adams, Francis Dana, Justice of the Massachusetts Supreme Court, presiding, opened in April, 1799. The attorneys for the defense maintained that the common-law principles of libel were repugnant to the Massachusetts Constitution; the prosecution insisted that the common law was perfectly consistent with the Massachusetts Constitution and with every principle of American liberty. Mr. Justice Dana, in his charge to the jury, declared that the doctrine advanced by the defense was even more hostile to public tranquillity than was the libel in question; and he concluded his charge with a political sermon against Jacobinism and all its works, even going so far as to say that the members of the Massachusetts legislature who had supported the Virginia and Kentucky Resolves were "worse than infidels" and abettors of "a traiterous enterprise to the government of this country."[20]

The jury promptly returned a verdict of guilty of publishing a libel — no surprise to Republicans, who had long since written off Massachusetts as the state "more degenerated from the love and the very principles of true liberty than any one of the Union." Abijah Adams was fined and sentenced to a month in jail, thus falling a victim, said the Republicans, to "that indefinite code of usurpation and barbarism, the English common law."[21]

After the conviction of Abijah Adams, the *Independent Chronicle* was sold to James White, a Boston bookseller. The Federalists rejoiced to see "an arm of Jacobinism wither and in its stead the rise of a powerful auxiliary to the cause of truth" — it being supposed that White was a stanch Federalist. The new editor proved, however, a disappointment to the champions of order; under his direction, the *Independent*

[20] *Springer's Weekly Oracle*, May 18, 1799. *Independent Chronicle*, March 7, 1799.

[21] *Aurora*, March 15, August 4, 1800.

Chronicle was open to both sides and only those articles were encouraged which contained reasoning instead of invective and answered "the objections made against the Administration, rather than exclaim *Jacobin* and Traitor."[22]

* * *

As Federalists pictured it, the majesty of the law was being invoked in the Sedition Act to defend the country against internal enemies. But more often, in actuality, partisan passions and personal resentments inspired the prosecutions under this act. The Sedition Act became a favorite way of striking down an enemy; the national welfare was merely a transparent covering for the settlement of personal grudges and party animosities.

Meanwhile, in the Vermont hills, reverberations of the trial and conviction of Matthew Lyon were still heard, even though that Republican hero had abandoned the Green Mountains for the greener pastures of Kentucky. Nathaniel Chipman, the Federalist boss, aspired to sew up the state completely, and since the Republican newspapers blocked his plan, he decided to eliminate or terrorize them into silence.

Anthony Haswell was a native-born New Englander of unimpeachable loyalty to his country, a Republican politician and editor, and postmaster general of the state of Vermont. He had made his newspaper, the *Vermont Gazette*, a Republican beacon in Federalist New England. As such, it attracted unwelcome attention from administration sympathizers: Haswell was threatened with tarring and feathering, having his house pulled down, and prosecution under the Sedition Act.[23]

To the crime of being a Republican editor — and it was so regarded in "high toned" Federalist quarters — Haswell added the equally heinous offence of having championed

[22] *Independent Chronicle*, May 13, 1799.
[23] John Spargo, *Anthony Haswell*, 55. Rutland, Vermont, 1925.

Matthew Lyon even after the Vermont congressman had been convicted of violating the Sedition Act. Haswell opened the *Vermont Gazette* to advertisements signed by Lyon's friends urging the purchase of tickets in a lottery to raise money for Lyon's "ransom." When Lyon was released from jail, Haswell headed the welcoming committee at Bennington and made a speech congratulating the newly re-elected member of Congress upon his escape "from the fangs of merciless power." "Let us," exclaimed Haswell on this occasion, ". . . follow the enthusiastic glow of liberty, till the minions of despotism tremble at the frown of democratic virtue, till the gewgaws of royalty cease to glitter in the western world, or levees and drawing-rooms cease to monkify the fashions of our rising nation."[24]

In October, 1799, almost a year after these events, Haswell was arrested by two deputy marshals on a writ containing no particulars of the charge of which he was accused: the writ merely directed that he be bought before the Circuit Court of the United States, then sitting in Vermont, "then and there to answer unto an indictment pending in said Court which was presented against him by the Grand Jurors." When Haswell asked the deputies what this meant, he received no answer. They were as silent, he later remarked, "as the midnight police officer of the French Bastille, the secret messengers of the Spanish Inquisition, or the mutes of the Turkish bowstring for strangling."[25]

The irony of this situation — as Haswell soon learned — was that he was indicted for publishing an advertisement signed by two subscribers to the fund being raised to pay Lyon's fine, and for reprinting in the *Vermont Gazette* the article on British influence that appeared originally in the *Aurora*. If this action were to serve as a precedent, American journalists

[24] Spargo, *Anthony Haswell*, 55. [25] *Ibid.*, 59.

were put under the necessity of scrutinizing for subversive implications all the advertisements they admitted into their newspapers. The advertisement in question was not seditious within the usual meaning of that word: it painted a harrowing picture of Lyon's suffering in jail "holden by the oppressive hand of usurped power, in a loathsome prison, deprived of almost the light of heaven, and suffering all the indignities which can be heaped on him by a hard hearted savage [his jailor, Fitch] who has to the disgrace of Federalism, been elevated to a station, where he can satiate his barbarism on the misery of his victims." Actually, this description was not greatly overdrawn, and the publicity given to Lyon's plight resulted in a marked improvement in his prison conditions.[26]

Haswell's trial took place in April, 1800, at Windsor, Vermont, a stanchly Federalist town. He was allowed a few days' continuance by Justice Paterson in order to procure the attendance of Secretary of War McHenry to prove that members of the administration had made a practice of appointing former Tories to office. McHenry refused to attend the trial; but, in any event, the outcome was a foregone conclusion. Justice Paterson's charge to the jury gave the defendant the benefit of no doubt; the jury promptly returned a verdict of guilty; and Haswell was fined two hundred dollars and sentenced to two months in jail. Truly a heavy punishment for having taken the wrong side in Vermont politics!

Yet when Haswell was released from Bennington jail on July 9, 1800, his sufferings did not perhaps seem in vain. As the prison doors swung open, the band struck up "Yankee Doodle," cannon roared, and the crowd cheered. The Fourth of July celebration had been postponed until Haswell was freed.

[26] Spargo, *Anthony Haswell*, 76, 86.

Even in darkest Connecticut, the Republicans rejoiced, a few rays of Jeffersonian light had begun in 1798 to penetrate the Federalist gloom. The land of steady habits boasted some of the most conservative newspapers in the country, and there were only a handful of opposition papers to contest their control of the public mind. Republican newspapers were held up in Connecticut post offices; stage drivers were reported to be bribed to destroy copies; on one occasion, a young army lieutenant, finding a Republican newspaper on a stage, tore it to bits, and the onlookers applauded his patriotism.[27] The *Hartford Courant*, professing to have discovered the list of subscribers of a rival Republican newspaper, threatened to publish their names, quite as though they were guilty of some crime.[28] A man who visited a Republican editor in jail was himself accused of being a Jacobin. An officeholder was said to have been deprived of his commission as justice of the peace for subscribing to a Republican newspaper "and other similar offences."[29]

Nevertheless, a few Republican editors continued to till this unpromising field, somehow managing to survive the long drought of readers and advertising and the unfair practices of their Federalist competitors. Chief among these Republican newspapers was the *Bee* of New Haven, edited by Charles Holt. To this slender sheet Connecticut Republicans pinned their hopes of breaking the Federalist domination of the press. Anxiously they watched its circulation figures, optimistically concluding that it "rises under persecution, and the awakened people of Connecticut stretch forth their hands

[27] *Aurora*, August 20, 1799. *Independent Chronicle*, November 19, 1798.

[28] J. Eugene Smith, *One Hundred Years of Hartford's Courant*, 74. New Haven, 1949.

[29] *Aurora*, November 6, 1799. *Norwich Packet*, June 13, 1799. *Bee*, November 21, 1798. Ephraim Kerby to Gallatin, June 8, 1801 (Gallatin MSS., New York Historical Society).

for the truths which it publishes, like travellers who had passed the sand parched deserts for the CUP."[30]

Acting upon the principle that "to be lukewarm in such a cause is to acquiesce in slavery," Holt's *Bee* stung the Federalists with charges of corruption, monarchism, malfeasance in office and warmongering.[31] But his most spectacular exploit in the field of propaganda was his attack upon Alexander Hamilton and the United States Army.

There were few things more deeply abhorred in rock-ribbed Connecticut than a standing army and a found-out adulterer. Holt managed to play upon both these prejudices. A large "provisional" army had been raised to combat the expected French invasion, and second in command of the army, next to Washington, was Major General (lately Colonel) Hamilton. Because of Washington's semi-retirement, it was arranged that Hamilton should be in active command of the army unless the French actually menaced American territory.

It was unthinkable, Holt wrote in the *Bee*, that the "sprightly and enterprising young farmers who by industry and economy may grow rich, become fathers of families, and men of great respectability" would consent to become soldiers in a standing army, the instruments of the ambition of some Caesar. Particularly when that Caesar promised to be Alexander Hamilton. "They will never," predicted Holt, "spend their best days in arms and vice, in order to glitter in regimentals, wear a sword and lounge in idleness as drones, unpitied and penniless. The best comment upon the recruiting service . . . is the appointment of Alexander Hamilton to command our army." President Adams had advised young men to study virtue and science — but if he had seriously intended this good counsel, he had put the wrong man in command of the army. "Are

[30] *Aurora*, November 23, 1799.
[31] *Independent Chronicle*, August 7, 1798.

our young officers and soldiers to learn virtue from General Hamilton?" asked Holt. "Or like their generals are they to be found in the bed of adultery?"[32]

With such a general, no wonder, said Holt, that the army was composed of "a band of disorganized, unprincipled and abandoned ruffians, a burden, a pest, and a terror to the citizens who are taxed for their support." No wonder that they committed atrocities upon helpless civilians, raping, shooting and looting until the people had more cause to dread their own soldiers than an invading foreign army. The only service rendered by these blackguards who wore the uniform of the United States was that they excited "in the breasts of citizens a natural and just abhorrence for standing armies, and perfect contempt for the creatures of which they are composed."[33] This army could be of no conceivable benefit to the people of the United States: only Hamilton, Schuyler, Wadsworth, Bingham — all the rich and powerful — stood to profit by war. But, asked Holt, "are our sons to fight battles that a certain class of men may reap the spoil, or enlarge their power and fortunes upon our destruction?"[34]

For several months after the publication of this outburst, no action was taken against Holt: "watched, inspected, and criticised by a thousand malicious eyes," he said of the *Bee*, "it has almost miraculously escaped the fangs of its powerful foes." As time passed, the Republican editor began to believe that he would escape prosecution altogether. For the guidance of his fellow editors, Holt disclosed the secret of his successful avoidance of the pains and penalties of the Sedition Act: bold, yet cautious, "the fear of the law constantly before his eyes," Holt said, he had "not withheld any necessary information from the people, though never so disagreeable to individuals in the highest station."[35]

[32] Quoted in *Richmond Examiner*, March 4, 1800.
[33] *Bee*, April 2, 1800.   [34] *Ibid.*, May 4, 1800.   [35] *Ibid.*, August 14, 1799.

Yet even as Holt wrote, the "fangs of power" were preparing to close upon him. It would have been truly remarkable had he escaped; he was guilty of discouraging enlistment in the army at a time of national emergency, an offence which no government can pass over lightly. Certainly, the Federalist administration was not disposed to suffer in silence Holt's attack upon the army and his libelous assault upon its commander. In October, 1799, he was indicted as "a wicked, malicious, seditious and ill-disposed person . . . greatly disaffected to the government of the United States," and charged with having written with intent to defame and bring into contempt the government, stir up sedition and discourage recruiting.

Holt's trial, which took place in April, 1800, in the Circuit Court of the United States, Justice Bushrod Washington presiding, attracted such a large crowd that it was necessary to adjourn to the meetinghouse to accommodate the spectators — here, a Republican sarcastically remarked, "to complete in the House of God the work of . . . *Religion and order*." Holt entered a plea of not guilty, resting his defense upon the unconstitutionality of the Sedition Act and his innocence of any evil intent in publishing the alleged libel — he had published, he said, only "moral arguments against the vices and abuses of military establishments, and an army confessedly useless, and subsequently abolished."[36] However, Mr. Justice Washington, in his charge to the jury, demolished Holt's defense by specifically upholding the constitutionality of the Sedition Act and pronouncing Holt's publication a seditious libel. Then, according to a Federalist account, the learned judge "explained and pronounced the law in such a mild, clear and masterly manner, as to satisfy all parties, even the prisoner himself, who was thereby prepared for a verdict of *guilty*." Holt was sentenced to six months in jail and fined two hun-

[36] *Bee*, May 21, 1800.

dred dollars; but in passing sentence, Mr. Justice Washington acted "in a manner so commanding, and still so dignified, as to make the prisoner blush for his crime, and be satisfied with the punishment inflicted." From this account, it would seem that Holt was led off singing the praises of Mr. Justice Washington and joyfully looking forward to a long term in prison where he might properly expiate his crime.[37]

If this were true, Holt's remorse must have been remarkably short-lived. The *Bee* suspended publication for a few weeks, but, with the aid of new capital, Holt was soon back in business, carrying on his editorial duties from his prison cell. The *Bee* lost none of its venom for Federalists and, with its aid, Jeffersonianism began to penetrate into the very stronghold of New England conservatism.

[37] *Massachusetts Mercury*, April 29, 1800.

CHAPTER VIII

ALTHOUGH the Sedition Act was intended to protect the reputations of the President and other Federal officials from libelous attack, the Vice President was left as a fair target for every kind of abuse. Never intended as a self-denying ordinance, the Sedition Act was not construed to mean that the Federalists were to cease maligning and whipping Jefferson; instead, during the entire existence of this law, honor and acclaim were to be won by blackening the reputation of the second officer of the United States government.[1]

As the law was then interpreted, John Adams was sacrosanct; Thomas Jefferson the butt of every man's malice. Federalist papers, complained the Republicans, contained "more corruption and filth than would fill the stables of a modern Augean," and most of it was shoveled onto Thomas Jefferson; but "when some bold truth is uttered by a Republican, they [the Federalists] send forth most pitiful yellings and yet they do not scruple to traduce and calumniate the purest characters of the Union."[2] No further proof was needed that this was purely partisan legislation intended not for the protection of the government but for the destruction of the

[1] At this time, the President and Vice President were not chosen from the same political party. The Electoral College chose these two officials without regard to party affiliation. Adams and Jefferson were elected President and Vice President in 1796. Beveridge, *Life of John Marshall*, II, 395.

[2] *Independent Chronicle*, September 13, 1798.

Republican opposition. "The *gag law*," said a Republican editor, "is either destitute of that impartial spirit which ought to characterise every law, or those to whom its execution is entrusted, are carefully blind to the aberrations of *federal* writers; when looking that way, as St. Paul says, "they see through a glass darkly."³ The only consolation left Republicans was that their leader was above the revilings of his enemies: Jefferson, they said, "neither has, nor needs a fence of the thorns and briars of the law round his character. . . . Let those men sanction sedition laws who need the protection of them."⁴

The complaint heard among Federalists that the great fish escaped the Sedition net, leaving only the lesser fry to satisfy the demands of justice, was largely occasioned by the fact that Thomas Jefferson went free. That the "Colossus of opposition," the "High Priest of Jacobinism," "the GREAT DEMO-CRATIC CHIEF of AMERICA," "a man, whose attachment, objects, religion, philosophy, and morals are wholly French," a "vain author, false prophet, and thorough-bred Frenchman," the tool of France and the "willing pander of her interests in the United States, and the beggar of her assistance to ruin his own country," and the chief instigator of a plot intended to bring about "the utter subversion of our own Government, the introduction of French *fraternity*, and the slavery of the American people" — that such a man should escape the penalties of the Sedition Act seemed to many Federalists a monstrous miscarriage of justice.⁵ When Jefferson was acclaimed as the colleague of Washington at the beginning of the Revolution, the Federalists replied that so was Benedict

---

³ *Bee*, May 1, 1799.
⁴ *Aurora*, May 16, 1800.
⁵ *Salem Gazette*, November 30, 1798. *Gazette of the United States*, July 19, September 4, December 20, 1798; May 14, 1800. *Russell's Gazette*, June 7, 1798. *Bee*, May 1, 1799. *Philadelphia Gazette*, March 24, 1800.

Arnold.[6] Apparently there was no more malicious Jacobin
in the United States: Alexander Hamilton regarded him as
the heart and soul of the "French faction" that aspired to
rule the country with French aid: "to be the proconsul of a
despotic Directory over the United States, degraded to the
condition of a province, can alone be the criminal, the ignoble
aim of so seditious, so prostitute a character."[7] It was supposed
by these Federalists that only Jefferson's want of nerve spared
them from these horrors: "He has," it was observed, "every
trait of a *Jacobin* but his courage; he has all the virtues of a
sans-culotte except his poverty."[8]

From the tone of the Federalist press, it seemed likely that
Jefferson would be among the first victims of the Sedition Act
and that the American people would be treated to the extraordinary spectacle of seeing the Vice President of the United
States in prison for libeling the President of the United States.
So certain was one Federalist newspaper that Jefferson was
doomed that it advised him to take the easy way out of suicide.
When he set off for Virginia in 1798, he was reminded of the
example of Ahithophel, who, finding that his advice was not
heeded and preferring death to disgrace, "saddled his ass, and
arose, and gat him home *to his house, to his city*, and put his
household in order, and hanged himself. . . ." This exemplary
conduct, it was pointed out, was "doing business like a man
who had a proper sense of his crime. I would to God that all
traitors would muster up courage enough to follow his example, for certainly the justice of this country lingers."[9]

Jefferson had long since resolved never to write for the
newspapers, and in 1799 he decided to write no more political

[6] *Gazette of the United States*, June 2, 1800.

[7] Hamilton, *Works* (Lodge), VI, 312.

[8] Robert G. Harper, *Observations on the Dispute Between the United States
and France*, Boston, 1798, 4, introduction. *Remarks on the Jacobiniad*, Boston,
1798, Part II, vi–vii.

[9] *Albany Centinel*, July 17, 1798.

letters, "knowing," as he said, "that a campaign of slander is now to open upon me, and believing that the postmasters will lend their inquisitorial aid to fish out any new matter of slander that can gratify the powers that be."[10] However, the damage had already been done: in a letter to Mazzei, the Italian liberal, which appeared in garbled form in American newspapers, Jefferson referred to the Federalist leaders as "men who were Samsons in the field and Solomons in the council, but who have had their heads shorn by the harlot England."[11] For less than this, men had been fined and imprisoned under the Sedition Act.

But John Adams never lent his authority to the plan of inflicting upon Jefferson the pains and penalties of the Sedition Act.[12] The President was better than his party: although he approved of both the Alien and Sedition Acts, he never advocated the prostitution of these laws to party purposes. Braintree was not the center of the inquisitorial court: it was to be found rather in the office of Secretary of State Pickering.

* * *

Under this vilification Jefferson did not lose his faith in the American people or cease to hope that "the reign of witches" would soon come to an end. "The disease of the imagination will pass over," he said in November, 1798, "because the patients are essentially Republicans. Indeed, the Doctor is now on his way to cure it, in the guise of a tax gatherer."[13]

Even an undeclared war costs money, and to fight France Congress was obliged to impose a stamp duty, a direct tax on

[10] Collections of the Massachusetts Historical Society, Boston, 1900, Seventh Series, I, 67–68.

[11] Jefferson, *Works*, VII, 77. *Gazette of the United States*, July 19, 1798.

[12] Jefferson's authorship of the Kentucky Resolves was not definitely known, although Federalists suspected that he had a hand in "the formation of those rallying-points of Sedition." *Columbian Centinel*, January 23, 1799.

[13] Jefferson, *Works*, VII, 310. *William and Mary Quarterly*, April, 1948, 147.

houses and slaves and a land tax, and to increase the customs
duties. The burden of these taxes created more resentment
against the Federalists than did the Alien and Sedition Acts;
and a loan of five million dollars on which the government
was compelled to pay 8 per cent interest gave color to the
charge that the administration was guilty of extravagance
and waste. It was still within men's memory how the Stamp
Act of 1765 had been "crammed down by the imps of Britain"
— even the name of a stamp tax was likely to make Americans
tremble for their liberty. But it was the land tax that produced
armed resistance — the abortive Fries's Rebellion in Pennsylvania. Certainly, to this extent Jefferson was right: it was the
tax collector rather than the Alien and the Sedition Acts that
most deeply stirred the people and turned them decisively
against the party in power.

But Jefferson grew impatient with waiting for the tax
collector to do his work: the "witches" were becoming more
arrogant and oppressive and the people seemed surprisingly
prone to acquiesce in their rule. Popular revulsion against
the Alien and Sedition Acts was, to Jefferson's way of thinking,
inevitable, yet it promised to take an unconscionable long
time in coming.

*   *   *

Madison proposed a toast to the Federal judiciary in 1798:
"may it remember that it is the Expositor of the laws, not the
Trumpeter of politics."[14] But the Republicans found that the
judges mixed such a generous amount of politics with their
law that they seemed to be nothing more than "a servile echo
of the executive." "An attempt to describe," said a Republican journalist, "in a volume of two or three hundred pages,
the crimes of the Supreme Court of the United States, would

[14] *Washington-Madison Papers*, edited by Stan V. Henkels, 153. Philadelphia, 1892.

be just like proposing to compress the Atlantic into a thimble."[15]

The entire Federal bench joined in the crusade against "Jacobinism" with such ardor as to raise grave doubts concerning its ability to conduct an impartial trial. In their charges to the juries, the judges often fanned political passions to white heat: when Justice Samuel Chase of the United States Supreme Court was asked whether he called his charge to the grand jury at Annapolis "a moral, a political, a religious or a judicial one," Chase replied that he thought it was a little of each.[16] Judge Lewis of New York, presiding at the trial of some young men accused of pulling down the sign of a Federal officer and attempting to destroy stamped paper, addressed himself in a forthright manner to the jury: "The Liberty Pole lads never received such a trimming as Judge Lewis gave them," reported the Albany *Centinel* — "he really labored to convince them of their error, and at the same time held out the rod of terror, as the only means to check such outrages. Whilst he was painting the melancholy consequences of opposition to the laws, the whole audience was in tears."[17]

The Federal judges defined patriotism by their own narrow partisan standards and interpreted seditious libel in such a way as to preclude ordinary political activity. Although the Sedition Act required proof of malicious intent, the judges inferred intent from the tendency of the publication to incite hatred against the government or its officers. This bad tendency test — the common-law test — leaves little room for freedom of discussion, because the judge and jury are apt to consider a point of view hostile to their own as likely to cause harm and, as Justice Holmes more recently said, "Every idea

[15] James T. Callender, *The Prospect Before Us*, Part II, Vol. II, 5. Philadelphia, 1800.

[16] *Report of the Trial of Justice Chase*, 63. Baltimore, 1805.

[17] *Albany Centinel*, July 2, 1799.

is an incitement." The only valid test in cases of this kind is whether the words and the attendant circumstances create a "clear and present" danger of wrongful acts. As long as there is no immediate danger of such acts, there ought to be no suppression of disagreeable truths. Instead, under the Federalist judges, intent to turn out the party in office was construed into intent to excite seditious acts.[18]

In ferreting out radicals, the judges were scarcely less zealous than Pickering himself. Justice Richard Peters of the Supreme Court confessed in August, 1798, that he was "uneasy under the movements of the internal Foes who are plotting Mischief," and he assured Pickering that he would leave no stone unturned "to get rid of a Set of Villains who are ready to Strike when they think the Crisis arrives." The judge was soon given an opportunity to make good his word. Near his country house outside Philadelphia he discovered some "Rascals . . . both Aliens and infamous Citizens" who seemed to be plotting mischief; one of them was "an English Democrat the worst, if possible, of all." Despite Justice Peters's eagerness to hale these incendiaries into court, he was unable to gather enough evidence against them to warrant an indictment. Rather than see justice defeated in this way, Peters expressed the hope that "those who are not for us would openly appear, and even in arms if they please. We could then manage them."[19]

The favorable answers of the grand juries to the Federal and state judges did not necessarily indicate, as the Republicans asserted, that all juries were packed; it is probably closer to the truth to say that the method of selecting jurors, together with the state of public opinion in the states in which most of these trials took place, ensured that the juries would

[18] Chafee, *Freedom of Speech*, 25. *Philadelphia Gazette*, February 2, 1799.
[19] Richard Peters to Pickering, August 24, August 30, 1798 (Pickering MSS.).

respond favorably to the exhortations of the judges. In any event, the juries were often found going out of their way to put themselves on record in support of the Sedition Act. "We feel ready," said the Grand Jury of Beaufort, South Carolina, to Judge Grimke, "by our example, to diffuse the laudable spirit and determination of repelling the abominable principles of French politics, and the horrible doctrine of Atheism by prostrating ourselves this day before the altar of our religion and our liberties, and in the all-seeing Eye of Heaven, make a Solemn Vow to defend with our Lives and our Interests our Religion and our Country."[20] In answering Judge James Iredell's charge, the grand jury at Trenton declared that the critical situation of the country rendered the Alien and Sedition Acts indispensable — the typical, if not invariable, opinion of these juries.

Although the judges were willing, the Federal judicial system was ill-equipped to enforce the Sedition Act or, indeed, any other act of the Federal government. Only one superior or circuit court of the United States was held in each state; and these circuit courts were presided over by the six justices of the Supreme Court, who were obliged to travel from one end of the country to the other. To relieve this pressure upon the justices, the Federalists proposed early in 1800 to reduce the number of justices of the Supreme Court to five and to confine them strictly to the business of the court, entrusting the holding of circuit courts to a new set of judges. The number of circuit courts was likewise increased. But these changes were effected too late to be of aid in enforcing the Sedition Act; and when the Jeffersonians came to power the Federalist additions to the national judiciary were swept away.

In the opinion of Republicans, the conduct of the Federal justices in the Sedition Act cases was a decisive argument

[20] *Newark Gazette* and *New Jersey Advertiser*, April 16, 1799. *Albany Centinel*, February 8, 1799.

against making the Supreme Court the final interpreter of the Constitution. Although the constitutionality of the Alien and Sedition Act was not carried to the Supreme Court, there can be no question what its decision would have been; it was probably for this reason — and because the Republicans wished to avoid creating a precedent that would enlarge the powers of the court — that no appeal was taken. Yet, had the Federal judiciary been of a different mind — had it been composed of Republicans — it is unlikely that Jefferson would have taken this opportunity of proclaiming the states themselves to be the final judges of the Constitution.

From the Federal judiciary, the Republicans had expected nothing less; but they were hardly prepared to find state judges echoing the thunder of their Federal colleagues against "Jacobins" and lauding the Alien and Sedition Acts as wise and necessary measures.[21] One of the most active watchdogs against subversives was Alexander Addison, a member of the Pennsylvania judiciary. At the time of the Whisky Rebellion, Addison had been distinguished by his opposition to the Federal government; but that event had produced a complete change in his political philosophy. This apostasy from Republicanism was traced by his political enemies to his meeting with Alexander Hamilton, by whose insidious charm, it was thought, he had been thoroughly corrupted.[22] From whatever cause, by 1798 Addison had come to be "as flaming as a *federalist*, as he was before a *democrat*."[23] His legal opinions were treasured by Federalists as gems of wisdom: of one of his charges to the jury it was said that "after the Sacred Oracles, it

[21] Many state judges upheld the Republican cause. Two notable examples were H. H. Breckenridge and Chief Justice McKean of Pennsylvania. *Porcupine's Gazette*, February 13, 1799. *Newport Mercury*, March 26, 1799.

[22] Alexander Addison to George Clymer, September 29, 1793 (Wolcott MSS. Com. Hist. Soc.).

[23] *Aurora*, July 25, 31, 1799.

should be the duty of Parents and Heads of Families, to read it to their Households: and that pupil who first can repeat it *memoriter*, will merit the highest honors of the school he belongs to."[24]

In western Pennsylvania, Addison was horrified by the radicalism of a Republican newspaper, the *Herald of Freedom*, published by the son of Israel Israel, the Philadelphia merchant whose friendship with Benjamin Bache had raised grave doubts of his loyalty. Addison set out to put young Israel behind bars and an end to the *Herald of Freedom*. At first he considered binding Israel over to the Federal court for publishing the Virginia and Kentucky Resolves, but finding that they had already appeared in the Philadelphia newspapers without occasioning resort to the Sedition Act, Addison concluded that he could hardly single out the *Herald of Freedom* for punishment. However, when Israel printed "an impious mock prayer for the President on the Fast day," Addison believed that the presumptuous Jacobin had laid himself open to an indictment. But here again he was disappointed: "I had hoped," he wrote Pickering, "that a Grand jury composed chiefly of men professors of religion would have presented him . . . but two Grand juries charged with it refused to find the Bill; sedition being with them a sufficient justification of impiety." And so the *Herald of Freedom* continued to flourish and the judge to lament the shortsightedness of even good men.[25]

Even the stoutest Federalists were obliged to admit that all was not quiet in "the West"; indeed, that region seemed almost as hostile to the Alien and Sedition Acts as it had been to the whisky tax. The Acts aggravated the very conditions they were designed to correct: Pickering was informed that in

[24] *Columbian Centinel*, January 1, 1799. Oliver Ellsworth to Pickering, December 12, 1798 (Pickering MSS.).

[25] Alexander Addison to Pickering, November 22, 1798 (Pickering MSS.).

western Pennsylvania the "terrible spirit of Jacobinism" was sweeping the country and that only force could hold it in check.[26] Summoned by the newspapers, five or six thousand people would assemble to hear orators who made a practice of "mounting on a Wagon or Stump, telling the People their Liberties were in danger, and declaring against Government for two hours and then proposing Resolutions when the minds of the people were inflamed."[27] As for the newspapers themselves, they printed libelous and seditious attacks upon the government and its officers without let or hindrance and were in consequence so popular that they threatened to put Federalist newspapers out of business.

Nor could the Federalists take comfort in the spirit prevailing in Virginia: indeed, in some respects, the trouble fermenting in the West took its rise from the Old Dominion — where, thanks to the Alien and Sedition Acts, many regarded the Federal government "as an enemy infinitely more to be guarded against than the French Directory."[28] "We look up to Virginia," said a Kentuckian, "as the head of a respectable opposition to the most diabolical laws that were ever attempted to be imposed on a free and enlightened people."[29]

A singularly weak breed of men — the natural prey of philosophers — seemed, in the opinion of the Federalists, to abound south of the Mason and Dixon line. How else could it be explained, they asked, that Virginians — "the greatest *aristocrats* in America" — espoused the cause of France and swallowed virtually the entire Jacobin creed?[30] Federalists had supposed that the gentlemen of America, North and South, would be united against demagogues who preached

[26] Alexander Addison to Pickering, November 22, 1798 (Pickering MSS.).
[27] Samuel McDowell to Arthur Campbell, August 29, 1798 (Pickering MSS.).
[28] Albert J. Beveridge, *The Life of John Marshall*, II, 395. Boston, 1916.
[29] *New Jersey Journal*, October 22, 1798, December 18, 1798.
[30] *Albany Centinel*, February 17, 1798.

liberty, equality and fraternity; yet these Southern planters seemed perversely bent upon working their own destruction. Naturally, they did not carry their admiration of French revolutionary doctrines to the point of trusting their Negro slaves "to engage in fraternal embrace" but neither did they seem to realize that, infected by the teachings of the philosophers, the slaves might take matters into their own hands.[31]

These signs of rising opposition in Virginia and the West did not at first seriously alarm the Federalists. Rather, they ascribed public discontent with the Alien and Sedition Acts to the want of "right information" among the people, regarding the nature and purpose of the Acts. Accordingly, they proposed in Congress to print forty thousand copies of the Alien and Sedition Acts to be distributed throughout the country. Although a bill for this purpose was favorably reported by a committee of the House, it failed of passage, some Federalists being of opinion that the text of these Acts did not furnish the best argument for silencing objections.

[31] *Albany Centinel,* July 17, 1798.

CHAPTER IX

FEAR of "Jacobinism" furnished the chief support for the Alien and Sedition Acts, and there was no lack of incidents to keep fear at fever pitch. To those versed in reading the signs, prodigies and portents were to be found on every hand. In Vermont, a blind child was acclaimed as a seer by hundreds of the awe-stricken rustics who came to hear his prophecies. Having foretold the outbreak of yellow fever at Philadelphia and crop failure in Europe, he undertook a more ambitious reading of the future. He came up with a vision calculated to make the hair of a Federalist stand on end. "He says," it was reported in the newspapers, "that before the year 1803, the Jacobins are to swarm in this country, to overthrow our present government and to put to death all the clergy and the religious of both sexes. That having effected this revolution, they will then fall out for the supremacy, and finally destroy each other with the sword; after which the present government will again be restored, and the country flourish for one hundred years, & c." The youthful prophet is not to be blamed: many of his elders, including some of the leaders of the Federalist Party, believed much the same thing.[1]

To these skittish patriots, even trivial events cast portentous shadows: the ordinary manifestations of political feeling took on the semblance of revolution and red terror. In Stamford, Connecticut, for example, a few Republicans burned Presi-

[1] *Telegraphe and Daily Advertiser*, June 16, 1800.

dent Adams in effigy — an incident, said a Federalist news-paper, which proved "the necessity of coercion, to extirpate the most infamous and dangerous sect, that ever polluted our system, and spread misery in the world."[2] In Williams-burg, Virginia, town and gown co-operated in consigning Adams's effigy to the flames.[3] In Philadelphia, a Frenchman overheard criticizing President Adams was immediately arrested. Over a hundred French uniforms were discovered in a house in Philadelphia; excitement ran high until the owner of the house, a Frenchman, when brought before the Mayor for examination, proved that he had been commis-sioned by Toussaint L'Ouverture to procure uniforms in the United States for the black troops fighting the French in St. Domingo.[4] In Andover, Massachusetts, a mysterious woman well supplied with money was observed traveling alone by stage. The natural deduction was that here was a man — presumably a French agent — disguised in woman's clothing.[5] From Norfolk, Virginia, it was reported that "a tall, lank, ill-looking fellow, with a large leather three-gable hat, strutted up and down our wharves, declaiming, with violent impreca-tions . . . that, *in a few days, he would have the command of a French privateer, with which he would set the Borough of Norfolk in a blaze.*"[6]

[2] The effigy read: "Those who venerate the intended Despot, may here pay their last homage to his remaining ashes." *Russell's Gazette*, June 21, 1798. *Massachusetts Mercury*, June 19, 1798.

[3] "I would sooner put a child of mine under the tuition of a common thief, than send him amongst this rascally seditious crew." *Country Porcupine*, August 13 and 15, 1798.

[4] *Pennsylvania Gazette*, May 1, 1799.

[5] Samuel Phillips to Pickering, May 10, 1799 (Pickering MSS.).

The stages running between Philadelphia and Pittsburgh were reported to be crowded with Frenchmen. "Do they flock there," it was asked, "to encourage another whiskey business?" *Salem Gazette*, September 18, 1799.

[6] *New Hampshire Gazette*, July 24, 1798. *Guardian: or New Brunswick Advertiser*, May 8, 1798.

Menaced by French agents, Irish revolutionaries and internal enemies, the Federalists believed themselves to be assailed from yet another quarter — the Society of Illuminati. Supposedly, this was a world-wide secret organization dedicated to the destruction of all religious establishments and existing governments. Many Federalists were firmly convinced that the French Revolution and the slave uprising in St. Domingo were the handiwork of this society; and they did not doubt that emissaries of the Illuminati were at work in the United States itself.[7] Jedidiah Morse, a New England Federalist, claimed to have a list of members of this organization which, if made public, would rock the country.[8] Although some ascribed Fries's Rebellion to the Illuminati — they had prepared the people for insurrection by "the insidious circulation of baneful and corrupting books, and the wonderful spread of infidelity, impiety and immorality" — it was more frequently lamented that the people were not fully aware of the designs of this organization.[9] If so, it was not owing to the lack of effort on the part of the clergy to put the people on their guard, whole sermons being devoted to the iniquities of the Illuminati and the horrors that awaited their triumph.

Federalists fed their fears with such best-sellers as *The Cannibal's Progress: or the Dreadful Horrors of the French Invasion, as Displayed by the Republican Officers and Soldiers, in their perfidy, rapacity, ferociousness and brutality, exercised towards the innocent Inhabitants of Germany*. Another favorite was Dr. Robison's *Proofs of a Conspiracy*, purportedly the inside story of the efforts of the Illuminati to wipe out religion and government. Here,

---

[7] *Gazette of the United States*, August 16, 1798. W. P. Cresson, *Francis Dana*, 370–371.

[8] Jedidiah Morse to Oliver Wolcott, April 22, 1799 (Wolcott MSS., Connecticut Historical Society).

[9] *Ibid.*

the doctrines of the Illuminati are described as being "so abominably wicked, as to be thought by some persons to exceed belief." But, the Doctor cautioned, horrors were the stock-in-trade of these fiends, and if skeptical readers "would retrace the characters of those monsters in human shape, which the French Revolution had cast up, they would see Weishaupts [the founder of the society] as thick as grass-hoppers." It must be admitted that Dr. Robison sorely tried the credulity of his readers: Weishaupt is accused of having debauched his sister-in-law, and of attempting to murder her and his illegitimate offspring — an incident which, however shocking to Americans, apparently caused hardly a ripple of surprise among the "pure republicans" of Paris. "If Professor Robison had alleged that the Illuminati would prey upon the carcasses of each other, as well as of the societies they should destroy," remarked a Federalist book reviewer, "all the connoisseurs at Paris would have acknowledged this picture, tho' faintly colored, to be a just likeness of the French Revolution."[10]

Of all the "Jacobin plots" claimed to have been unearthed by the Federalists, none caused greater stir than the celebrated "Tub Plot." For a brief time, this mysterious affair seemed to have proved at one stroke the Federalists' contention that the Alien and Sedition Acts were essential to the defense of the country. Yet, a few weeks later, the Federalists were happy to forget the whole incident; they would have been even happier had the Republicans likewise been willing to bury the "Tale of the Tubs."

Early in 1799, Pickering was informed by Joseph Pitcairn, United States consul at Hamburg, that one Matthew Salmon, a mulatto and former deputy to the French National Convention, had taken passage in the *Minerva*, a Danish ship, for Charleston, South Carolina. Salmon — the consul had reason

[10] *Salem Gazette*, August 28, 1798.

to believe — was carrying, concealed in tubs with false bottoms, dispatches from the Directory. Pickering concluded that here at last was tangible evidence of a French-engineered plot to overthrow the government of the United States. His imagination ran far ahead of the bare facts sent by Pitcairn: Salmon, he assumed, being a mulatto, had been sent by the Directory to stir up an insurrection among the Negro slaves of the South. Accordingly, he wrote in hot haste to Governor Rutledge of South Carolina and to the officials of the port of Charleston to arrest this incendiary upon arrival.[11]

When the *Minerva* dropped anchor in Charleston Harbor, the government was ready for the worst: the ship was boarded by a boatload of armed officials, resolved to save the country from subversives or to die nobly in the attempt. On board, they found not only Salmon but four other French citizens, two whites, two mulattoes and one white woman, all traveling on Swiss passports. They found more: tubs with false bottoms, containing documents written in French. At this point, it was said that "the horrors of guilt were depicted strongly on the countenances of the guilty wretches, and their bodies shook with fear and trembling."[12] For a moment, they were in danger of being incontinently thrown overboard, but the more ardent patriots were restrained and the suspected French agents were hustled off to prison where they were questioned and their papers examined by General Pinckney.[13]

It was at this juncture that the story "broke" in the American press. General Pinckney and Governor Rutledge were enthusiastically acclaimed as the saviors of the Republic: had it not been for their providential discovery of this latest ex-

---

[11] Henry William De Saussure to Pickering, February 5, 1799; Pickering to De Saussure, January 4, 1799; Pickering to Joseph Pitcairn, March 7, 1799; Pickering to R. G. Harper, March 21, 1799 (Pickering MSS.).

[12] *Philadelphia Gazette*, March 6, 1799.

[13] *Albany Centinel*, March 8, 1799. *Carolina Gazette*, May 9, 1799.

ample of French turpitude, "throats might have been cut: Carnage and Devastation roaming thro' our Land, and our City one Pile of Ruins."[14] Solemn thanks were returned in the Andover meetinghouse "for the wonderful discovery of a French plot."[15] This narrow escape was held to prove that the Federalists had been right from the beginning: "Americans! Unite, rally round your government," exhorted a Federalist newspaper, "look on Frenchmen with the eye of suspicion, and prepare to meet them as enemies, with the sword: and BEWARE OF FRENCH EMIGRANTS."[16]

Amid all this hullabaloo, the Republicans remained surprisingly calm; the "Tale of the Tubs," they insisted, was "founded on a *false bottom*," an idle tale "fabricated to fill the vacancies of barber-shop conversation," "a trick of the Tories to delude honest Americans." Who, they asked, could seriously believe that the Directory would select a handful of whites and mulattoes to overthrow the government of the United States?[17]

Republicans professed to see much significance in the fact that a woman was included in this singular party of travelers and that she had fallen into the hands of General Pinckney. Pinckney's name had once before been linked with a Frenchwoman: during the X Y Z negotiations he had been involved with a "diplomatic lady" who acted as go-between for Talleyrand. On this slender foundation, the Republicans concocted a tale of unrequited love calculated to make Pinckney regret that his name had ever been mentioned in connection with the Charleston voyagers. The lady of Paris and the lady awaiting trial in Charleston as a French agent were, the Republicans

[14] *Newport Mercury*, March 26, 1799.
[15] *Independent Chronicle*, April 8, 1799.
[16] *Philadelphia Gazette*, March 6, 1799. *Springer's Weekly Oracle*, March 18, 1799.
[17] *Independent Chronicle*, March 18, April 8, 1799.

maintained, the same. In Paris, Pinckney and Marshall, the two Federalist members of the commission, had carried their intimacy with the young lady far beyond diplomatic niceties; indeed, it was suggested that if they had had half the success in upholding the rights of their country that they had met with in Paris boudoirs they would have gone down in history as the greatest of American diplomats. But their success in this limited sphere of operations had proved the young lady's undoing: about to become a mother, she had been cast out by her father. When she had appealed to Marshall and Pinckney to take her with them to America, they had slipped out of the country. Betrayed and deserted, she appealed to a kindhearted ship captain to give her passage to the United States, but no sooner did she arrive in Charleston than she was arrested as a spy and "a few tender and affectionate cards, which had been addressed to her by her lovers, and which she carried along with her passport, were twisted into bills of treason; two or three small trunks containing wearing apparel, which constituted all her property, were, with the same facility, framed into tubs of seditious papers." With her she carried "a helpless infant, the only known benefit procured to the United States from the embassy of Pinckney, Marshall and Gerry."[18]

These canards were permitted to stand without refutation by the government because the publication of the truth would have injured the State Department's policy of cultivating friendly relations with Toussaint L'Ouverture, who was engaged at this time in a struggle against the French in St. Domingo. Actually, the Charleston travelers, far from being agents of the Directory, were hostile to the ruling group in France; their intention was to proceed from Charleston to St. Domingo, there to stir the colored population to arms by pro-

[18] *Aurora*, March 7, 21, April 1, 1799. John Wood, *Administration of John Adams*, 186–187.

ducing documentary proof of the plans of the Directory to reduce them again to a state of slavery.[19]

The "Tub Plot" became a byword among Republicans; and whenever the Federalists claimed to have unearthed fresh evidence of French villainy, the "Tale of the Tubs" was called to mind. "We hear daily of plots," said a Republican newspaper. "Tub plots — fire plots — itinerant Jacobin plots — Talleyrand plots," but all were mere fabrications of the Federalists. Certainly this incident proved that as propagandists, the Federalists were no match for the Republicans.[20]

*   *   *

Nevertheless, war with France, at which all these alarums and excursions pointed, did not eventuate; there was no formal declaration of war, and, after the summer of 1798 when the Alien and Sedition Acts became law, there was a gradual but steady easing of the crisis. Thus, officially at least, the country remained at peace, and the Alien and Sedition Acts were forced to stand unsupported and unsanctioned by formal and declared war. Inevitably, therefore, these Acts, when war failed to come, began to appear more and more like a Federalist plot to establish tyranny at home by crying "crisis" when no real crisis existed.

Yet these Acts were always defended by the Federalists as war measures, justified by the right of self-preservation; and certainly, in the summer of 1798 when they were enacted, war with France seemed inevitable. Both on land and sea, the United States was getting on a war footing; hostilities had already begun in the Atlantic and West Indies; and President

[19] Henry Knox to Washington, July 29, 1799 (Washington MSS., LC.). Pickering to John Adams, March 19, 1799; to Edward Stevens, July 13, 1799 (Pickering MSS.).
[20] *Aurora*, August 15, 1799. *Independent Chronicle*, March 28, 1799.

Adams had sworn never to send another diplomatic mission to France unless given positive assurances by the Directory that it would be treated with respect.

In the summer of 1798 President Adams left Americans in no doubt that the administration had all but abandoned hope of peace. "I cannot cry PEACE! PEACE! when there is no peace," he exclaimed. ". . . To me there appears no means of averting a storm, and, in my opinion, we must all be ready to dedicate ourselves to fatigues and dangers."[21] The United States, he said, was "on the point of being drawn into the vortex of European war"; there was "no alternative between war and submission to the Executive of France"; and the prospect of a change of policy on the part of France was so dim "as to render further negotiation not only nugatory, but disgraceful and ruinous."[22] He could only hope that war, when it came, would be "a holy war" in which Americans would fight as courageously as in '76. In the meantime, he assured the people, the honor and independence of the United States were in safe hands: he would never send another minister to France "without assurances that he will be received, respected and honored, as the representative of a great, free, powerful and independent nation."[23]

So bellicose did the President seem in June 1798 that Alexander Hamilton began to fear that the country might be forced into a premature declaration of war against France.[24] He deplored the "intemperate and revolutionary" sentiments expressed by Adams: "it is not for us," he cautioned, "particularly for the government, to breathe an irregular or violent

[21] *Gazette of the United States*, May 22, June 18, July 30, 1798.

[22] *New Hampshire Gazette*, July 17, 1798. *Salem Gazette*, June 26, 1798. John Ward Fenno, *Desultory Remarks*, 13–14. John Adams, *Works*, IX, 203.

[23] John Adams, *Works*, X, 10–11. Oliver Wolcott to William L. Smith, November 29, 1798 (William L. Smith MSS., LC.).

[24] Hamilton to Wolcott, June 5, 1798 (Wolcott MSS., Connecticut Historical Society).

spirit."[25] Knowing Hamilton as they did, the Republicans suspected that he was egging the President into war; they did not dream that it was Hamilton who sought to cool the President's ardor for a showdown with France.

As events were soon to make unpleasantly clear to Hamilton, the President — despite his sword rattling — had no desire to wage a land war against France. From his early days, Adams had been a big-navy man, and when in 1798 he spoke of war it was naval war that he had in mind: "Floating batteries and wooden walls," he declared, "have been my favorite system of warfare and defence for this country."[26] On May 23, 1798, he exhorted the young men of Boston: "To arms then, to Arms especially by sea."[27] He cooled perceptibly, however, at the suggestion of a large army and land fighting against the French; and when Hamilton was forced upon him as the second in command of this army, the President began to show signs of wishing to call off the dogs of war.

From war might accrue many benefits to the Federalist party if not to the nation itself. War would enable the administration to act decisively against the French faction, thereby eliminating all opposition to the party in power. "It would cut off the cankering, poisonous *sans culottes* connexion," it was said, "and leave the country once more sound and really independent"; it would "fix the Thomases, the timid and injudiciously cautious. None would dare to plead the cause of that perfidious nation"; "traitors and sedition-mongers, who are now protected and tolerated, would then be easily restrained or punished."[28] It would also have cut off the hope

[25] Hamilton, *Works* (Lodge), X, 288. John Jay, *Correspondence and Public Papers*, edited by Henry P. Johnston, IV, 242. New York, 1893.

[26] *Gazette of the United States*, September 14, 1798.

[27] John Adams, *Works*, IX, 194.

[28] *Gazette of the United States*, June 20, July 2, 1798. *Columbian Centinel*, November 7, November 21, December 5, 1798. Mary Elizabeth Clark,

of peace which, during the entire crisis, hampered the war effort and finally produced President Adams's peace mission to France. If war had only been declared, said Theodore Sedgwick, "we might have hanged traitors and exported frenchmen" and acted in that wholly arbitrary and ruthless manner that some Federalists found so congenial.[29]

War thus beckoned and yet the Federalists could not bring themselves to take the plunge. From a military point of view, there were many considerations that counseled caution: Great Britain, the natural ally of the United States in a war with revolutionary France, was in grave danger of being beaten to its knees; in which event, the United States would be obliged to encounter alone the power of the French fleet and army. Nor were our military and naval preparations sufficiently advanced to afford much hope of successful resistance against the massive attacks that France was capable of delivering.

Moreover, an immediate declaration of war might have jeopardized the lives of the American ministers still in France. And even after Marshall and Pinckney left France, Gerry remained behind to carry on negotiations with Talleyrand, by whom he had been convinced that his departure would be the signal for a declaration of war.

The hope thus held out by Gerry's presence in France that the dispute would be peacefully settled made him exceedingly unpopular in Federalist circles; his efforts to make peace brought upon him a far heavier load of obloquy than is usually allotted to a warmonger.[30]

Peter Porcupine in America, 132–133. Allan Nevins, *American Press Opinion*, 27–28. Lodge, *George Cabot*, 169.

[29] James Hillhouse to Jonathan Trumbull, June 21, 1798 (Trumbull MSS., Conn. Hist. Soc.). John Ward Fenno, *Desultory Reflections*, 17. *Report of the American Historical Association . . . 1896*, I, 808. Washington, 1896. *Rufus King*, II, 515.

[30] Richard Peters to Pickering, August 30, 1798 (Pickering MSS.). *Writings of John Quincy Adams*, edited by W. C. Ford, II, 277. New York, 1917. *Correspondence between John Adams and William Cunningham*, 104. Boston, 1823.

The failure of the United States to declare war upon France came, some Federalists later complained, from giving too much weight to the opinions of John Marshall. In the summer of 1798, Marshall returned to the United States and was enthusiastically welcomed as one of the heroes of the X Y Z negotiations. As an expert on French affairs, Marshall was immediately questioned by the Federalist leaders as to the intentions of the Directory, whether for peace or war with the United States. The Virginian assured his colleagues that a declaration of war by France could be expected at any moment.[31] "Having taken their Measures," he said, the Directory "would in his opinion sacrifice one Hundred Thousand men sooner than recede one *Step*." In a public address to the officers of the New Jersey militia, he declared that "it seems to remain only for our country to try the LAST RESORT" and that the United States ought to resolve "to enforce, by the SWORD, those injured rights which the milder means of negotiation have failed to secure."[32] He left no room to doubt that war was inevitable and that it would come at France's initiative.

To support this opinion, Marshall could cite much recent European history: the fate of Switzerland, Venice and the Netherlands and the eagerness of many revolutionists to win world domination for France. What Marshall failed to see was the unpredictableness of French foreign policy. In the space of five years, Americans were to be given two striking instances of how unfathomable this policy could be: the French peace efforts of 1798–1800 and the sale of Louisiana to the United States by Napoleon in 1803.

Some Federalists would have welcomed a call from the President for a declaration of war, thus shifting the onus from

[31] James Hillhouse to Jonathan Trumbull, June 21, 1798 (Trumbull MSS., Conn. Hist. Soc.).
[32] *Salem Gazette*, July 3, 1798.

the Congress to the Executive; but no such summons came from the President. Despite the President's bold front, said the warhawks, his nerve failed him at the critical moment; and his shortcomings left the Federalists without "an imposing, firm leader, to direct their measures, and to whip in the stragglers from party and duty."[33] Left to themselves, the Federalists in Congress were unable to agree upon any policy other than national defense: although a motion for a declaration of war against France was made in Congress, the party did not wholeheartedly support it. At a caucus of the Federalist members of the national legislature, Jefferson heard that the question of war or peace was lost by five votes.[34]

But, above all, the state of public opinion in the United States made a declaration of war a serious risk to the political party that embarked upon it. The Federalists admitted that the people had "been kicked by France into some spirit"; but that they were ready for war before every possibility of peace had been exhausted, few were willing to say. Even some Federalists who usually professed indifference to public opinion were reluctant to precipitate offensive war in 1798 because they were not sure of popular support. Hamilton opposed both a declaration of war and a British alliance on the ground that public opinion, while disposed to approve measures for resisting aggression, could not yet be relied upon to go the length of declaring war upon France and entering into a foreign alliance. Much as they feared Jacobinism and resented the indignities offered the United States by France, a large part of the people clung to the hope that peace could be made with the Directory. "Everything should be done to inform the people and cause them to see things as they are," said John Jay, but he admitted that the people were not yet

[33] George Gibbs, *Memoirs*, II, 70.
[34] Jefferson, *Writings*, I, 282. Madison, *Writings*, VI, 325, 328. Pickering to Rufus King, April 26, 1798. *Rufus King*, II, 352–353.

ready to face what he regarded as the "realities" of the international situation.[35] "I believe that in our country," said John Quincy Adams, "the government can never carry through any war, unless the strong unequivocal and decided voice of the people leads them into it. The impulse must go from the circumference to the center. I have seen hitherto no such spirit, notwithstanding all the provocations, indignities and injuries we have received."[36]

Under these circumstances, the Federalists could do no more than wait for France to declare war. Certainly in this course there were undeniable advantages, always provided, of course, that France did not fail to make itself the aggressor.

From the viewpoint of the Federalist warhawks, the crisis was all too quickly passed: in July, 1798, the coastal waters of the United States had swarmed with privateers and picaroons — ships manned by "a banditti of negroes, mulattoes and outlaws" acting without commissions. But by November, 1798, not a hostile flag was to be found off our shores; the naval actions of the undeclared war with France were mostly fought in the West Indies or in the Atlantic, hundreds of miles from the coast of the United States.

The Directory wanted no war with the United States in 1798. It aimed only at securing a reorientation of American foreign policy in France's favor; a cash donation to permit Talleyrand and other high officials to live in the lavish style to which they were accustomed; and a loan to keep France's war machine running. Between inflation and the competition of war profiteers, keeping a mistress in Paris was no longer easy.

Only a declaration of war or aggravated acts of hostility by France could have united the American people after the passage of the Alien and Sedition Acts; but instead, Talleyrand

[35] John Jay, *Correspondence and Public Papers*, IV, 245.
[36] John Quincy Adams, *Writings*, II, 301.

got off his high horse and assured the United States that it was all a mistake: he had never authorized X Y and Z to blackmail the American negotiators; and by devious means he let it be known that he was willing to resume negotiations. As proof of the Directory's good intentions, the West India corsairs were brought under control; corrupt Admiralty judges were recalled; and the embargo on American shipping was lifted.[37]

Among Federalists, the prevailing opinion was that these overtures indicated not that the Directory wanted peace but that it was still playing its game of dividing Americans by making pacific promises which it had no intention of honoring. As they saw it, France was never more dangerous than when holding out the olive branch; and they resolved not to be caught in the trap laid by Talleyrand, "the cloven footed *Judas.*" "There is more to be dreaded from the pacific proffers of that infamous power than from their most active and open enmity," said the *Albany Centinel.* "AMERICANS, FORGET NOT THE FATE OF SWITZERLAND."[38]

Nevertheless, President Adams, finding that his party was unable to decide whether it should have peace or war, preferring instead a middle state, open to the inconveniences of both, determined to resolve the dilemma by taking the Directory at its word and sending a peace mission to France. In February, 1799, without prior consultation with his Cabinet, he submitted his proposal to the Senate and, over the opposition of a large part of the Federalist party, sent the emissaries to France in November, 1799.

The Hamiltonian wing of the Federalist party, far from celebrating this triumph, regarded peace with France as a greater evil than war. For his distinguished service to the

[37] Hamilton, *Works* (J. C. Hamilton), VI, 357–359.
[38] *Albany Centinel,* May 3, 1799. Henry William De Saussure to Pickering, November 26, 1798 (Pickering MSS.).

cause of peace, they were prepared to punish John Adams
by demoting him to Vice President; and if the old gentleman
had any objections to playing second fiddle he could retire
to Braintree and cease to meddle in politics altogether.[39]
Indeed, their hatred of Adams became so uncontrollable that
they wrecked the Federalist party in order to punish him for
his transgressions.

While the Federalists quarreled among themselves, the
events of war between England and France were settling their
problems for them. The victory of Nelson at the Nile — celebrated among the Federalists by toasts of "Buonaparte to the
Crocodiles, and Destruction to the Infernal Republic" — put
an end to all talk of a French invasion of the United States.
Although Hamilton declared that the army must still be kept
at full strength — "the aspect of Virginia was threatening,
and . . . he had the most correct and authentic information
that the ferment in the western counties of Pennsylvania was
greater than previous to the insurrection of 1794" — Federalist congressmen, better judges than he of public opinion,
decided that the time had come to reduce the size of the
armed forces.[40] On the motion of Robert G. Harper, Congress
voted to disband the provisional army by the summer of
1800. Hamilton, a general without a war, was thus in danger
of finding himself in the even more deplorable position of a
general without an army.

*　　*　　*

The war at sea went on, but from beginning to end it was
a strictly limited warfare on the part of the United States.
Although the treaty of alliance with France (dating from 1778)
was abrogated and American vessels were authorized to cap-

[39] *Porcupine's Gazette*, May 7, 1799. John Ward Fenno, *Desultory Reflections*,
55.

[40] Henry Adams, *Gallatin*, 223. General Drayton's *Notes of Conversation
with Hamilton*, 1799 (Hamilton MSS., LC.). *Rufus King*, III, 162–163.

ture French armed vessels and to recapture their American prizes, the taking of unarmed French ships was not permitted, nor the fitting out of privateers to prey indiscriminately upon French shipping. In short, the war was confined as far as possible to reprisals at sea and national defense at home.

The reduction of the army, together with French military reverses in Europe and the Near East, signalized the ending of the crisis that had gripped the country since the publication of the X Y Z dispatches. It might seem, therefore, that it would have been the part of wisdom for the Federalists to welcome this happy turn of events and to claim that they had preserved peace with honor. As Hamilton said, although the United States had not taken the boldest and most energetic course open to it — outright war with France — "yet, considering the prosperous state of French affairs when it was adopted, and how many nations had been appalled and prostrated by the French power, the conduct pursued bore sufficiently the marks of courage and elevation to raise the national character to an exalted height throughout Europe."[41]

[41] Hamilton, *Works* (Lodge), VII, 332.

CHAPTER X

VIEWED as a whole, the Naturalization, Alien and Sedition Acts appeared to Republicans as the entering wedge of a complete system of tyranny. Jefferson expected that if they went down, the Federalists would press for a Senate and President for life, and then demand an hereditary monarchy. Americans would awake one day to find themselves the slaves of a despotic government: Congress would assume a general guardianship over morals; it would supervise education; and it would establish a state religion. The transformation of liberty-loving Englishmen into wretched slaves (as the Republicans portrayed them) offered a dreadful parallel to events in the United States: "Has not the British Bull," they asked, "formerly a most obstinate and sluggish beast, been tamed by degrees?"[1] Working with even greater dispatch, the Federalists seemed about to pinion the American eagle. Jefferson remarked upon "the singular phenomenon" that the government of the United States had become in ten years "more arbitrary, and has swallowed more of the public liberty than even that of England." Oppressed and degraded as they were, the English, said Jefferson, "blush and weep over our sedition law."[2]

In the meantime, in preparation for the final extinction of liberty, the Federalists seemed bent upon investing the Presi-

[1] *Aurora*, April 3, 1799, January 20, 1800.
[2] Jefferson, *Writings*, VII, 311.

dent with unprecedented powers and making him the oracle of all wisdom. "Federalism," it was said, "has determined that there shall be but one standard of opinion among us, and that, as *infallibility* is chased away from Rome, it shall take up its abode in the Vatican in Market Street."[3] Americans must bow down and worship the plump little man in knee breeches and accept his word as law — or face the consequences of his sovereign displeasure. "This," exclaimed a Republican, "is that AWFUL SQUINTING foreseen by Patrick Henry. . . . An army of 50,000 mercenaries, at the devotion of some future enterprising President, aided by a sedition bill and other accumulated terrors, with the influence of hope from an enormous patronage, will subject America to executive despotism."[4]

In Republican newspapers, the Federalists were made to appear as arrogant aristocrats, aping their British counterparts in waging war upon the Rights of Man and intent upon establishing a full-fledged tyranny in the United States. One journalist pictured them seriously debating "whether thinking could be called sedition"; another predicted that "to laugh at the cut of a coat of a member of Congress will soon be treason"; a third warned that it would be declared seditious "to speak irreverently of his Brittanic majesty, or any of his royal brats"; and all agreed that the press would soon be put under a censorship worse than Russia's.[5] "The Embassy to Turkey ought not to create any astonishment," observed the *Aurora*. "There has for some time been an evident *predilection* for Turkish Politicks! Our Ambassadors to Russia and Turkey may send some *models* of the *knout* and

[3] *Aurora*, May 10, 1798.

[4] *The Prospect Before Us*, I, 83. *Bee*, April 3, 1799. *Aurora*, March 15, 1800. *Richmond Examiner*, December 10, 1798. *Greenleaf's New Daily Advertiser*, July 20, 1798. *The Proceedings of the House of Representatives*, 1779, 24.

[5] *Greenleaf's New Daily Advertiser*, July 16, 20, 1798. *Time Piece*, July 13, 1798. *Annals of Congress*, IX, 2435.

Bow-string, in order to see how they will *fit* into our new penal code." In handbills distributed among the Pennsylvania Germans they were told: "If you do not humbly submit to the Sedition Bill you will have chains on your necks and be handcuffed."[6]

Almost as much as they dreaded the Alien and Sedition Acts themselves, Republicans feared the interpretation of the Constitution made by the Federalists in order to uphold the legality of those acts. For if the Federalist practice of broadly construing the powers of the Federal government were followed, that government might become one of unlimited powers, endowed with authority in all cases whatsoever and restrained by no force other than its own will. Given power to pass any law it deemed necessary and proper to promote the common defense and general welfare, the Federal government became a master rather than a co-partner of the states; hence Madison's opinion that the Sedition Act was "the offspring of those tremendous pretensions, which inflict a death-wound on the sovereignty of the States."[7] The "necessary and proper" clause of the Constitution became "a grant of new powers to Congress," and this, to the Republicans, meant unvarnished despotism.

According to the strict construction of the Constitution favored by Republicans, the government of the United States was a government of enumerated, specified powers. It could not be endowed with new powers by implication; its realm of authority was plainly designated in the Constitution, and the Constitution must be exactly adhered to at all times. They denied that the government of the United States possessed an inherent right of self-preservation by which the Alien and Sedition Acts were justified; admit this power, they

---

[6] *Aurora,* February 13, 1799, July 17, 1800. St. George Tucker, *A Letter to a Member of Congress,* 31. *Porcupine's Gazette,* July 22, 1799.

[7] Madison, *Writings,* VI, 333. *Annals of Congress,* X, 421.

said, and the sovereignty of the states was annihilated and the government became consolidated and uncontrollable.

The Alien Act was attacked as unconstitutional on two counts: as an enlargement of the powers of the Chief Executive, and as an unwarranted extension of the authority of the Federal government over aliens. Jealousy of executive power was one of the cardinal principles of the Jeffersonians. Champions of congressional supremacy, they had unsuccessfully resisted Hamilton's efforts to concentrate power in the executive branch; but they had never before been confronted with such a sweeping delegation of authority as was made by the Alien Act. Both the Alien Enemies Act and the Alien Act gave the President power to remove from the country suspected aliens. No overt act by an alien was necessary: as the Republicans said, the crime consisted in incurring the suspicion of the President. Moreover, no directions were laid down in these acts to enable foreigners to distinguish between guilty and innocent conduct. In the plenitude of his power, said a Republican, if the President "dislikes the face of a man, if he squints, if he be wry-necked . . . if he fails to make his obeisance as he passes, or to shout 'long live the President' when he appears in public, all these *may* be grounds of suspicion, for which the President will not be accountable to any one but himself." William Livingston declared that he, for one, would "disdain to enjoy the liberty which depended upon the will of *one man*" — yet this was the very system established under the Alien Act.[8]

By Republican constitutional theory, resident aliens were wholly within the jurisdiction of the states; the Federal gov-

[8] St. George Tucker, 25. *Aurora*, June 13, July 2, 1798. *The Proceedings of the House of Representatives*, 1799, 20. The Jeffersonians also denounced the Alien Act as an unconstitutional deprivation of liberty without due process of law, a violation of the Fifth Amendment. This objection cannot be sustained.

ernment had no right to touch their persons and property. This constitutional objection was given added force by the apprehension felt in the Southern States that the Alien Act menaced the institution of slavery. Baldwin of Georgia predicted that if this bill became law, "Congress would again be appealed to by the advocates for an abolition of slavery," and that the President would be authorized to send all slaves out of the country as undesirable aliens. One of the reasons for the unpopularity of the Alien Act in the South was the persistence of this belief that the President had been given authority to deport slaves.[9]

As upholders of the implied and inherent powers of the national government, the Federalists found sanction for the Alien Act in the right of Congress to defend the country against foreign aggression. Self-preservation was the higher law — a power with which every government was endowed. If, asked Otis, we find "men in this country endeavoring to spread sedition and discord; who have assisted in laying other countries prostrate; whose hands are reeking with blood, and whose hearts rankle with hatred towards us — have we not the power to shake off these firebrands?" These acts were no violation of the Constitution, said Timothy Pickering, the Secretary of State, "for he must be ignorant indeed who does not know that the Constitution was established for the protection and security of American citizens, and not of intriguing foreigners."[10] True, no hostile army had yet appeared; but French agents and Irish and English malcontents were at work, corrupting American opinion — and "those who corrupt our opinion," said Judge Addison, ". . . are the most dangerous of all enemies."[11]

The Federalists were right in assuming that the Federal

[9] *Philadelphia Gazette*, February 2, 1799.
[10] Pickering and Upham, *Life of Pickering*, III, 475.
[11] *Pennsylvania Gazette*, February 20, 1799.

government possessed the right of deporting aliens: the admission of foreigners to asylum is not an absolute right but a revocable privilege; and the grant as well as the revocation is at the discretion of the government. As a Federalist congressman said, it was a right "which every man exercises in his own house, by turning out of it, without ceremony, any person whom he thinks dangerous to the peace and welfare of his family."[12]

The constitutionality of the Alien Act aside, it is apparent that the United States was turning its back upon the ideal, repeatedly affirmed since the Revolution, of serving as a refuge to the oppressed of all nations. In the Declaration of Independence, George III had been castigated for doing what the Federalists now did in the name of national security: "he has endeavored to prevent the population of these States, for that purpose obstructing the laws for the naturalization of foreigners, refusing to pass others to encourage their migration hither."

* * *

Of these "crisis" measures passed by the Federalist-dominated Congress, the Sedition Act seemed by far to strike the sharpest blow at freedom. Apparently, the Federalists had begun in the manner of all would-be despots: "Whoever should overthrow the liberty of the nation," it was observed, "must begin by subduing the liberty of speech; a thing terrible to public traitors." "The first born of American rights," said John Taylor of Caroline, "was the free examination of public servants"; deprive Americans of that right and all their freedom would be forfeit.[13]

[12] *Albany Centinel*, April 12, 1799. Kelly and Harbison, *The American Constitution*, 196–197. Chafee, *Freedom of Speech*, 240.

[13] *Time Piece*, July 4, 1798. *Aurora*, May 10, 1799. *Independent Chronicle*, July 5, 1798. *Greenleaf's New Daily Advertiser*, July 17, 1798. *The Proceedings of the House of Representatives*, 1799, 7–8, 15, 21. Simms, *Life of John Taylor*, 76.

No Republican doubted that such an inroad upon the liberties of American citizens was flagrantly unconstitutional. William Livingston declared that the Sedition Act was a breach of the Constitution "compared with which, he looked upon war, pestilence, and every other calamity, as of trifling consequence." Macon of Virginia charged that although previous laws of Congress had sometimes violated the spirit of the Constitution, now, for the first time, the letter had been directly violated. "If this bill was passed," he declared, "he should hardly think it worth while in future to allege against any measure that it is in direct contradiction to the Constitution."[14] Jefferson considered it "as merely an experiment on the American mind, to see how far it will bear an avowed violation of the Constitution"; if it were not successfully challenged, the Constitution would be little more than a scrap of paper.[15]

*   *   *

On the score of unconstitutionality, the Republicans seemingly had an impregnable case against the Sedition Act. The First Amendment to the Constitution declares that "Congress shall make no law respecting an establishment of religion, or prohibiting the free exercise thereof; or abridging the freedom of speech, or of the press; or the right of the people peaceably to assemble, and to petition the government for a redress of grievances." From this, it would appear that the Bill of Rights had effectively tied the hands of the Federal government from interfering in any way with the freedom of the press and of speech. So the Republicans assumed; but here, as elsewhere, the Federalists insisted that there was more in the Constitution than met the eye.

[14] *Abridgment of the Debates of Congress*, II, 308.
[15] Jefferson, *Writings*, VII, 283.

Despite the First Amendment, Harrison Gray Otis could say in Congress that he had never expected to hear the constitutionality of the Sedition Act denied: he was prepared to hear "the most elaborate harangues in favor of the liberty of the press, and on the right which ought to be allowed to censure men and measures, and such popular topics; but he did not foresee any objection arising from the Constitution." Otis exclaimed that he and his fellow Federalists would never consent to violate that sacred instrument: their purpose, rather, was "to preserve it against the attempts of invidious and dangerous aliens" and domestic foes.[16] Even Luther Martin, the champion of democratic rights in the Constitutional Convention, pronounced the Alien and Sedition Acts constitutional.[17]

As in the case of the Alien Act, the Federalists justified the Sedition Law by citing the power of Congress to provide for the common defense and general welfare, and the inherent right of every government to act in self-preservation. It was passed at a time of national emergency when, as a member of Congress said, "some gentlemen say we are at war, and when all believe we must have war." "Threatened by *faction*, and actually at *hostility* with a foreign and perfidious foe abroad," the Sedition Act was held to be "necessary for the safety, perhaps the existence of the Government." Congress could not permit subversive newspapers to "paralyze the public arm, and weaken the efforts of Government for the defense of the country."[18] The wiles of France and its adherents were as dangerous as its armies: "Do not the Jacobin fiends of France use falsehood and all the arms of hell," asked William Cobbett, "and do they not run like half famished wolves to accom-

---

[16] *Abridgment of Debates of Congress*, II, 317.
[17] *Philadelphia Gazette*, January 12, 1799.
[18] *Columbian Centinel*, January 1, 1799. *Albany Centinel*, July 20, 1798. *Annals of Congress*, X, 917. *The Alarm*, 11–12; Philadelphia, 1798.

plish the destruction of this country?"[19] If Congress had failed to take every precautionary measure against such danger, the blood of the Republic would have been upon its hands.[20]

From these lengthy declamations delivered by both sides upon the sanctity of the Constitution and the purity of their intentions it might be supposed that the Constitution was in safe hands, regardless of whether Republicans or Federalists administered the government. "No one," a Congressman observed, "will be found to say he is willing to violate the Constitution."[21] Nevertheless, each party believed that the other was preparing shamelessly to violate that consecrated instrument of government.

* * *

Despite their vigorous opposition to the Sedition Act, the Republicans were not willing to leave the press altogether free; one point of difference between them and the Federalists was that the Republicans regarded the punishment of libels and seditious speech and writings as a province of the states rather than of the Federal government. Nathaniel Macon declared that the "liberty of the press was sacred" — but he meant only as against the Federal government, not against the states. Indeed, as he added, "the States have complete power on the subject." William Livingston, whose speech against the Sedition Act made him a hero to Republicans, advised the victims of libels, whether government officials or private citizens, to look for redress to the state courts — where, he remarked, "every man's character is protected by

---

[19] *Albany Centinel*, April 12, 1799. *Newark Gazette*, September 14, 1798; *Aurora*, March 3, 1800. *New Jersey Journal*, March 17, 1799. *Greenleaf's New Daily Advertiser*, February 8, 1799.

[20] *Porcupine's Gazette*, August 22, 1799. *Gazette of the United States*, April 14, 1800. *Annals of Congress*, X, 409.

[21] *Annals of Congress*, VIII, July 5, 1798. Speech of Francis Dana.

law, and every man who shall publish a libel on any part of the Government is liable to punishment." Even in the case of a libel upon the President, the offense ought to be tried in a state court.[22] In the Republicans' crusade against the Sedition Act, there was concern for states' rights as well as for civil liberties.[23]

* * *

The most forceful statement of the constitutional objections to the Alien and Sedition Acts was made in the Virginia and Kentucky Resolves, drawn up by Madison and Jefferson late in 1798. Here the Acts are pronounced unconstitutional — a manifest usurpation of power by the Federal government. The Bill of Rights is held to debar Congress from restricting in any way the freedom of the press, and there is no common law in the United States (save that expressly adopted by the states) that can serve as the foundation for an enlargement of the sphere of Federal authority. The powers of Congress are defined in the Constitution and they must be construed with exact regard to the letter: "any powers inherent, implied, or expedient are obviously the creatures of ambition; because the care expended in defining powers would otherwise have been superfluous." What Americans have most to dread is a consolidated government, because such a government, by its very nature, becomes a despotism; for if no bulwark remains against "the passions and the powers of a majority of Congress," liberty cannot exist. Although Jefferson and Madison declare that they are sincerely anxious for the preservation of the Union, yet they make no concealment of their fears that these acts "may tend to drive these States into revolution and blood, and will furnish new calumnies against Republican governments, and new pretexts for those who

---

[22] *Abridgment of the Debates of Congress*, II, 317–318.
[23] Madison, *Works*, VI, 333. Simms, *Life of John Taylor*, 77.

wish it to be believed, that man cannot be governed but by a rod of iron."

To these familiar doctrines, Jefferson and Madison added a new conception of the nature of the union and a novel remedy for the ills suffered under the Alien and Sedition Acts. For the first time, the theory was put forward that the Federal government was created by a compact between the states: "we, the people" acceded only as states. In consequence, the Federal government is not the final or exclusive judge of the extent of the powers delegated to it by the states: "as in all other cases of compact among parties having no common Judge, each party has an equal right to judge for itself, as well of infractions as of the mode and measure of redress." And so the Virginia and Kentucky Resolves propose that the states associate themselves in opposition to the Alien and Sedition Acts by pronouncing them void and of no force. This procedure seemingly avoided the pitfall of unilateral action by a state against the Federal government; but in response to Jefferson's wishes, the legislature of Kentucky adopted a second set of resolutions in 1799 in which it was declared that "a nullification, by those sovereignties, of all unauthorized acts done under color of that instrument, is the rightful remedy." Thus the states became not only the legitimate judges of the Constitution but the executors of their decisions with regard to the constitutionality of Federal laws.

At the same time that the Resolves were adopted, a bill was introduced into the Virginia legislature arraying the state judges against the Federal government.[24] This bill provided that any person arrested under the Alien or Sedition Acts could be set at liberty by a Virginia judge. If this bill

---

[24] A bill introduced into the Kentucky legislature would have made it a high misdemeanor for any citizen of the state to inform or aid in the prosecution of alleged violations of the Alien and Sedition Acts. Alexander Campbell to Pickering, December 8, 1798 (Pickering MSS.).

became law, exclaimed a Federalist, "the government of the United States must protect itself or yield to the force of Virginia. Such open hostility cannot and must not be passed over in silence."[25] Over the opposition of John Taylor, the bill was laid aside; and, although the Republican leaders later attempted to persuade the Virginia judges openly to support the Virginia Resolves, they declined to commit themselves in its favor.[26]

As could easily have been foreseen, the Virginia and Kentucky Resolves brought forth a quick reaction from the Federalists.[27]

These "treasonable resolutions . . . calculated to subvert the constitution, and to introduce discord and anarchy" were intended, said the Federalists, "in plain French, to stop, or rather break down, the wheels of the Federal Government at one stroke." Alexander Hamilton branded them as "an attempt to change the government" — as a signal proof of his contention that only by dividing the large states would the Federal government be secure against their designs upon its authority.[28] Unquestionably, they *were* a challenge to the Federal government: Theodore Sedgwick of Massachusetts called them "little short of a declaration of war."[29]

Every reply from the states that answered Virginia and Kentucky unequivocally rejected the principles advanced by Madison and Jefferson: in every case, the claim of right in the state legislatures to declare an act of Congress unconstitutional was repudiated as an "unwarrantable doctrine" by the state legislatures themselves. Most, indeed, took this opportunity to

[25] *Albany Centinel*, February 5, 1799.

[26] *Columbian Centinel*, September 4, 1799.

[27] Fifty-eight members of the Virginia House of Delegates signed a protest to the Virginia Resolves. The protest was probably written by John Marshall.

[28] Hamilton, *Works* (Lodge), X, 335. *Columbian Centinel*, January 23, 1798. *American Eagle*, January 21, 1799. *Porcupine's Gazette*, January 26, 1799.

[29] *Rufus King*, II, 518.

praise the Alien and Sedition Acts as necessary "at this crisis" and "conducive to the public welfare." The Pennsylvania House of Representatives rebuked Virginia and Kentucky for attempting "to excite unwarrantable discontents, and to destroy the very existence of our government"; and in most of the replies, the position of the Supreme Court as the final expositor of the Constitution was explicitly upheld.[30]

On the other hand, if it were Virginia's purpose in passing these Resolves to "call to her all the malcontents, all the villains, all the United Irishmen, from every part of the continent," some Federalists were prepared to say good riddance. At least, the rest of the union would no longer be troubled by these "home-bred incendiaries" and "imported patriots" — they would all be in Virginia poisoning the minds of the common people and the slaves and preparing for the advent of liberty, equality and fraternity.[31]

While rejoicing in this "stern and sharp reproof given to the seditious Virginians," some Federalists did not conceal their chagrin that the affair had ended so tamely.[32] They had hoped for better things from Virginians: after so much vaunting and vainglory, they supposed that some form of overt resistance would follow. This would give the Federalists an opportunity to try out their brand-new army. Since the

[30] Only the states north of the Potomac answered Virginia and Kentucky. These states were largely under Federalist control; the Republican states to the south were silent. This created the appearance that the Resolves, and particularly the remedy they proposed, were overwhelmingly rejected. There was, however, some support for the Resolves in the state legislatures. Hardly touched upon in the discussion was the doctrine put forward in the Resolves that the Federal Constitution was the result of a compact between the states. *Annual Report of the American Historical Association . . . 1912*, 535–536. *Philadelphia Gazette*, January 25, 1799. *American Historical Review*, V, 53–54, 236–237.

[31] *Albany Centinel*, February 12, 1798. *Porcupine's Gazette*, January 29, 1799.

[32] George Cabot to Pickering, February 15, 1799 (Pickering MSS.). *Albany Centinel*, Feburary 5, 1799.

French showed no eagerness to fight, perhaps the "French faction" in the United States would oblige. Uriah Tracy of Connecticut lamented that Jefferson and his followers were not more mettlesome: "I had wished," he said, "that all the discontented would have made an effort, at this time to overturn the federal Government." A little bloodshed promised to "establish the Government with more advantage, than if no opposition had ever occurred."[33]

From the reports coming out of Virginia, Uriah Tracy seemed likely to have his wish even to the final gratification of seeing bloodshed. The words "dissolution of the union" were heard in Virginia; John Taylor of Caroline advocated disunion in preference to submission to the "monarchical" Federalists; and even Jefferson, confident of the good sense of the American people and the ultimate triumph of the "true principles of our federal compact," declared that he was ready to destroy the Union "rather than give up the rights of self-government which we have reserved, & in which alone we seek liberty, safety & happiness." Fortunately for the Republican party, Madison restrained his leader's impatience. Clearly, at this juncture, Madison was the conservative, Jefferson the extremist. Whereas Madison did not believe individual states justified in declaring Federal laws null, void and of no effect, Jefferson advocated nullification by a single state and was willing to consider the final and irreparable step of disunion.[34]

Even more ominous was the rumor that the Virginians were stockpiling arms, calling up the militia, establishing

[33] Uriah Tracy to Trumbull, January 2, 1799 (Trumbull MSS., Conn. Hist. Soc.).

[34] *William and Mary Quarterly*, April, 1948, 160, 165–166. Adrienne Koch, *Jefferson and Madison*, New York, 1950, 209. Although Taylor probably did not say that it was "unwise" to remain longer in the Union (as a misreading of his manuscripts has led some to believe) he certainly did not exclude the possibility of secession.

armories, and taxing the people — "an unequivocal proof how much they are in earnest," said Hamilton — apparently with a view to armed conflict with the Federal government.[35] Justice James Iredell of the United States Supreme Court believed that war was imminent — but, he added, "there is a respectable minority struggling in defence of the general government, and the government itself is fully prepared for any thing they can do, resolved, if necessary, to oppose force to force."[36] Jefferson was among this "respectable minority": armed resistance to the Federal government, he said, was what the Republicans had most to fear — "this is not the kind of opposition the American people will permit."[37]

Actually, these war preparations that so deeply alarmed the Federalists had been begun in 1798 or earlier and were intended to restore the long-neglected defenses of Virginia. As protection against a threatened French invasion and the much more real danger of Indian attacks on the frontier, three arsenals, each containing ten thousand stands of arms, were ordered to be established and the governor was authorized to erect an arms plant in Richmond.[38] But, regardless of the original purpose of these armaments, there can be little doubt that John Taylor of Caroline was ready for all eventualities including armed conflict with the Federal government. Taylor was reported to fear that the members of the Virginia legislature might be prosecuted under the Sedition Act for signing the Virginia Resolves. An ardent advocate of strengthening Virginia's military defenses, he was certainly not alarmed by the prospect of a French invasion; indeed,

[35] *The State Gazette and New Jersey Advertiser*, August 13, 1798. *Rufus King*, III, 147–148.
[36] Griffith J. McRee, *Life and Correspondence of James Iredell*, II, 543, 577. New York, 1857–1858.
[37] Jefferson, *Writings*, VII, 354.
[38] *The Centinel of Freedom*, February 19, 1799. *The State Gazette and New Jersey Advertiser*, August 13, 1798.

that hazard had from the beginning been dismissed by the Republicans as a mere Federalist bogey.[39]

These stories of war preparations in the Old Dominion galvanized Major General Hamilton into action. Hamilton was in the unhappy position of a general with no one to fight except his fellow citizens. Making the best of this turn of fate, he now urged that the Sedition Act be rigorously enforced and that Federal authority be upheld in every part of the Union. Although Hamilton was not in full agreement as to the expediency and justice of the Alien and Sedition Acts, the opposition of Virginia and Kentucky resolved his doubts and misgivings. *The Federal government, right or wrong* seems to have been his guiding principle. Moreover, he did not overlook the fact that a victory of the general government over the largest and most disaffected state in the union would go far towards determining the final outcome of the struggle between the states and the nation. To that end, he set down detailed instructions how a bloodless decision could best be reached with Virginia. "When a clever force has been collected," he wrote, "let them be drawn toward Virginia, for which there is an obvious pretext, then let measures be taken to act upon the laws and put Virginia to the test of resistance. This plan will give time for the fervor of the moment to subside, for reason to resume the reins, and, by dividing its enemies, will enable the government to triumph with ease."[40] Manifestly, Hamilton did not understand Virginians: it is much more likely that the approach of a Federal army would have strengthened the hand of John Taylor and other extremists than that it would have led to submission.

Fortunately for the peace of the country, the administration

---

[39] *New Jersey Journal*, December 18, 1798. *Albany Centinel*, February 5, 1799. *Gazette of the United States*, February 1, 1799. D. R. Anderson, *The Life of William B. Giles*, 69–70.

[40] Hamilton, *Works* (Lodge), X, 340–342.

did not attempt to indict the members of the Virginia legislature who had voted for the Virginia Resolves or to carry out Hamilton's plan of coercing the Old Dominion into submission. On the other hand, serious consideration was given by the administration to the idea of bringing Governor James Garrard of Kentucky to the bar of Federal justice. Garrard was guilty of making what Pickering called "a very impudent and inflammatory speech" against the Alien and Sedition Acts.[41] "Though a Governor may say much with impunity," it was observed, "thanks to the wisdom of Congress, we have a SEDITION LAW" — which set limits to what he might say without incurring the penalties of the law.[42] Having been informed that Garrard was not a citizen, Pickering gave some thought to the feasibility of applying the Alien Act against him. But Garrard proved to be a citizen, the Department of State lost interest in the case, and the Governor of Kentucky remained a free man.

But at least, the Federalists had the satisfaction of issuing, through Congress as well as through the Northern state legislatures, counterblasts to the Virginia and Kentucky Resolves. A committee appointed by the House of Representatives to consider petitions against the Alien and Sedition Laws submitted its report early in 1799.[43] This report was a rousing vindication of the Acts in question and a scathing denunciation of those who had the temerity to protest against them. Such fault-finding, the committee pointed out, was no more justified than were complaints against the army and navy, loans and

[41] Pickering to Rufus King, December 14, 1798 (Pickering MSS.).
[42] *Albany Centinel*, January 29, 1799.
[43] Petitions against the Alien and Sedition Acts were referred by the House to a special committee; had the House as a whole considered these petitions, its work would have suffered. Gallatin introduced petitions signed by eighteen hundred citizens of Pennsylvania against the Alien Act; Livingston of New York presented the remonstrance of the Irish resident in the United States against the same measure.

taxes — all were measures made necessary by the critical state of our relations with France. While many of those who took exception to the Alien and Sedition Acts were no doubt acting out of ignorance and misconception, the committee detected in some of the petitions a "style of vehement and acrimonious remonstrance" — a sure indication of "the principles of that exotic system which convulses the civilized word." Thus the Alien and Sedition Acts were made to appear as a barrier to the introduction of those baleful principles in the United States; and the petitions themselves were made to prove that a quarantine upon foreign ideas was more necessary than ever. France, the committee reminded Americans, had not renounced its designs upon the independence of the United States; its agents still worked underground, sapping the foundations of law and order; and too many Americans were still willing, unwittingly or otherwise, to play the French game.[44]

Had the only objective of Madison and Jefferson been to procure the speedy repeal of the Alien and Sedition Acts, they would have been well advised never to broach the remedy suggested by the Virginia and Kentucky Resolves. Despite their eloquent and moving arraignment of the Acts in those Resolves, the antidote they proposed probably injured the Republicans' chances of repealing them. By injecting a new and not wholly popular issue into the dispute, Jefferson and Madison played into the Federalists' hands. After the publication of these "mad and rebellious resolves," Federalists could say that the Republicans aimed at virtually destroying the authority of the central government at a time of national crisis.[45] Let the Republican doctrines prevail, exclaimed the administration leaders, and the United States would fall an

[44] *Annals of Congress*, IX, 2890. *Greenleaf's New Daily Advertiser*, February 21, 1799.
[45] *Rufus King*, III, 13. Hamilton, *Works* (J. C. Hamilton), V, 460–461.

easy victim to the Directory — a consummation supposed to be devoutly wished by Jefferson. For this reason, it was said that the Resolves had produced "good rather than an evil, by confirming the doubtful in the importance of a firm, energetic head to the Union, sufficiently strong to control the whole." In short, at least for the duration of the crisis, the cure proposed by the Republican leaders seemed, to most Americans, to be worse than the disease.[46] And so the Republican leaders deliberately kept them in the background during the presidential campaign of 1800.

But the Virginia and Kentucky Resolves were not the product merely of the Alien and Sedition Acts, nor were Jefferson and Madison thinking solely of the repeal of those hated laws. Rather, the Resolves took their origin in the Republicans' largely unsuccessful opposition to Hamilton's program of centralizing power in the Federal government and systematically weakening the states. The Republican leaders were therefore seeking to erect an impregnable constitutional barrier against encroachments by the central government upon the authority of the states. That authority was conceived in the broadest terms; and, just as Hamilton had sought to ensure the sovereignty of the Federal government by making it master over the states, so Jefferson, at this point in his career, would have made the states the dominant partner and awarded them the final voice in interpreting the Constitution.

The outcome of the elections of 1799 revealed that the Federalists rather than Jefferson and Madison had more correctly gauged the temper of the country. Unpopular as the Alien and Sedition Acts were in many quarters, the Virginia and Kentucky Resolves — particularly as a program of action — failed to provide an effective basis of opposition. Even in Virginia, a Republican acknowledged, "the people fearing

[46] *Philadelphia Gazette*, May 6, 1799. *Norwich Packet*, June 13, 1799. *American Historical Review*, V, 53–54, 56, 244.

disunion as the worst of evils have therefore thought it better even at the risk of bad laws, to elect men who would never consent to a dissolution of the federal compact." Aaron Burr, while praising the literary felicity of the Resolves, admitted that "in the honest love of Liberty, [they] had gone A LITTLE TOO FAR."[47] The North Carolina House of Representatives — which in December, 1798, had voted that the Alien and Sedition Acts were unconstitutional — refused to go along with its neighbors in the proposal that the states take countervailing action against the Federal government.[48] Partly for this reason, in 1799 the Federalists won the largest majority in Congress they had ever held, gaining two seats in New England, four in South Carolina and Georgia, and four in Virginia. For the first time since Hamilton's financial measures had alienated the South, the Federalists appeared to be a truly national party.[49] As a result of this election, Jefferson admitted that any "reformation in the public proceedings which depends on the character of Congress" had been postponed for at least two years.

Clearly, the best hope of ridding the country of the Alien and Sedition Acts lay, as Jefferson himself admitted, in relying upon the people to "bear down the evil propensities of the government, by the constitutional means of election and petition" rather than in summoning the states to take action of

[47] *Gazette of the United States*, April 29, 1799. *Virginia Magazine of History and Biography*, XXIX, 263–264. Richmond, 1921. *Rufus King*, II, 543.

[48] *Columbian Centinel*, February 4, 1799.

[49] Jefferson, *Writings*, VII, 396. In Pennsylvania, however, where the Alien and Sedition Acts became an issue in the gubernatorial contest of 1799, James Ross, the Federalist candidate, was defeated by Chief Justice McKean, a Republican. The Federalists charged that McKean had said that he wished "twenty thousand of the United Irishmen would come over to the United States, that in his opinion, they were the only men that understood true liberty." McKean denied making this statement but he put himself on record as a warm friend and admirer of the Irish — and they did not let him down at the polls. *Aurora*, August 13, 15, 1799.

dubious constitutionality.[50] The Federalist majority in Congress was small and the party's hold upon public opinion might be broken at any time by events in Europe. As John Marshall said, had opposition to the Acts "been confined to ordinary and peaceable and constitutional efforts to repeal them," the Federalists might not have been able to withstand the attack. There was good reason to believe that this approach was making progress: at a meeting of four hundred citizens of Essex County, New Jersey, where the Alien and Sedition Acts were freely debated, it was almost unanimously agreed that the Acts were unconstitutional, and a remonstrance to that effect was sent to the New Jersey legislature.[51]

Indeed, in 1799 and early in 1800, the Federalists warded off only with considerable difficulty two Republican attempts to repeal the Alien and Sedition Acts. In 1799, by prearrangement, they refused to answer the Republican speakers: when Gallatin and others rose to speak, "after a little while of common silence," said Jefferson, "they began to enter into loud conversations, laugh, cough, &c." until the Republican orators were drowned out.[52] Nevertheless, in the final vote, the Federalist margin of victory was alarmingly small.

In the spring of 1800, a resolution for the repeal of the Sedition Act actually passed the House of Representatives; but an amendment, proposed and carried by the Federalists, to the effect that the common-law principles of seditious libel were henceforth in effect, led to the defeat of the resolution as amended.[53] Clearly, the Federalists lacked the sanction of overwhelming support for the Alien and Sedition Acts either in popular or congressional opinion.

[50] Jefferson, *Writings*, VII, 354.
[51] *Newark Gazette*, January 2, 1799. *Massachusetts Mercury*, February 22, 1799. *Independent Chronicle*, September 22, November 12, 1798. *Greenleaf's New Daily Advertiser*, February 13, 14, 21, 1799.
[52] Jefferson, *Works*, VII, 370–372. *Aurora*, February 28, 1799.
[53] *Gazette of the United States*, May 10, 1800.

The failure of the Virginia and Kentucky Resolves to free the country of the Alien and Sedition Acts strengthened the Federalists' conviction that public opinion — at least that of "the sober part of the community" — was on their side. Active opposition to these laws seemed to be confined to a small part of the country; and as John Rutledge, Junior, said, "in those sections of our country where clamors have been raised against this law, everything is disliked and everything is abused which emanates from the Federal Government." "All this bustle about the alien, sedition and tax bills," said the *Salem Gazette*, "arises wholly from foreigners, and from those who have been in the habit of venting their spleen against the Government in publications of evil tendency, and from those who were inclined to seditious practices. These men are *materially* interested; therefore their objections ought to be received with caution."[54]

But it did not follow that the Federalists, buoyed up on the tide of this seemingly successful experiment in "energetic" government, were willing to admit any relaxation in the laws. Even granting that the "sober part of the community" was behind them, there remained that more numerous part of the community that was neither sober, nor wise, nor good, nor rich. Upon them, the Federalists looked as through a glass darkly. "Public opinion has not been ameliorated," said Hamilton: "sentiments dangerous to social happiness have not been diminished. . . . Among the most numerous class of citizens, errors of a very pernicious tendency have not only preserved but have extended their empire."[55] And, to add to his misgivings, it seemed that the Federalists were becoming soft and complacent, whereas the Republicans were growing more daring and enterprising in their efforts to undermine the established order.

[54] *Annals of Congress*, X, 932. *Salem Gazette*, November 30, 1798.
[55] Hamilton, *Works* (Lodge), X, 229–330.

CHAPTER XI

Of the Federalist leaders, only John Marshall actively opposed the Alien and Sedition Acts after their passage. Marshall, who returned to the United States from his mission to France at almost the same moment that Congress was engaged in passing these laws, declared that if he had been a member of Congress at that time he would have voted against them and that "had they been opposed on their principles by a man not suspected of intending to destroy the government or of being hostile to it, [the laws] would never have been enacted."[1]

Nevertheless, Marshall did not break wholly with his party; he tempered his criticism with many reservations and questioned the expediency rather than the principle of the Acts. He did not believe that they were "fraught with all those mischiefs ascribed to them"; nor did he regard them as inimical to freedom. It was rather that they served no useful purpose and were "calculated to create unnecessary discontent and jealousies when our every existence as a nation may depend on our union." Even so, he admitted that the Republicans carried partisanship to such lengths that "had they [the Alien and Sedition Acts] never been passed, other measures would have been selected" for raising a hue and cry against the administration. He did not advocate the repeal of the Acts: they would expire of themselves, he pointed out; but he left no

[1] *New Jersey Journal*, October 22, 1798.

doubt that he would oppose any attempt to revive them. Finally, it was Marshall who led the fight in the Virginia legislature against the Virginia Resolves and who wrote the report for the minority of the House of Representatives against those resolves.[2]

Although Marshall opposed these controversial laws largely on grounds of expediency, this did not spare him from the resentment of his fellow Federalists. Cries of astonishment and grief arose from the friends of "order" that one of the principal pillars of Federalism in Virginia had thus crumbled into dust. Marshall's friends were staggered that he who had bitter personal experience of the workings of French Jacobinism, and who had even been in its lair in Paris, could find objections to laws designed to combat Jacobinism at home. "I suppose," said John Quincy Adams, "this is the way of putting the foot into the stirrup of opposition, and if he (Marshall) goes to Congress we shall soon find him full mounted galloping with the best of them" — that is, with Jefferson, Madison and Gallatin.[3]

Marshall's kindlier critics ascribed his dereliction to a quixotic devotion to liberty and to an overweening desire for popularity at any price. "Hence it is," said Theodore Sedgwick, "that he is disposed on all popular subjects to feel the popular pulse and hence results indecision and an expression of doubt. . . . He is disposed to express great respect for the sovereign people, and to quote their opinions as evidence of truth." George Cabot, a Massachusetts businessman-politican, believed that allowance ought in all charity to be made "for the influence of the atmosphere of Virginia which doubtless makes every one who breathes it visionary, & upon

[2] John Marshall to Pickering, August 11, 1798 (Marshall MSS., LC.).
[3] John Quincy Adams, *Writings*, II, 397. *Annual Report of the American Historical Association . . . 1912*, 530.

the subject of Free Government incredibly credulous."[4] Marshall, according to this view, was altogether "too much guided by the refinements of theory" and expected the world to be governed by the rules of logic, quite forgetting that the evil passions of men had to be restrained by energetic government.[5] Even so, Marshall was not past saving, could some New England iron be infused into his Virginia softness. But, as a New Englander observed, it would always be a matter of regret that Marshall had been born on the wrong side of the Potomac: "I sometimes have been led to think," said George Cabot, "that some of the Virginia Federalists are little better than half-way Jacobins"; their opinions would never "prove sound according to New England ideas."[6]

With this opinion, Fisher Ames was in wholehearted agreement. Ames — in whose eyes even Harrison Gray Otis was a dangerous moderate — declared that "the moderates are the meanest of cowards, the falsest of hypocrites. The other side has none of them, though it abounds in every other kind of baseness." This Massachusetts Federalist was ready to write off Marshall as a bad risk to the party: — "Excuses may palliate — future zeal in the cause may partially atone — but his character is done for."[7]

Obviously, there existed a strong disposition to make the Alien and Sedition Acts the party line and to tolerate no deviations — which was to be expected from men who were doing their utmost to establish uniformity of opinion in the country as a whole.[8] Yet, as a Virginia Federalist, the white

[4] *Rufus King*, III, 237. George Cabot to Pickering, October 31, 1798 (Pickering MSS.).

[5] *Rufus King*, III, 9, 163, 183.

[6] Lodge, *George Cabot*, 125.

[7] Fisher Ames, *Works*, I, 246. Warren, *Jacobin and Junto*, 117–118. *Rufus King*, III, 69.

[8] *Pennsylvania Gazette*, February 20, 1799. *Albany Centinel*, February 28, July 31, 1799. *Salem Gazette*, November 30, 1798.

hope of Federalism in the South, and as "the man whose great and commanding genius was to enlighten and direct the national councils," Marshall could not be read out of the party without producing schism. One of the most glaring weaknesses of Federalism was its sectional character: except in South Carolina, it had made few converts in the South. To cast out Marshall was to relinquish the best hope of making Federalism a power to reckon with south of the Potomac; and this, few except the most doctrinaire were willing to do. And so Marshall remained a Federalist in official good standing, "cherished as a most precious acquisition to the cause of order, morality, and good government" but privately censured as one of the weak-kneed brethren.[9]

* * *

As time went on, a querulous note was heard among Federalist stalwarts. Few ventured to criticize the Acts themselves, for they were held beyond reproach; but their enforcement seemed lax and inefficient. It was accounted a signal failure of these Acts that hardly a Jacobin had been brought to a right way of thinking; as Noah Webster said, "the sedition law has left room enough for lying and misrepresentation with impunity to satisfy any common enemy to the truth."[10] The country was supposedly swarming with traitors and disaffected persons, yet, it was pointed out, few have "graced a halter, and few have been imprisoned." Presumably these Jacobins were still at liberty to undermine the government and churches of the United States; "I am almost delirious at seeing our once happy Country disordered by such infamous instruments," exclaimed a Federalist.[11] Only about twenty-five persons were indicted under the Sedition Act and of these hardly

[9] Lodge, *George Cabot*, 185. *Rufus King*, III, 163.
[10] *Massachusetts Mercury*, June 18, 1799.
[11] *Albany Centinel*, December 14, 1798. Allan McLane to Pickering, February 8, 1800 (Pickering MSS.).

a dozen were ever brought to trial. The suppression of a few newspapers and the jailing of a few editors were not, the Federalists well knew, sufficient to stop the flood of subversive matter pouring from the presses. More heroic measures were required to put the country beyond the reach of the "French faction," and there were not a few Federalists ready to take such measures even at the cost of destroying civil liberties.

With the proposition that the Alien and Sedition Acts ought to be more rigorously enforced there was general agreement among Federalists. "The only thing that is wanting to establish their complete popularity," said the *Hartford Courant*, "is a prompt and faithful execution of them. If several hundred intriguing, mischief-making foreigners, had been sent out of the country twelve months ago, and a few more Matthew Lyons had been shut up in prison for their seditious libels, we should not have had so many *Duanes, Burkes, Bees*, and a host of other villains, filling the country with falsehoods, slanders, and factions."[12] Federalists were convinced that they had been too lenient, although erring on the side of mercy was hardly a characteristic to which they could lay claim. Having laid on the rod without improving the culprit, it was now necessary to try coercion in earnest: "enough has been done for the fools," said a Federalist ex-member of Congress, "and as to the knaves, nothing will do them any good, but the whipping post and the gallows": short of hanging, there was no sovereign cure for Jacobinism.[13] Providence, he did not doubt, had reserved special punishment for them in the world to come, but even so, castigation ought not to be dispensed with: "it is but a small addition to the punishment that awaits them, but very useful in this world, and particularly in this country."[14]

[12] Quoted in *Porcupine's Gazette*, July 31, 1799.
[13] *Albany Centinel*, February 26, April 5, 1799. Upham and Pickering, Life of Pickering, III, 475.
[14] John H. Morison, *Life of Jeremiah Smith*, 135–137.

To carry forward this good work, it was urged that teeth be put in the laws; let every opposer of the Alien and Sedition Acts suffer prosecution as a traitor or, as Thatcher of Massachusetts advised, let the Sedition Law be made perpetual: "every press," he declared, "ought to be considered as a million of tongues, and ought to be guarded with a million of guards."[15] Some excitable Federalists advocated a nation-wide burning of seditious books: *Common Sense*, *The Age of Reason*, *Political Justice* and the *Aurora* were a few titles specially recommended for the fire. Since the Jacobin presses were working overtime turning out new handbooks of revolution, it seemed advisable that "a sort of perpetual and vestal fire should be kept up in some convenient place" for the benefit of citizens who felt urged to toss in a volume or two.[16] Harrison Gray Otis would have employed the Sedition Act against all associations, including the Masons: "The spirit of association," he warned, "is a dangerous thing in a free government, and ought carefully to be watched."[17] Freedom itself, he might well have added, is a dangerous thing — but the Federalist leaders would have made sure that the American people escaped that particular peril.

* * *

With the Alien Act, the administration seemed to have begun a war of nerves against aliens in the United States: with this law suspended over their heads, few foreigners could feel wholly secure in their persons or property. Rather than submit to this state of affairs they would, predicted the Republicans, "fly from a land of inquisitors and spies" and find refuge among the more hospitable and humanitarian Hottentots.[18]

[15] *Annals of Congress*, IX, 2902–2903.
[16] *Gazette of the United States*, June 24, 1800.
[17] *Newark Gazette*, June 18, 1799. *Albany Centinel*, December 14, 1798.
[18] *Aurora*, June 8, 1798. A letter from George Nicholas, 12. Philadelphia, 1799

Jefferson supposed that Volney, the French savant who had escaped the guillotine by fleeing to the United States, was intended to serve as the principal victim of the Alien Act.[19] Volney was suspected of plotting to put Louisiana in the hands of the Directory, but he later ridiculed these Federalist charges. How, he asked, could it suppose that "a single solitary Frenchman" could carry out a scheme of such magnitude? Besides, he said, he regarded the idea as "visionary and delusive, and dreaded it as tending to embroil us with the United States, and to strengthen their bias towards England"; in fact, when he returned to France, his views on Louisiana, so contrary to those of the Directory, made him an object of suspicion.[20] However, Volney did not rely upon his innocence to protect him against Federalist rancor; in the spring of 1798 he quietly left the country.

It is true that the passage of the Alien Act coincided with the departure from the United States of a considerable number of French refugees, but too much can be made of this coincidence.[21] That Volney and other French nationals left the country at this time was not necessarily owing to the Alien Act: the United States and France were on the brink of war and in that event few Frenchmen wished to remain in this country where they would become subject to the Alien Enemies Act and perhaps to even more drastic legislation. Also, France was beginning to relax restrictions upon the return of émigrés; and with the restoration of diplomatic and commercial rela-

[19] *Annual Report of the American Historical Association . . . 1896*, 807. Washington, 1896.

[20] C. F. Volney, A View of the Soil and Climate of the United States, vii–viii, Philadelphia, 1804.

[21] The Federalists were careful to point out that the Alien Act affected only those aliens deemed inimical to the national security. Their advice was to "go home and mind your business as a peaceable man, and John Adams will never know there is such a man as you in the world. He can only know you by your deeds; take care they are not evil, and you are not in danger." *Albany Centinel*, April, 1799.

tions between the United States and St. Domingo, many French subjects were eager to return to that island. The State Department closely screened all applicants for passports to St. Domingo, granting them only to such former residents as were acceptable to the government of Toussaint L'Ouverture and who did not seem likely to counteract American policy toward the government of that island.[22]

Except for Volney, the Frenchmen living in the United States whom the government regarded as most dangerous to the national security remained in this country. True, some took cover, but that hardly made them less a menace to the internal security of the Republic. Instead of forcing them out, the Naturalization and Alien Acts stimulated aliens to become citizens. James Callender, the Republican journalist whom Jefferson supposed to be one of the intended victims of the Alien Act, escaped its penalties by hurrying to the nearest naturalization office.

Of the suspected French agents in the United States none was more feared than General Jean Baptiste Collot. Accused of intriguing with Westerners to set up an independent French-sponsored state, of plotting to make Spanish Louisiana a French base of operations in the Western Hemisphere, and of seeking to revolutionize the United States itself, Collot stood high on the government's list of candidates for the attention of the Alien Act.[23]

Although President Adams had little faith in the effectiveness of the Alien Act, he declared himself to be "always ready and willing to execute the Alien Law" upon Collot. Even though the United States was, at Adams's insistence, engaged in peace negotiations with France, the President saw no impropriety in taking action against such a "pernicious and

[22] Pickering to Olway Byrd, July 19, 1799; Pickering to Edward Stevens, July 13, 1799 (Pickering MSS.).
[23] Pickering to Elisha Boudinot, August 13, 1799 (Pickering MSS.).

malicious Intriguer"; "On the contrary," said Adams, "it is more necessary to remove such an Instrument of Mischief from among our People, for his whole Time will be employed in exciting corrupt divisions, whether he can succeed or not."[24]

But even after the President had sanctioned the use of the Alien Act against Collot, there remained the problem of tracking down the elusive general. Although he was reported to have left the country, actually he was hiding in Newark. He was living under an assumed name, but he incurred the suspicion of some vigilant Federalists by subscribing to the *Aurora* — the certain mark of a democrat and disorganizer — and by talking against Washington and Adams. Among other things, he was reported to have remarked that "if there was War between France & this country, he would be one of the first to step forward & plunder the property of certain Individuals."[25]

But after President Adams undertook to send a peace mission to France, the Federalists who had been active in ferreting out General Collot, and collecting evidence against him, lost heart in their work. Elisha Boudinot, a New Jersey Federalist, wrote in discouragement to Pickering: "Perhaps as it appears we are going to return to our *dear Sister's* [France's] *warm embraces again*, all this may be unnecessary and this Spy may appear triumphant and in a capacity to take revenge on his enemies."[26] Meanwhile, the witnesses against the general displayed unexpected reluctance to testify. As a result, no action was taken against Collot and he later left the country of his own free will.

Nor was any other French national made to suffer under the Alien Act. When it was learned that Letomb, the French consul, had, in pursuance of instructions from the Directory,

[24] John Adams to Pickering, August 13, 1799 (Pickering MSS.).

[25] John Doughty to Elisha Boudinot, August 22, 1799; Elisha Boudinot to Pickering, August 7, 1799 (Pickering MSS.).

[26] Elisha Boudinot to Pickering, August 26, 1799 (Pickering MSS.).

sought to bribe members of Congress, Pickering was eager to expel him. He proposed to take equally drastic action against the French representative at Philadelphia who, he was informed, planned "to rally every sort of Devil from the Mississippi to the Delaware" and to make his house "the scene of all sorts of seditious deputations."[27] Pickering would not have permitted French consuls or other persons suspected of plotting against the country "even to breathe the air of the United States." Much to the disappointment of the Secretary of State, however, President Adams refused to permit the Alien Act to be invoked against French consular agents. "There is a respect due to public Commissions," said the President, who had himself served as United States minister to Great Britain, "which I should wish to preserve, so far as may be consistent with Safety." He was not averse to letting Letomb and others know that the government wished them to leave the country.[28]

If the administration expected to frighten Irishmen out of the United States by threatening them with the penalties of the Alien Act, it showed remarkably little understanding of the courage and hardihood of the Irish revolutionaries. Not a single Irishman is on record as leaving these shores in consequence of the Alien Act; even such marked men as Hamilton Rowan stood their ground.[29] And if the Alien Act had been enforced against them, Jefferson was prepared to turn Virginia into a refuge: he wrote Rowan that, come what would, safety could be found in Virginia where "upright judges" would afford protection "from any exercise of power unauthorized by the Constitution of the United States." "Habeas Corpus," said Jefferson, "secures every man here, alien or

[27] *Annual Report of the American Historical Association . . . 1912*, 447. *Russell's Gazette*, June 14, 1798. Mr. Van Polamen's Information, May 14, 1799 (Pickering MSS.).

[28] John Adams to Pickering, August 13, 1799. Pickering to Adams, October 4, 1798.

[29] *Independent Chronicle*, July 3, 1800.

citizen, against everything which is not law, whatever shape it may assume."[30]

While the Alien Act was thus lapsing into the status of a dead letter, the Federalists were lamenting that such a promising piece of legislation had fallen stillborn from the statute books. Foreigners seemed destined to possess themselves of the good American earth, particularly that part of it that lay west of the Appalachians. "Kentucky is all alien," mourned Fisher Ames: the scourings of Europe — debtors, criminals and "men who are averse to the wholesome restrictions of society" — were peopling the country; even the Indian savages might justly complain of the class of people they were being forced to associate with.[31] In the East, the situation was equally alarming: "If some check is not applied to their [the 'foreigners'] enormous and growing influence," Joseph Hopkinson predicted, "the day of their triumph is not far distant. The time approaches when the American knee shall bend before the foot-stool of foreigners, and the dearest rights and interests of our country await on their nod."[32]

The ultimate justification of the Alien Act was that it was necessary to the defense of the country against foreign aggression — but, asked Gallatin, "is that a measure of general defence, which has diminished the confidence in government, and produced disunion amongst the states and amongst the people?"[33] Its propagandistic value to the Republicans was out of all proportion to any small benefits it had achieved: as a Federalist admitted, "in many parts of the union, it has been used as a pretext and instrument to inflame the passions of the people, destroy the peace of the country, destroy respect for the laws, and relax the authority of the government; and,

[30] Jefferson, *Writings*, VII.

[31] Fisher Ames, *Works*, I, 247. *Albany Centinel*, February 12, 1799.

[32] *What Is Our Situation?*, 21–22.

[33] *The Proceedings of the House of Representatives, 1799*, 20.

in one state [Virginia], to produce such a commotion as threatens an insurrection, if not a separation from the Union."[34]

Altogether the Alien Act had to be set down as a failure, and its cost to the Federalists had been high. Whatever measure of the foreign-born vote they might have won from the Republicans had been irretrievably lost; suspicion of Federalist policies had among naturalized citizens been converted into outright hatred. The Germans, the Irish, the French — powerful groups in the United States — regarded the Federalists as their sworn enemies; and they voted accordingly. In New York State, in 1800, it was reported that about fifteen hundred naturalized Frenchmen, who had never voted before, cast their ballots for Republican candidates.[35] In the precarious balance of parties, the vote of these groups represented the margin between victory and defeat.

By the same token, the Act administered a serious setback to the war effort, inasmuch as it discouraged recruiting among the Irish and other foreigners who always composed a large part of the American army. Major General Hamilton, it was said, might raise an army of twenty thousand officers, but he would have to beat the hedges for privates.

*　　*　　*

On June 25, 1800, the Alien Act expired, unhonored and unsung. No Federalist orator commemorated its passing, but neither were the members of that party ready to confess their error in having brought it into the world. Republicans called it "a monster that must forever disgrace its parents" but the Federalist fathers were still disposed to believe that the failure lay in the execution rather than in the original conception.[36]

[34] *Pennsylvania Gazette*, February 20, 1799.
[35] John Rutledge to Oliver Wolcott, October 15, 1800 (Wolcott MSS., Conn. Hist. Soc.). *Greenleaf's New Daily Advertiser*, February 22, 1799.
[36] Madison, *Writings*, VI, 320.

CHAPTER XII

WITH Jefferson aspiring to the presidency in 1800, the Federalists relied upon the Sedition Act to save the country from a "Jacobin plot" "to destroy our present government, to place Jefferson in the chair of state, and to spread anarchy and confusion through the nation."[1] They saw no hope of salvation unless "the strong arm of Federalism should be stretched forth, to crush the demon of faction, and blast the feverish hopes and insidious schemes of deluded men."[2] It was, therefore, hardly coincidental that at this time three of the leading Republican journalists — William Duane, Thomas Cooper, and James T. Callender — were added to the list of victims of the Sedition Law.

The death of Benjamin Bache had wonderfully cheered the Federalists; but their joy was soon tempered by the realization that the *Aurora* was not dead. After Bache's death, William Duane took over the paper and with it Mrs. Bache, whom he married in 1800. If anyone could make the Federalists regret the untimely end of "Lightning Rod, Junior," it was William Duane.

Duane was an Irishman who, brought to the American colonies before the Revolution, went to India before next settling in England as a printer. In 1796, hounded by the authorities, he came to the United States and connected him-

[1] *Philadelphia Gazette*, May 24, 1800.
[2] *Gazette of the United States*, May 14, 1800.

self with Benjamin Bache and the *Aurora*. These brief facts of his biography enabled the Federalists to stigmatize him as "a wretch who was with the Enemy during the whole of our struggle for Independence, and who is still a base foreign emissary."[3]

In this so-called "Reign of Terror," the Sedition Act was not the only rod held over Republican editors — the mob was ready to step in when the law seemed too slow or ineffectual. James Lyon, a Republican editor, was attacked by "the aristocratical banditti of George-Town"; the Republican printer at Reading, Pennsylvania, was dragged from his office and whipped; and, before his death in 1798, Benjamin Bache was beaten and his office wrecked.[4] Occasionally, Federalist editors were given the same treatment, but most of the mobs of this period were composed of Federalists wearing the insignia of the black cockade. Dueling pistols were essential equipment for members of the newspaper profession: political differences were not infrequently settled on the dueling ground. In these encounters, however, it was not always the Federalist who walked off the field: in Petersburgh, Virginia, the editor of the Virginia *Republican* cut down his man at the first fire.

For the first six months of his editorship of the *Aurora*, Duane escaped the Sedition Act, but the Federalist mob atoned for this oversight. In May, 1779, he was attacked by a mob of civilians and army officers and was knocked down and soundly kicked, preparatory to receiving a coat of tar and feathers. But hearing the noise of the fracas in Duane's office, "the Democrats assembled, and the Macedonian heroes vanished in the Shade."[5]

[3] *Gazette of the United States*, June 16, 1800. A. C. Clarke, *William Duane*, 15.
[4] *Mirror of the Times*, October 18, 1800. *The Telegraphe and Daily Advertiser*, September 25, 1800.
[5] John Wood, *Administration of John Adams*, 195. John Beckely to William Irvine, May 17, 1799 (Irvine MSS., Pennsylvania Historical Society).

A more serious disturbance occurred when, on a Sunday early in 1799, Duane, Dr. Reynolds and several other Irish-Americans went to St. Mary's Roman Catholic Church in Philadelphia and posted petitions against the Alien Act to be signed by the members of the congregation. At this point, according to Republican accounts, "the alarm of sedition and treason was sounded in the Church: the pious priest dropped the bible, and out rushed the federal mob," knocking down Duane and his friends and ripping the petition from the walls. The Federalists swore, however, that the riot was begun by Duane and Reynolds when they assaulted the churchgoers with a "most seditious and inflammatory petition." For thus "prophaning the temple of the Most High," said the Federalists, "they were deservedly kicked and pummeled"; and this incident afforded the champions of law and order "a better argument in favor of the Alien Bill than a thousand pamphlets and speeches." But when Duane and his companions were tried for seditious riot in the state courts, they were acquitted.[6]

In July, 1799, Duane, as the Federalists said, "grown bold in calumny and falsehood from too long delay in noticing his crimes," declared in the *Aurora* that the British were calling the tune for administration policies and that the British minister in Philadelphia had spent eight hundred thousand dollars in the election of 1798 in bribing congressmen and their constituents.[7] As a result, he asserted, the British minister exerted more influence upon the government than did the veterans of the Revolutionary army. A secret alliance between the United States and Great Britain was being forged; already the two governments had agreed upon "measures of aggression and insult . . . calculated for the dismemberment of

[6] *Columbian Centinel*, February 20, 1799. *Connecticut Journal and Weekly Advertiser*, February 21, 1799. John Wood, *Administration of John Adams*, 194.
[7] *Albany Centinel*, August 4, 1799. *Aurora*, August 2, 1799.

France." These charges, he declared, were not based upon rumor and hearsay but upon documentary proof.[8]

That this was seditious libel of the rankest sort was the immediate response of the administration; the only question in the minds of Adams and Pickering was how Duane should be punished. As a foreigner and "base foreign emissary," Duane could be proceeded against under the Alien Act; as the publisher of seditious libel, he was open to prosecution under the Sedition Act.[9] Pickering at first favored employing the Alien Act, but the President was of the opinion that Duane's offense was so heinous that both Acts ought to be brought into play. "If Mr. Rawle [the district attorney] does not think this paper libellous, he is not fit for his office," Adams exclaimed; "and if he does not prosecute it, he will not do his duty. . . . The matchless effrontery of this Duane merits the execution of the alien law. I am very willing to try its strength upon him."[10] Pickering soothed the distracted President with assurances that Duane would be punished and that the *Aurora* would not be permitted to transgress again. District Attorney Rawle was ordered to examine every issue of the *Aurora* and to institute prosecutions under the Sedition Act for every breach of the law.[11]

On July 30, 1799, less than a week after the publication of his "British influence" article, Duane was arrested by a Federal marshal on a warrant issued by Richard Peters, Associate Justice of the Supreme Court. For a man facing prosecution under the Sedition Act, Duane seemed remarkably unworried. "Neither persecution nor any other peril to which bad men may expose him," he declared, "can make him swerve from the cause of republicanism, or prove himself unworthy to be

[8] *Aurora*, July 24, 1799.
[9] *Gazette of the United States*, June 16, 1800.
[10] John Adams, *Works*, IX, 3–5.
[11] Pickering to Adams, August 1, 1799 (Pickering MSS.).

the successor of the descendent of Franklin."[12] Moreover, he continued to assert that he had not published anything he could not prove: "We have it in the handwriting of John Adams," he said, "that British influence has been employed in the appointment of an officer of importance under the federal government."[13] Much too optimistically, as the event proved, Federalists set this down as the bravado of a cornered Jacobin.

But when Duane came up for trial at the autumn session of the Circuit Court of the United States sitting at Norristown, Pennsylvania, the case against him collapsed. Mr. Justice Peters wrote Pickering an ambiguous account of this unexpected turn of events: "We are all to much chagrined," he said, "to say much about the Circumstances or the Consequences. . . . We do not say anything about the true Reason of our breaking up."[14] Instead, the court explained that there was an error in the proceedings, and that a sufficient number of jurors had not been procured. The best that could be done was to bind over Duane and several other defendants to appear at a special court to be held in January, 1800, but Justice Peters admitted that it was very doubtful if this special court would ever be summoned and the prosecution of Duane resumed.[15]

Duane owed his reprieve to the fact that Justice Peters had learned that the Republican editor was making no idle boast when he claimed to have documentary evidence in John Adams's handwriting of British influence. Several years before, John Adams had written a letter to Tench Coxe, then Hamilton's assistant in the Treasury, in which he asserted that the Pinckneys of South Carolina were seeking the aid of

[12] *Aurora*, March 29, 1800. *Richmond Examiner*, May 2, 1800.

[13] *Albany Centinel*, October 22, 1799.

[14] Richard Peters to Pickering, October 23, 1799 (Pickering MSS.).

[15] Pickering to Stephen Higginson, December 23, 1799. Richard Peters to Pickering, October 23, 1799. William Schaacke to Jeremiah Wadsworth, October 23, 1799 (Wadsworth MSS. Conn. Hist. Soc.).

the British court to procure important posts in the Federal government. Tench Coxe had subsequently turned against Hamilton and Adams and joined the Republicans; and in 1799 he turned over this letter to Duane as political propaganda.[16]

With this letter in his pocket, Duane was in a position to cause the Federalist leaders serious embarrassment. He deliberately held the letter as "a rod over the old man's back," threatening to publish it in the *Aurora* if the Federalists made trouble.[17] Emboldened by his escape from prosecution, he smote the Federalists so vigorously that they cried out that "in any other country, his conduct would tend much to his *final elevation*." Every morning, they lamented, he concocted "a double stock of lies for his chaldron" and served it up for the delectation of the reader of the *Aurora*.[18]

But Duane pressed his advantage too far; his journalistic license did not extend to all branches of the Federal government. By means he never disclosed (the Senate was meeting in secret), Duane learned that a bill for settling disputed elections of the President and Vice President had been introduced into the Senate. This bill provided for the establishment of a tribunal composed of seven members of the Senate and six of the House of Representatives; meeting behind closed doors, this body was to have final powers in deciding which of two or more candidates with equal votes in the electoral college should carry off the palm of the presidency. The *Aurora* loudly cried fraud — it was the work, said Duane, of the Federalist caucus, acting "in the perfect spirit of a *jacobinical*

[16] *Albany Centinel*, October 22, 1799. W. C. Ford, Jefferson and the Newspaper, 58. *Proceedings of the Massachusetts Historical Society*, Second Series, XX, 266. Boston, 1907.

[17] Letters from William Cobbett to Edward Thornton, edited by G. D. H. Cole, 121–122. New York, 1937.

[18] Uriah Tracy to Trumbull, December 16, 1799 (Trumbull MSS., Conn. Hist. Soc.). *Gazette of the United States*, June 18, 1800.

conclave" by which seventeen Senators out of forty dictated laws to the United States; and the purpose of these Federalist enemies of the rights of man was to deprive Thomas Jefferson of the Presidency.[19]

The Senate — particularly the Federalist members — took a serious view of this accusation, especially because it was true. Unquestionably, the majority party was seeking to ensure the election of a Federalist president in 1800; but, as an administration supporter admitted, if this should be proved, "the Senate ought to be hanged, I mean the Federal part of the Senate." Some Federalists had talked of hanging William Duane, but they had never supposed that he would hang them.[20]

Duane was therefore summoned to the bar of the Senate for questioning. But before he agreed to attend, he asked his good friends Alexander Dallas and Thomas Cooper, an English radical who had fled England, to act as his counsel. Both Dallas and Cooper declined to serve on the ground that rules of procedure laid down by the Senate did not permit an effective defense, the Senate having barred all proof that might be offered in justification of the assertions made by Duane. In the opinion of these two Republican attorneys, the Senate had prejudiced the case, leaving no ground upon which the defense could stand. "I will not degrade myself," said Thomas Cooper in a letter to Duane published in the *Aurora*, "by submitting to appear before the Senate with their *gag in my mouth*." The Senate's claim of a right to summon any individual to its bar, he denounced as a new form of Federalist tyranny: "where rights are undefined, and power is unlimited — where the freedom of the press is actually attacked, under whatever intention of curbing its licentiousness, the melancholy period

[19] *Aurora*, March 27, 1800. *Gazette of the United States*, May 10, 1800.
[20] Uriah Tracy to Trumbull, March 18, 1800 (Trumbull MSS.). *Gazette of the United States*, July 19, 1800.

cannot be far distant when the citizens will be converted into a SUBJECT."[21]

With the leading Republican lawyers unwilling to handle his case, Duane told the Senate that he held himself "bound by the most sacred duties to decline any further voluntary attendance upon that body." He therefore left them "to pursue such measures in this case as in their wisdom they may deem meet." Then, in self-vindication, he published in the *Aurora* the entire correspondence between himself, Dallas and Cooper.[22]

To the Federalists, Duane's defiance of the United States Senate was an attempt to array the people against their own government. "No culprit," said a Federalist newspaper, "ever manifested such determined impudence. In plain language, he told his excellency the Vice-President, that he looked upon the Senate as a gang of sharpers who meant to lay traps for his ignorance; that unless he were permitted to be attended by a lawyer, up to their designs, he was fearful they would make a sacrifice not only of himself, but immolate the liberties of his fellow-citizens."[23]

Despite the outcry of the Federalist press, the Senate was evenly divided on the question of arresting Duane for contempt. It was Jefferson who, as the presiding officer of the Senate, broke the tie by casting his vote in favor of apprehending Duane. The warrant for his arrest was signed by Jefferson as President of the Senate: Duane was served with process and taken into custody by the sergeant at arms. He stood accused of having published scandalous, malicious and defamatory assertions against the Senate, "tending to defame

[21] *Aurora*, March 25, 27, 1800. James T. Callender, *American Annual Register*, Philadelphia, 1800, 143.

[22] *Aurora*, March 27, 1800.

[23] *Philadelphia Gazette*, March 25, 28, 1800. Uriah Tracy to Trumbull, March 18, 1800 (Trumbull MSS.).

the Senate of the United States, and to excite against them the hatred of the good people of the United States."[24]

But no further action was taken by the Senate; and, when Congress adjourned in the spring of 1800, Duane was still at liberty. The administration then tried a new tack: Duane was indicted under the Sedition Act for his libel upon the Senate. This action was still pending when Jefferson was elected to the Presidency. The new President ordered the suit against Duane under the Sedition Act dismissed; but to preserve the legal rights of the Senate, he directed that a new suit be brought against Duane. As the Republicans expected, the grand jury refused to indict the journalist, and thus Duane's long period of jeopardy was brought to an end.[25]

Because Duane, Dallas and Cooper were all foreign-born, their defiance of the Senate was regarded as particularly heinous. If "foreign mercenary caitiffs," a "motley mixture" of "Irish and English fugitives," could thus insult the legislature with impunity, it was time for the Republic to confess its impotence and resign itself to an early dissolution. "Just Heavens!" exclaimed a Federalist newspaper — "To what are we coming, when our soil, our laws, our government, our sovereignty are thus usurped and trampled under the feet of wandering vagabonds."[26]

Dallas escaped prosecution for his part in Duane's encounter with the Senate but Thomas Cooper was not let off so lightly. The administration had long had its eye on Cooper; Adams and Pickering had even gone into the question whether he ought to be prosecuted under the Alien or Sedition Act. Much to Pickering's disappointment, it was found that

[24] Columbian Centinel, April 15, 1800. Aurora, March 25, 1800. Gazette of the United States, May 10, 1800.
[25] Clarke, William Duane, 17–19. Proceedings of the Massachusetts Historical Society, XX, 263. W. C. Ford, Jefferson and the Newspaper, 93–94.
[26] Russell's Gazette, April 17, 1800.

Cooper had become a citizen, thereby spoiling a rare opportunity for putting the Alien Act, threatened with atrophy from long disuse, into execution. In August, 1799, as a result of the discussions between the President and his Secretary of State, Pickering instructed William Rawle, the United States District Attorney for Eastern Pennsylvania, to institute proceedings against Cooper as a violator of the Sedition Act.[27]

In June, 1799, Cooper, as editor of the Northumberland, Pennsylvania, *Gazette*, had let his readers infer that Adams was a power-mad despot — an enemy of popular sovereignty, the rights of man, and a friend of the moneyed men and aristocrats — who hoped to rivet his despotism upon the country by means of the Sedition Act and a standing army. Later printed in handbills and distributed by Cooper's good friend, Dr. Priestley, this *Address to the People of Northampton Country* was widely circulated in Pennsylvania during the campaign of 1779 which saw the Republican, McKean, elected over his Federalist opponent. Stung to the quick, Adams exclaimed that "A meaner, a more artful, or a more malicious libel has not appeared. As far as it alludes to me I despise it. But I have no doubt it is a Libel against the whole Government and as such ought to be prosecuted."[28]

Dr. Joseph Priestley, with whose name Cooper's was frequently associated, was a nonconformist minister and English scientist, one of the leading chemists in England, whose advanced views on religion and government had led some to suspect that he was attempting "to decompose both Church and State" with chemical formulae. As a friend of the French Revolution he was marked down by a Birmingham mob: his chapel was burned and his house was wrecked. England was no place for a French sympathizer who wished to lead a quiet

[27] Pickering to Adams, August 1, 1799; Charles Hall to Pickering, July 26, 1799 (Pickering MSS.).
[28] *Ibid.*

life; and so, in 1794, Priestley settled in Northumberland County, Pennsylvania, where he tried to avoid giving offense to the Federalist administration.

Finding the President in a mood for chastising Jacobins, Pickering suggested that the Alien Act be brought to bear against Dr. Priestley, who, not having become a naturalized citizen, was still amenable to its penalties. The Secretary of State had so often followed a promising lead only to discover that his quarry had taken out citizenship papers that he felt almost an affection for Dr. Priestley who, whatever else might be said of him, played the game fairly. From Pickering's point of view, therefore, Dr. Priestley was eminently qualified to become the first victim of the Alien Act.[29] But some curse seemed to lay upon that Act that always prevented it from being put in force, no matter how pressing the occasion. In this instance, it was President Adams who upset Pickering's plans: remarking that Priestley was "weak as water" and as unstable as the wind and that his influence was "not an Atom in the World," Adams concluded that he was more to be pitied than feared. Tom Cooper, the President went on, was the real villain of the piece: that rash, ungovernable, malicious man had led Priestley into mischief.[30]

And so Dr. Priestley was permitted to remain in the United States, living quietly out his last years on his farm in Pennsylvania. Pickering lamented the singular blindness of justice that permitted such things to be; but he was soon presented with an even more glaring instance of failure of the law that took his mind off Dr. Priestley's crimes. Having couched his attack upon President Adams in a fanciful "If I were President" vein, Cooper apparently had not committed a sufficiently flagrant breach of the Sedition Act to warrant prosecution; in any event, the government dropped its case against him.

[29] Pickering to Charles Hall, August 1, 1799 (Pickering MSS.).
[30] Adams to Pickering, August 13, 1799 (Pickering MSS.).

But when Cooper, having once slipped through Pickering's fingers, joined forces with Duane against the United States Senate, the administration resolved to punish him at all costs. This meant raking up old scores and reading the files of old newspapers, but Pickering did not fail to produce the needed evidence. In November, 1799, six months before Duane's quarrel with the Senate came to a head, Cooper had written a campaign document in which — as did all good Republicans — he forcefully condemned the policies of the Adams administration. More in sadness than in anger, he pointed out that Adams had proved to be a worse president than anyone could reasonably have expected when he first took office. Apparently Adams was then merely "in the infancy of political mistakes"; with maturity, his mistakes had become more frequent and more egregious. He had ended by saddling the country with a standing army, a navy, and a heavy debt; and he had delivered up to the British an American seaman (Jonathan Robbins) accused of being a deserter from the British navy — an act which Cooper pronounced to be "a stretch of authority which the monarch of Great Britain would have shrunk from; an interference without precedent, against law and against mercy!"[31]

This may or may not have been seditious libel but it served the purpose of an administration bent upon putting Cooper behind bars. Less than two weeks after his letter to Duane was published in the *Aurora*, Cooper was indicted on a charge of violation of the Sedition Act. The government moved with a dispatch that might, under different circumstances, have been flattering to Cooper: within six weeks of the publication of his letter he was lodged in the Philadelphia prison.

With Samuel Chase, Associate Justice of the Supreme Court, presiding, Cooper's trial opened on April 19, 1800, after a short postponement to give the defendant time to

[31] American Eagle, May 1, 1800.

secure official copies of Adams's speeches in order to prove the truth of the charges made in his alleged libel. Justice Chase believed that the defendant's purpose was merely to delay the proceedings and embarrass the court; and he seems to have acted throughout on this assumption. Cooper insisted that the presence of the President together with that of many high-ranking members of the administration and members of Congress was essential to his defense; he was particularly eager to bring Adams into court "to make this man confess, or deny, whether he was the author of certain publications, which Mr. Cooper had quoted as his."[32] Pickering was another key defense witness: on the strength of his testimony, Cooper expected to prove the truth of his contention that one of the assailants of Benjamin Bache had been rewarded with a diplomatic appointment. He also asked that the Secretary of State bring to court "the dates and salaries of the various Embassies and diplomatic agents from the United States at the courts of Prussia, Russia and Turkey."[33]

Cooper's defense was that his writings did not have and were not intended to have a seditious effect: he had made no attack upon the private character of the President; his concern was only with public measures. If freedom of discussion of the President's policies was not allowed, said Cooper, the people could not vote intelligently: hearing only one side of the controversy, they might be kept in the dark as effectually as though the United States were a despotic monarchy. This, Cooper exclaimed, was the question raised by the Sedition Act: Was the United States in the process of being converted into some form of authoritarian state? "Is it a crime to doubt the capacity of the President? . . . Have we advanced so far on the road to despotism in this republican country,

---

[32] James T. Callender, *The Prospect Before Us*, II, Part II, 5. *American Eagle*, May 1, 1800. *Aurora*, June 10, 1800. *Annals of Congress*, X, 930.
[33] Thomas Cooper to Pickering, April 15, 1800 (Pickering MSS.).

that we dare not say our President may be mistaken?" In Great Britain it was held that the King could do no wrong; were Americans, in belated imitation of this outworn doctrine, to establish the dogma of presidential infallibility?[34]

In conducting his own defense, Cooper found himself blocked at every point by the rulings of Mr. Justice Chase. When he read passages from a book containing loyal addresses to President Adams, the court refused to admit this as legal evidence. When he called witnesses to prove his good character and his high opinion of John Adams as a man — by which he hoped to show that it had not been his intention to bring the President into contempt — Mr. Justice Chase refused to permit them to be examined on the ground that the private opinion of the defendant was immaterial to the offense with which he stood charged. Moreover, by his rulings, Chase made it virtually impossible for Cooper to make truth a defense. This much-vaunted amelioration of the common law was, in practice, no defense at all. If the defendant undertook to prove the truth of his remarks about the President, Chase declared, "he must prove it to the marrow. If he asserts three things, and proves but one, he fails; and if he proves but two, he fails in his defence, for he must prove the whole of his assertions to be true."[35] Among other things, he was forced to prove that Jonathan Robbins was a native-born American and was forcibly impressed by the British — such a manifest impossibility as to make a travesty of the principle of truth as a defense. Despite this handicap, Cooper made a speech lasting three and a half hours, punctuated by bickerings with the court and a long pause to regain his strength. In one instance, at least, Chase showed proper consideration for the defendant: when Cooper pleaded faintness, the judge said that he "would pa-

---

[34] Wharton, *State Trials*, 662–669. *American Eagle*, May 1, 1800.
[35] Wharton, *State Trials*, 676. *The Telegraphe and Daily Advertiser*, April 25, 1800.

tiently wait until the Defendant refreshed himself and was able to resume his defence."[36]

Mr. Justice Chase's charge to the jury sounded more like the address of a public prosecutor than a calm and judicious summing-up of the evidence and exposition of the law. He pronounced Cooper's strictures upon the President to be the boldest attempt to poison the minds of the people he had encountered in his long career of hunting Jacobins. Of Cooper's charge that the President had saddled the country with a standing army, Chase declared that this was calculated to destroy the people's confidence in the government. Cooper had said that under Adams's auspices the credit of the United States government had sunk so low that it was forced to borrow money at 8 per cent: "I cannot suppress my feelings," exclaimed the justice, "at this gross attack upon the President." But the most serious accusation made by the defendant, in Mr. Justice Chase's opinion, was that the President had influenced a court of justice in the case of Jonathan Robbins; this he branded as an aspersion upon the character of the President.[37]

The jury was apparently deeply impressed by these charges; after twenty minutes' deliberation it brought in a verdict of guilty. In its account of the trial, the *Aurora* declared that "the jury being well selected for the purpose, were taken up to Dunwoddy's tavern to consider of their verdict, which did not take longer than was necessary to prepare and drink their punch."[38]

Before sentencing Cooper, Mr. Justice Chase asked him if he had anything to say — to which Cooper replied that "not being conscious of having *set down aught in malice*, he therefore had nothing to say in extenuation." This answer was not pleas-

[36] *American Eagle*, May 1, 1800.
[37] Wharton, *State Trials*, 672–676. *Aurora*, June 10, 1800.
[38] *Aurora*, June 10, 1800.

ing to the court: Cooper had not struck the proper note of contrition and supplication. It was apparent to Justice Chase that the defendant was an unreconstructed Jacobin and yet the justice was troubled in his mind about imposing a heavy fine, much as he believed Cooper deserved it. Chase had heard that the Republican party made a practice of indemnifying all victims of the Sedition Act for fines assessed against them: if this were true, said Chase, he would "go to the utmost extent of the power of the court. . . . We do not wish to impose so rigorous a fine as to be beyond a person's abilities to support, but the government must be secured against these malicious attacks." Cooper replied that he was not a party writer — he had "higher and better motives, than a party could suggest" — and that while he had many offers of financial aid from friends, he had no assurance that his fine would be paid. "If the court should impose a fine beyond my ability to pay," said Cooper, "I shall accept it without hesitation; but if the fine be within my circumstances to discharge I shall pay it myself." This earned him no favor from the court: he was sentenced to pay a fine of four hundred dollars and to serve four months in prison.[39]

As reported in the Republican press, Cooper's trial was a parody of justice, with the defendant himself appearing as "the amiable hero of some pathetic Romance." The verdict was alleged to have been decided upon before the trial began; the jury was packed with "high toned" Federalists; and the court conducted itself like "a Turkish tribunal." Samuel Chase bore the brunt of this criticism: in the course of the trial and particularly in his charge to the jury, he was said to have revealed "all the zeal and vehemence that might have

[39] *Aurora*, June 10, 1800. James T. Callender, *The Prospect Before Us*, II, Part II, 5. *Gazette of the United States*, May 3, 1800. *Collections of the Massachusetts Historical Society*, Seventh Series, I, 76. *Massachusetts Mercury*, May 2, 1800.

been expected from a well fee'd lawyer, all the bitterness of a vindictive personal enemy, and all the rudeness and brutality of Chase; and *little Peters* [Judge Richard Peters] *growled in concert.*" Between them, these two "abandoned pimps of power" succeeded in sending an innocent man to prison. Chase acquitting himself in a manner "the most arbitrary, high handed, and tyrannical that ever disgraced the judiciary of any country having the least pretensions to freedom."[40]

Among the Federalists, on the other hand, Samuel Chase gained new stature as a result of the Cooper trial. Let the Jacobins rage, they said; his judicial behavior was "conspicuous for its lenity and justice, its urbanity, as well as dignity, its temperateness as well as its fortitude."[41] The learned justice himself offered to answer his critics in a court of law. Declaring that he had been libeled, Chase invited his traducers to reveal themselves and stand trial to prove the truth of their charges. However, since Chase's unknown assailants were "not disposed to enter into controversy in the *Federal Court*, with a Judge of that Court, under the existing practice of packing juries," Chase said he was willing to meet his enemies in the Supreme Court of Pennsylvania. The only answer he ever received to this challenge was the dry remark that juries could be packed in state as well as in Federal courts.[42]

* * *

Fresh from his triumph over Cooper, Chase turned his attention to Virginia. As yet, no trial under the Sedition Act had taken place in the Old Dominion; indeed, in the entire region south of the Potomac, there had not been a single

[40] Callender, *The Prospect Before Us*, II, Part II, 5. *Aurora*, July 22, 1800.
[41] *Gazette of the United States*, May 3, June 17, 1800. *Massachusetts Mercury*, May 20, 1800. *Aurora*, July 22, 1800.
[42] *Gazette of the United States*, June 17, 1800. *Aurora*, July 22, 1800. *Massachusetts Mercury*, June 13, 1800.

instance of its enforcement. This oversight Chase intended to correct by bringing to trial the most abusive and the most irresponsible of the Republican journalists.

James Thomson Callender was a Scotsman who had come to the United States with the powerful recommendation — to Republicans — of having been expelled from Great Britain. In their eyes, his crime was only that "his manly, just and rational sentiments were too formidable to be any longer rated with impunity by that corrupt and corrupting government."[43] His writings fostered every American prejudice against the former mother country. The British parliamentary system he pronounced to be a "mass of legislative putrefaction"; the House of Commons seldom transacted business until a majority were half drunk; the contradictory orders issued relating to American shipping he ascribed to "the predominance of port." "For," he added, "to call the leaders of the British cabinet scoundrels would imply a degree of consistency and of consequence which they hardly possess."[44] Above all, as the passionate foe of British imperialism, he appealed strongly to men who scarcely twenty years before had rebelled against "British tyranny." The special merit of this "discerning philosopher" was that he exposed all the "horrible enormities" committed by his countrymen upon subject peoples. This he did with such an eye for telling detail that one admirer urged that he take up the subject of the death of an estimated fifty thousand American prisoners of war at the hands of the British. "His penetrating eye, and deep incisive pen," it was observed, "could easily penetrate, and explain, the horrid tale."[45] This was an assignment which Callender would have relished, but the necessity of exposing

[43] *Independent Chronicle*, August 23, 1798.

[44] *Porcupine's Gazette*, February 11, 1799. James T. Callender, the *American Annual Register*, 1797, 140–141.

[45] *Independent Chronicle*, August 23, 1798.

the horrors perpetrated by President Adams and the Federal party left him no leisure for such research.

Like Thomas Paine, Callender believed that government was the badge of lost innocence, but, unlike Paine, he never departed from this position: rather, he became a philosophical anarchist to whom all government was an evil, "a contrivance of human villainy." Every government, he maintained, was corrupt; office holders were thieves and villains and "the object of every government always had been, and always will be, to squeeze from the bulk of the people as much money as it can get."[46] It was therefore hardly surprising that he should regard the government of the United States as a "conspiracy against the welfare of the people."[47]

In the United States, before the enactment of the Alien and Sedition Acts, Callender found himself in a congenial atmosphere: the quarrel of the Republicans and Federalists had reached a pitch of rancor reminiscent of the political struggle in Great Britain. But in this country the press was comparatively free, vituperation was one of the liveliest and most highly prized arts in the young Republic, and the Federalists furnished ample scope for the talents of a skilled calumniator. From his experience as an English journalist, Callender had acquired a vocabulary rich in invective; and he had come naturally by a censorious temper that permitted him to see evil in all men and good in none. In his *Political Progress of Britain*, he inveighed against "the ruffian race of British Kings," most of whom, he said, were "deserving of a gibbet"; William Pitt he termed a "hardened Swindler"; and the Prince of Wales was labeled a murderer. In this spirit, he fell to the task of vilifying Washington, Hamilton, Adams and the lesser lights of the Federalist party.[48]

[46] James T. Callender, *The Prospect Before Us*, II, Part II, 94–95.
[47] *Richmond Examiner*, February 6, 1801.
[48] Callender, *American Annual Register*, 140.

Callender justified his acerbity on the ground that he was merely echoing the tone assumed by Republican politicians when dealing with their Federalist colleagues. John Taylor of Caroline, for example, said that Congress had repeatedly violated the Constitution and that Secretary of State Pickering ought to be confined in a madhouse. "With such a specimen of frankness," remarked Callender, "it will hardly be said that my stile is a great deal broader than that of Mr. Taylor."[49]

Callender's fantasies bore little resemblance to reality: George Washington was not a cheat, a liar, and a would-be dictator who would have gladly destroyed American liberty in his quest of power; Hamilton was not a monarchist, pining for an American king; and John Adams was not a "hoary-headed incendiary" bent upon precipitating war between the United States and France. In Callender's world, every conservative was an inveterate enemy of the rights of man, deserving of a speedy and, if possible, painful liquidation. He was totally innocent of any sense of responsibility; if he had a code of professional ethics, he certainly did not live by it. And yet, Jefferson encouraged him, aided him financially, and regarded him as one of the most redoubtable of the Republican journalists. And so he was: a republican evangelical, hurling fire and brimstone at all who denied the true faith of revolutionary France, his zeal, as Jefferson perceived, could be turned into good account in driving the Federalists from office.[50]

Alexander Hamilton, whose practice of frankly speaking his mind made him peculiarly vulnerable to attack, became Callender's favorite target. He was called "the *Judas Iscariot* of our country," a man whose ideas were "so perfectly British and monarchical, that it seems inconceivable how he ever

[49] Callender, *The Prospect Before Us*, I, 4. Callender, *American Annual Register*, 135. *Massachusetts Mercury*, April 25, 1800.
[50] W. C. Ford, *Jefferson and the Newspaper*, 91.

came to fight, as he did, for the American revolution."[51] He
was pictured sighing over the fate of the Bastille, and pining
to re-erect that vanished emblem of oppression in the United
States. But the greatest disservice done by Callender to
Hamilton was to force the former Secretary of the Treasury,
in order to preserve his reputation for financial integrity, to
confess publicly his illicit love affair with Mrs. Reynolds.[52]
This, to Callender, was one of the triumphs of his journalistic
career. Of Hamilton's confession, he wrote exultingly to Jefferson: "If you have not seen it, no anticipation can equal the
infamy of this piece. It is worth all that fifty of the best pens
in America could have said against him."[53]

Second only to Bache, Callender was the kind of thorn in
the flesh of the Federalist party that the Sedition Act was
designed to remove. Fully aware of what his enemies intended,
Callender left Philadelphia and took the road to Virginia,
where he was assured of protection by some of the leading
Republicans of the state. But in escaping the Sedition Act, he
ran afoul of the Virginia Vagrant Act. At best, his appearance
was not prepossessing: one unfriendly critic described him as
"a little reptile, who, from outward appearances seems to have
been born for a Chimney sweep"; another portrayed him as
"a dirty, little toper with shaved head and greasy jacket, nan-
keen pantaloons, and woolen stockings."[54] The protracted
drinking bouts in which he frequently engaged certainly did
not make him seem any less down-at-heels. It was therefore
not wholly surprising that he was picked up near a distillery
near Leesburgh, Virginia, as a vagrant. When he loudly protested that he was a gentleman, albeit somewhat the worse for

[51] Callender, *The History of the United States for 1796*, 110. Philadelphia,
1797. *The Examination of the Conduct of the Executive of the United States*, 65.
Philadelphia, 1797. *Gazette of the United States*, September 11, 1795.
[52] Callender, *The History of the United States for 1796*, 115, 205–207.
[53] W. C. Ford, *Jefferson and the Newspaper*, 90.
[54] *Porcupine's Gazette*, February 11, 1799.

liquor, and that he had come to Virginia at the express invitation of Senator Mason, the authorities were pardonably incredulous. However, Senator Mason put all doubt to rest by hurrying to Leesburgh to secure the release of his friend and fellow Republican.[55] Although Callender's presence in Virginia delighted Jefferson and other high Republicans, others felt that it was a disgrace to the Old Dominion. "If an antiquated Virgin of acknowledged *ancient dominion*," remarked a Federalist newspaper, "should desert her family and friends, fall in love with foreigners of every description, whether a French fiddler, a Maître du Hop, an Irish LYON, or a scald-headed, lousy Scotch candidate for Botany Bay" (Callender was actually turned out of Congress for being covered with lice and filth), "and even go so far as to take the latter *into keeping*, is she a Virgin? I say she is a ———."[56] Callender, said a Virginia Federalist, was "a dreadful calamity. . . . If the General Government or Executive would lend their aid and take him from us we should think it a National blessing."[57] Failing such aid, an effort was made to run him out of the state: an anti-Callender Association was formed in Richmond and plans were laid for a tarring-and-feathering party. But Callender's friends swore that if an attempt were made "to drum Callender out of town, there would not be a house left standing in the brick row" and that the country people would be called in to finish the work of destruction.[58] The Federalists thought better of their plan of disposing of Callender and he was permitted to remain in Richmond and to pursue his journalistic work with the *Richmond Examiner*.

[55] *Gazette of the United States*, August 9, 1799. *Columbian Centinel*, August 18, 1799. *Aurora*, August 3, 1799.
[56] *Gazette of the United States*, June 19, 1800.
[57] John B. Walton to Pickering, January 19, 1800 (Pickering MSS.).
[58] *Virginia Argus*, August 2, 6, 1799. *Aurora*, August 3, 1799.

With Callender goading the Federalists from the privileged sanctuary of Virginia, it began to be seen that Jefferson would achieve his objective of making the Old Dominion a haven for journalists and others fleeing the Alien and Sedition Acts. Unsuccessful in effecting a coalition of the states against the hated Acts, Virginia would help to nullify them in practice. Secure in the knowledge that he enjoyed the patronage of the Vice President, Callender took a bold tone indeed. "Let us," he exclaimed, "by one grand effort, snatch our Country from that bottomless vortex of corruption and perdition which yawns before us." He welcomed every attempt to enforce the Sedition Act: "The more violence, the more prosecutions from the Treasury, so much the better. You know the old ecclesiastical observation, that *the blood of the Martyrs was the seed of the church.*"[59] Callender little knew how soon he would be himself included among the martyrs.

Yet it must be acknowledged that Callender invited martyrdom. In *The Prospect Before Us* (read and approved in manuscript by Jefferson), Callender described the administration of John Adams as "one continual tempest of malignant passions. As President he has never opened his lips, or lifted his pen without threatening or scolding. The grand object of his administration has been to exasperate the rage of contending parties, to calumniate and destroy every man who differs from his opinions." He compiled a catalogue of "presidential felonies": a standing army, a large navy, high taxes and a French war. Washington and Adams, he declared, raised "an affected yelp against the French Directory; as if any corruption could be more venal, more notorious, more execrated than their own." According to Callender, the only limit upon President Adams's career of profligacy and corruption was his stupidity: "this federal gem, this apostle of the parsons of Connecticut, is not only a repulsive pedant, a

[59] *Richmond Examiner*, May 2, 1800.

gross hypocrite, and an unprincipled oppressor, but . . . in private life, one of the most egregious fools upon the continent." Future historians, Callender predicted, "will enquire by what species of madness America submitted to accept, as her president, a person without abilities, and without virtues: a being alike incapable of attracting either tenderness, or esteem."[60]

While Chase was presiding over the circuit court at Annapolis, a Federalist admirer sent him a copy of *The Prospect Before Us,* with the more offensive passages underlined. Chase is thereupon said to have declared that "It was a pity they had not hanged the rascal." It was not a mistake of which Chase himself would have been guilty.[61]

Callender was promptly indicted under the Sedition Act and it was observed that when he appeared for trial he had lost some of his customary brazenness. Facing Justice Chase — a sobering spectacle to the most hardened offender — he seemed "very much alarmed, and wished to make some concessions to the court." The justice, on the other hand, was not at all inclined to make concessions to Callender, and he began by denying the journalist's plea for a long postponement of the trial in order to bring defense witnesses to Richmond. He was ready, Chase said, "to allow every fair opportunity, but would not suffer justice to be eluded."[62] To this end, he overrode the objections of one of the jurors who pleaded prejudice against Callender; he refused to permit John Taylor of Carolina to give evidence on the political views of President Adams and his alleged partiality to Great Britain; and he browbeat Callender's counsel till they threw up the case and left the courtroom. Perhaps he did not display, as was later said, "an

---

[60] *Aurora,* June 17, 1800. *Report of the Trial of Justice Chase,* 84–86.

[61] *Report of the Trial of Justice Chase,* 43.

[62] *Virginia Federalist,* June 16, 1800. *Report of the Trial of Justice Chase,* 36, 71.

indecent solicitude unbecoming even in a public prosecutor" to convict Callender, but certainly the defendant was given little opportunity to prove the truth of his charges against Adams.[63]

Callender's counsel grounded their case upon the unconstitutionality of the Sedition Law and demanded that this question, among others, be submitted to the jury. This Chase refused to permit; although he had always maintained that the jury had a right to decide the law as well as the fact in criminal cases, it had no right to determine the constitutionality of any statute of the United States. With this ruling from the bench, Callender's defense collapsed: at six o'clock in the evening of the same day on which the trial had opened, the jury brought in a verdict of guilty.

The next day, in passing sentence upon Callender, Mr. Justice Chase read the journalist a lecture in his best style, presumably to provide matter for meditation in the long months ahead. President Adams, the judge informed Callender, was a great and a good man in whose hands "the American people had repeatedly confided their most important concerns and dearest interests." Therefore, to libel Adams was to impugn the wisdom of the sovereign people. And yet Callender had seen fit to paint Adams's character "in blacker colors than *Sejanus* himself" — a crime which no country in the world could tolerate. This brought Chase to his favorite theme — the distinction between freedom and licentiousness of the press. If permitted free reign, he declared, the press would corrupt public opinion and destroy the morals of the people — with the result that government itself would be destroyed. On the other hand, if safeguards were erected against libel and sedition, freedom of the press might be enjoyed "in

[63] John P. Kennedy, *Memoirs of the Life of William Wirt*, I, 80–81. Philadelphia, 1849. *Report of the Trial of Justice Chase*, 58. *The Telegraphe and Daily Advertiser*, June 9, 1800. *Richmond Examiner*, June 14, 1800.

the fullest extent to every rational and valuable purpose, without its licentiousness." After thus exhorting Callender to recognize the enormity of his crime and to mend his ways, Chase imposed upon him a fine of two hundred dollars and sentenced him to nine months in jail.[64]

The principal results of Callender's imprisonment were to give him a halo and sufficient leisure to write the second volume of *The Prospect Before Us*. It is quite apparent that Chase's advice was lost upon Callender: instead of meditating upon his own sins, he continued to ponder the iniquities of John Adams — no doubt, a vastly more congenial subject. Nor did prison sweeten his disposition or make him more just to his enemies. John Adams he now pronounced to be a "despicable attorney," "a wretch whose soul came blasted from the hand of nature," "the blasted tyrant of America," "a hoary headed incendiary," a "ruffian" who deserved "the curses of mankind," a man of such ungovernable temper that on one occasion he hurled his wig to the floor and stamped on it.[65]

Against the second volume of *The Prospect Before Us* no action was ever taken. The Federalists could only deplore that Jefferson, a candidate for the presidency of the United States, should aid and abet a man obsessed by hatred of all those in positions of authority. It augured ill for the future of the Republic: "Dismal indeed will be *The Prospect Before Us*," they groaned, "should the view of men, who patronize a *miscreant* like *this*, ultimately prevail."[66]

But at least Federalists had the satisfaction of putting Callender behind bars, and there he remained until he was pardoned by President Jefferson. A fund was raised among Cal-

---

[64] *Aurora*, June 13, 1800. *Gazette of the United States*, June 17, 1800.

[65] Callender, *The Prospect Before Us*, II, Part II, 76–77, 81.

[66] *Salem Gazette*, March 4, 1800. Madison, *Writings*, VI, 420–421. James Sprunt Historical Monograph No. 3, 131. Chapel Hill, North Caronlia, 1912.

lender's friends to reimburse him for the cost of his fine, and Jefferson contributed fifty dollars to what he supposed was a worthy cause. But Callender, disappointed in his expectations of favors from the new administration, turned against Jefferson the same venom he had once directed against Adams and Hamilton. Among the numerous derelictions of which he accused Jefferson was that of fathering most of the mulattoes at Monticello.

Callender's career as a character assassin came to a timely end: in a drunken seizure he fell off a ferry and was drowned.

CHAPTER XIII

WITH Cooper, Duane and Callender either in prison or under indictment, it might be supposed that the Federalists would take a more cheerful view of their situation. Nevertheless, this was the season of Federalist discontent, when disillusionment, despair and internal dissension began to weaken the morale of the party and to prepare it for defeat and eventual extinction. And while the Federalists fell out among themselves, the Republican newspapers took the opportunity of making the Sedition Act as much of a nullity as ever the Alien Act had been.

No act of Congress gave the Republicans more ammunition with which to attack the administration. Largely for this reason, the Republicans were able to recover from the setback they had received by the publication of the X Y Z dispatches: "Lock Jaw Federalism" provided them with the issues and the slogans by which they regained their prestige as the guardians of American freedom. More than this a political party could hardly ask: that its adversary should stumble into such a pitfall when it seemed about to carry all before it.

If the purpose of the Sedition Act had been to multiply Republican newspapers and to increase vastly their circulation, it could be accounted an unqualified success. In 1798, there were less than a score of Republican newspapers out of a total of two hundred; by 1800 there were at least fifty newspapers supporting Jefferson. In preparation for the presidential campaign of 1800, the Republicans established four new newspapers in Virginia alone.[1]

Nor was there any reason to believe that the Sedition Act had raised the tone of the opposition press: Federalists were still obliged to withstand the same barrage of scurrility and vilification of which they had complained in 1798. Indeed, it was questionable whether matters had not become worse: as a Federalist leader said in 1800, "the News Papers have heretofore been abandoned beyond all former example; but there is now an effort to concentrate all the mischievous men & designs in the Union, thro' the medium of the press. . . . The press has become a most daring nuisance to society. No purity of character, no integrity of motive can screen a man from detraction of the most gross and abusive kind."[2] One Republican newspaper, the *Time Piece* of New York, had been put out of business; the *Farmer's Weekly Museum* of Walpole, Connecticut, had changed from a Republican to a Federalist sheet; and several newspapers had been temporarily suspended while their editors served time in jail. By imprisoning editors, the Federalists seemed merely to have afforded them more leisure for writing and to have added venom to their pens. All the most influential Republican newspapers were flourishing and their circulation had increased under persecution. Thus, after two years of struggle, the Federalists found themselves back where they started; their only achievement had been to stir up a nest of hornets.[3]

Some Federalists were losing their faith in the efficacy of a law which, instead of discouraging and intimidating Republi-

[1] *Aurora*, September 21, November 23, 1799. *Bee*, December 18, 1799. *Massachusetts Mercury*, August 28, 1800. *Salem Gazette*, February 28, 1800. Smith, *100 Years of Hartford's Courant*, 74–75.

[2] Jonathan Trumbull to James Hillhouse, March 3, 1800; Uriah Tracy to Jonathan Trumbull, March 18, 1800 (Trumbull MSS., Conn. Hist. Soc.).

[3] *Aurora*, September 21, 1799. *Massachusetts Mercury*, August 22, 1800.

cans, seemed only to multiply the newspapers and adherents of that party. For this reason, Richard Harison, United States District Attorney for New York, recommended that William Durrell, a printer found guilty of libeling the President — for which he had been sentenced to four months in jail and a fine of fifty dollars — be freed. "He appears very poor at present," Harison wrote Pickering, "has a large Family to maintain, and has a considerable Time since he discontinued his News paper" — moreover, he had merely copied the libel from another newspaper. Harison also advised entering a nolle prosequi in the cases of Mrs. Ann Greenleaf, proprietress of the *Argus*, and Jedediah Peck, a member of the New York legislature, against whom proceedings were pending.[4]

Certainly there were not enough prisons in the country to hold the newspaper writers, the politicians and the plain citizens guilty of violating the Sedition Act in the campaign of 1800. The character of John Adams was given a going-over that might have led an innocent bystander to suppose that he was being tried for treason, murder, robbery and other assorted crimes and misdemeanors instead of merely running for the presidency of the United States. Alexander Hamilton was rolled in the mire by both the Republicans and the Federalist followers of President Adams. Pickering was accused, among other crimes, of having pilfered five hundred thousand dollars while serving as Commissary General of the United States.[5] When a fire broke out in the Treasury office, Oliver Wolcott, the Secretary of the Treasury, was denounced as "the felonious burner of public offices and records."[6] Yet hardly a voice was raised in favor of reviving the Sedition Act; there were already enough Republican "martyrs" to

[4] Richard Harison to Pickering, April 10, 1800 (Pickering MSS.).
[5] *American Eagle*, July 3, 1800.
[6] *Annals of Congress*, X, 957. *American Eagle*, July 3, 1800. *Richmond Examiner*, February 6, 1801.

make the outcome of the election highly doubtful to the Federalists.

If it was no longer dangerous to be known as a Republican and to express Republican principles, said William Duane, it was owing to the courage of the press which had upheld constitutional freedom "in despite of open threats, of frequent danger, of the persecutions of power, and of unconstitutional laws."[7] It is true that for their deliverance Americans could also thank the internal strife that split the Federalist party into warring factions.

Pickering's dismissal from the Cabinet in May, 1800, for obstructing the President's efforts to make peace with France, eliminated the chief Jacobin hunter from the government. With Pickering's retirement, the Sedition Act became an orphan of the storm that rent the Federalist party, neglected and almost forgotten — except by Justice Samuel Chase.

Although the Federalists had been accused of "worshipping at the Presidential shrine," they were largely engaged after 1800 in wrecking the altar and tearing down the idol. For the moment, the Hamiltonian wing of the Federalist party seemed to have become "the most seditious men in the Union"; certainly their strictures upon John Adams and his policies had hardly been surpassed by the Republicans' most "seditious" condemnations of the President.[8] In the last days of their power, the Federalists gave a convincing demonstration that they could libel the Chief Executive as flagrantly as had the Republicans and that they, too, would not submit to being gagged when it came to expressing their political opinions.

Had President Adams been of a persecuting temper, he could hardly have asked for a better opportunity for gratifying his rancor; instead, he refused to enforce the Sedition Act,

[7] *Aurora*, September 21, 1799.
[8] *Philadelphia Gazette*, September 16, 1800.

even against Alexander Hamilton, whom he hated. He blamed Hamilton for the Alien and Sedition Acts and repented that he had ever signed them. Thus Adams joined that small group of Federalists who recognized their error, even though it was too late for anything but repentance: "There is danger of proscribing, under imputations of democracy," he said, "some of the ablest, most influential, and best characters in the Union."[9]

It is ironical that Alexander Hamilton, to whose energy and vision the Federalist party was deeply indebted for its existence, should have contributed largely to its ruin. His resentment towards Adams for flouting his advice and pursuing an independent policy towards France completely overpowered his none too keenly developed political sense. While Jefferson and his followers thundered at the gates, Hamilton was busy nursing a scheme to trick Adams out of the presidency and to award the prize to Charles Cotesworth Pinckney. The impulse to put pen to paper, which to Hamilton was almost always an irresistible temptation, proved his undoing: in a letter addressed to a select circle of Federalist leaders (but which, owing to Aaron Burr's vigilance, was made public), Hamilton dwelt upon the "disgusting egotism, the distempered jealousy and the ungovernable indiscretion of Mr. Adams's temper" and "the unfortunate foibles of a vanity without bounds and a jealousy capable of discoloring every object."[10]

When Thomas Cooper was released from prison, he found the Federalists themselves committing the very offense — and with even greater vindictiveness — for which he had been sentenced to jail. But what disturbed him most was that they were libeling the President with complete impunity; apparently no one thought of resurrecting the Sedition Act to

[9] John Adams, *Works*, IX, 87.
[10] Bernard C. Steiner, *The Life and Correspondence of James McHenry*, 476. Cleveland, 1907.

silence the Federalist enemies of John Adams. This, Cooper exclaimed, was the final proof of the injustice of the Sedition Act: there was one law for Republicans, another for Federalists. If each were equal before the law, he reasoned, surely Alexander Hamilton would not be permitted to publish his "candid" character studies of President Adams.[11]

Although it was exceedingly doubtful if he could do much to make Hamilton suffer as he himself had suffered, Cooper resolved to make the effort; and while he did not succeed, he at least embarrassed the Federalists and showed up the Sedition Act for what it was — a partisan law which ran only against those so unfortunate as to belong to the wrong political party. Cooper went to New York to ask Hamilton if he were in truth the author of the libel upon President Adams that had been ascribed to him; and if Hamilton's answer was "Yes," Cooper intended to institute against him "a prosecution under the detestable act of Congress, commonly known by the name of the 'Sedition Law.' " But Hamilton was in Albany, and he declined to be drawn into a correspondence with Cooper, which prompted the latter to add to his indictment of the Federalist leader the charge that he was no gentleman.[12]

Yet, as the time approached when the Sedition Act would expire by law, the Federalists found it increasingly difficult to make the parting. Despite its imperfections, it was still their darling; their only regret was that "the little monster," as Republicans called the Sedition Act, had not been given more opportunity to use its claws. Harrison Gray Otis declared in Congress that "very material benefits would have

[11] *Epitome of the Times*, December 1, 1800. *Aurora*, December 6, December 31, 1800. *Philadelphia Gazette*, December 5, 1800. *Annual Report of the American Historical Association . . . 1912*, 675. Dumas Malone, *Thomas Cooper*, 138–141.

[12] *Gazette of the United States*, December 31, 1800. *Albany Centinel*, December 5, 1800.

flown from it had ten prosecutions been instituted where one has been; had three or four venal presses, set up with foreign money, and conducted by incendiary emigrants, been crushed and silenced."[13]

However misplaced this affection for the Sedition Act might be, and however vain these regrets that it had not been more rigidly enforced, it was hardly to be expected that the Federalists would attempt to renew its life. The Republicans would shortly come into office, and, with the Sedition Act still on the statute books, they might turn its full force against the critics of the Jeffersonian administration. Nevertheless, the Federalists made a determined effort to keep the Sedition Act; and, although the Republicans successfully prevented its re-enactment, in the final vote in the House of Representatives (where the Federalists mustered almost their entire strength) it received more votes than had the original act of July 14, 1798.[14]

This devotion to the Sedition Act surprised even Jefferson, inured as he was to the vagaries of Federalist policy. "I had expected," he wrote, "that some respect to the palpable change in public opinion would have produced moderation, but it does not seem so."[15] The friends of order seemed to be flying in the face of accumulated evidence that from every point of view the Sedition Act was a failure. As John Quincy Adams said, it was "an ineffectual attempt to extinguish the fire of defamation, but it operated like oil upon the flames." It had hastened the downfall of the Federalist party; it had not succeeded in shaping the course of public opinion; and it had "disgusted a large portion of the American people." This was undeniable; yet the Federalists seemed resolved to go down with their errors, as well as their principles, intact.[16]

---

[13] *Annals of Congress*, X, 957–958. [14] *Ibid.*, 975–976.
[15] *Collections of the Massachusetts Historical Society*, Seventh Series, I, 82.
[16] W. C. Ford, *Jefferson and the Newspaper*, 88.

In seeking to perpetuate the Sedition Act, the Federalists were not, however, acting out of mere perversity; there was sound reason for their stand on this issue. They were resolved, above all, to make no deathbed repentance: consistency and the stiff upper lip to the end. Moreover, it was clear that if they could but transmit the Sedition Act to the Republicans, they would embarrass and confuse the incoming administration; Jefferson, if he remained true to his principles, would be reluctant to invoke this Act against his political enemies. For this reason, Harrison Gray Otis was prepared "to give to the new Administration the means of protection that have been provided for their predecessors" — by which he meant that he was willing to hand the poisoned chalice to Jefferson.[17]

Nor is it extraordinary that the Federalists, if they were to be punished for libel and sedition, preferred to take their medicine from the Federal government rather than from the states. In falling victims to their own law, they would at least have the satisfaction of confirming the principles for which they had fought. It was no small victory to compel Jefferson to act through the Federal government, thereby upsetting what the Federalists supposed were his plans "to paralyze the General Government, and confide all power to the State courts."[18]

Furthermore, so convinced were the Federalists of the rightness of their cause that they assumed that if truth were admitted as a defense — as it was under the Sedition Act — few, if any, of them would be convicted of libeling Jefferson. Nothing they could say about him would be as awful as the truth. And so, said Otis, "We may want this law as a coat of armor to defend us from persecution." Robert G. Harper assured his colleagues that with the Sedition Act on the statute books, the Federalists could carry on opposition to the Repub-

[17] *Annals of Congress*, X, 957–958.
[18] *Ibid.*, 948.

lican administration: "not a factious, profligate and unprincipled opposition, founded on falsehood and misrepresentation, and catching at the prejudices of the moment,"
such as the Republicans had engaged in, "but a manly, dignified, candid and patriotic opposition, addressed to the good
sense and virtue of the nation, and resting on the basis of
argument and truth."[19]

A few weeks before the question of renewing the Sedition
Act was taken up by Congress, the Federalists had been given
a foretaste of what they might expect under the common-
law law of libel as enforced in the state courts where, it was
well known, the Jeffersonians intended to carry their cases.
In December, 1800, John Ward Fenno was fined two thousand, five hundred dollars in a Pennsylvania court for libeling
a Republican. The amount of this fine was compared by dis-
traught Federalists with the two-hundred-dollar fine imposed
upon Abijah Adams for publishing a libel on the Massachusetts legislature and with the fines assessed by Federalist
judges under the Sedition Act. "What a difference there is
between the chance of a Federalist among Jacobins, and of a
Jacobin among Federalists!" they exclaimed. "The boasted
friends of the liberty of the press inflict a tenfold more severe
punishment, when their characters are canvassed."[20]

Moreover, Benjamin Rush, a Republican, sued William
Cobbett for libel and won a verdict of five thousand dollars in
damages in the Pennsylvania courts — despite the fact that
Cobbett's counsel was Robert G. Harper, one of the leading
Federalist lawyers in the country. As a result of this reversal,
Cobbett was obliged to sell his printing press and return to
England.

Many Federalists were dismayed to see "this intrepid
foreigner" whose "talents and abilities were a terror to all

[19] *Annals of Congress*, X, 939–940, 957–958.
[20] *Gazette of the United States*, December 15, 1800.

French philosophers" — one of the few Englishmen who, coming to the United States, seemed to prefer his own country to the French Republic — banished and ruined. In New York, before his departure for England, with new prosecution confronting him, Cobbett was assured by Alexander Hamilton that he (Hamilton) "should think himself honoured in defending me. He behaved with great kindness and assured me that I had nothing to fear from injustice in New York."[21] That was as much as Jefferson had ever told fugitives from the Alien and Sedition Acts in Virginia.

In view of Jefferson's narrow margin of victory in the presidential election of 1800, it cannot be said that the Federalists were cast out of office by a whole people rising up in wrath against profaners of the temple of liberty. Yet the Federalists lost control of Congress as well as the presidency, and the unpopularity of the Alien and Sedition Acts certainly contributed to their overthrow. It was not, however, until after the panic engendered by "Jacobinism" was over that the full import of these measures became clear. And so the Federalist party went down, not in the fullness of honor and with its ideals held high, but in obloquy and contempt. It had gambled everything on laws designed to perpetuate its control of the government of the United States; when those laws failed to achieve their purpose, the party was bankrupt. Much of the Federalists' social and political philosophy was outmoded in 1800; but it was the immorality of their public conduct and their disregard of the basic freedoms of Americans that completed their ruin and cost them the confidence and respect of the people.

*   *   *

[21] *Gazette of the United States*, April 14, 1800. *Cobbett-Thornton Letters*, 25, 72–73. *Aurora*, August 5, 1800. *Greenleaf's New Daily Advertiser*, December 18, 1799.

After Jefferson's election to the presidency, he pardoned all still serving terms for violating the Sedition Act, declaring that he considered that law "to be nullity as absolute and as palpable as if Congress had ordered us to fall down and worship a golden image." Yet Jefferson was no advocate of a "licentious" press; like Hamilton and Adams he believed that the press ought to be restrained "within the legal and wholesome limits of truth." He differed from the Federalists chiefly in insisting that this restraint be imposed by the states rather than by the Federal government; his scruples against the Sedition Act were based in part on constitutional grounds. Moreover, during his presidency, finding himself "a fair mark for every man's dirt," he expressed the opinion that "a few prosecutions of the most prominent offenders would have a wholesome effect in restoring the integrity of the presses. Not a general one," he cautioned, "for that would look like persecution; but a selected one."[22] It remained his boast, however, that his administration had not resorted to a Sedition Law, nor did he attempt to destroy the Federalist party by means of unjust laws. Instead, particularly during the early part of his administration, he gave the freedom of the press a fair trial. But at the end of his career, thoroughly disillusioned by the manner in which Americans had abused that freedom, he said that "Nothing can now be believed which is seen in a newspaper. Truth itself becomes suspicious by being put into that polluted vehicle." Things had come to such a pass, he lamented, that the only part of a newspaper that could be relied upon were the advertisements.[23]

While Jefferson was President, prosecutions were instituted in the state courts against Federalist (and against some Republican) editors for seditious libel. In most of these cases,

---

[22] W. C. Ford, *Jefferson and the Newspaper,* 84, 106–109. *Virginia Magazine of History and Biography*, LI, 124. April, 1943.

[23] Ford, *op. cit.*, 109–110.

the charge was libeling the Chief Magistrate. It was now the Federalists' turn to champion the freedom of the press: Hamilton, who in 1799 had demanded the assumption by the Federal government of jurisdiction over all common-law libels, in 1804 gave a definition of freedom of the press that has been incorporated into many state constitutions. Liberty of the press, said Hamilton, is "the right to publish, with impunity, truth, with good motives, for justifiable ends though reflecting on government, magistracy, or individuals." Had the Federalists acted on this principle in 1798, no stigma would have been cast by History upon their name.[24]

*   *   *

Without doubt, liberty of speech and of the press lies at the heart of all liberty: "where men cannot freely convey their thoughts to one another, no other liberty is secure."[25] In every society worthy to be called free there is an untrammeled play of public opinion; immunity from criticism is the privilege of no government officials; and the right of arguing about ideas is jealously guarded.

This is the kind of society envisaged by the first amendment to the Constitution; freedom of speech and of the press is the first article of the Bill of Rights. The Federalists who were responsible for the enactment of the Sedition Act had little comprehension of this ideal; their thoughts ran in channels which lead not to freedom and democracy but to an authoritarian slough of despond.

Every administration facing a diplomatic crisis such as that which gripped the country in 1798 must weigh in the balance the imperative necessity of safeguarding the nation, and the hardly less imperative necessity of permitting men to search

[24] Duniway, *The Development of Freedom of the Press in Massachusetts*, 146–149, 157.

[25] William Ernest Hocking, *Freedom of the Press*, 1947, 53.

freely for the truth. Without freedom of discussion, without the right of examining the methods and objectives of the party in power and criticizing its acts, democracy becomes an empty name. Unity of purpose, however essential to the existence of the nation, cannot be achieved by suppressing this freedom; but it can be realized in a democracy where common standards are accepted and where the principles of the Bill of Rights are maintained.

The issue, then and now, is the same: "Whether the state can punish all words which have some tendency, however remote, to bring about acts in violation of law, or only words which directly incite to acts in violation of law."[26] In the Sedition Act cases, the tendency of words to produce acts against the peace and security of the community was stretched to its utmost latitude. Likewise, judges and juries, in their willingness to presume evil intent on the part of Republican writers, largely nullified the safeguards erected by the Sedition Act itself. Criticism of the President and Congress — in which every American indulges as his birthright — was severely punished; yet this practice manifestly has only a remote tendency to injure and bring into contempt the government of the United States. In short, much that has become commonplace in American political life was put under the ban by the Federalist lawmakers and judges of 1798.[27]

"There is a tide in the affairs of nations, of parties, and of individuals," said John Marshall about the time Jefferson became President. "I fear that of real Americanism is on the wane."

Marshall was mistaken: the best was yet to come. In the Alien and Sedition Acts, American freedom had survived one of the severest attacks destined to be leveled against it in the name of "real Americanism."

[26] Chafee, *Freedom of Speech*, 25.
[27] *Ibid.*, 30, 38, 56, 204.

B I B L I O G R A P H Y

MANUSCRIPT SOURCES

Albert Gallatin MSS., New York Historical Society.
Alexander Hamilton MSS., Library of Congress.
William Irvine MSS., Historical Society of Pennsylvania.
Rufus King MSS., New York Historical Society.
Robert Liston Correspondence, Henry Adams Transcripts, Library
  of Congress.
James Madison MSS., Library of Congress.
John Marshall MSS., Library of Congress.
Timothy Pickering MSS., Massachusetts Historical Society.
William Plumer MSS., Library of Congress.
William L. Smith MSS., Library of Congress.
Jonathan Trumbull MSS., Connecticut Historical Society.
Peter Van Schaack MSS., Library of Congress.
George Washington MSS., Library of Congress.
Oliver Wolcott MSS., Connecticut Historical Society.
Domestic Letters of the Department of State, X and XI (1797–1799), the
  National Archives, Washington, D. C.

NEWSPAPERS: 1798–1800

Albany Centinel.
American Eagle.
Aurora or General Advertiser.
Bee.
Carolina Gazette.
Centinel of Freedom.
Columbian Centinel.
Country Porcupine.
Democratic Republican and Commercial Daily Advertiser.

Epitome of the Times.
Federal Galaxy.
Gazette of the United States.
Greenleaf's New Daily Advertiser.
Guardian: or New Brunswick Advertiser.
Impartial Herald.
Independent Chronicle.
Lancaster Journal.
Massachusetts Mercury.
Mirror of the Times.
New Hampshire Gazette.
New Jersey Journal.
Newark Gazette.
Newport Mercury.
Norwich Packet.
Oracle of Dauphin and Harrisburgh Advertiser.
Pennsylvania Gazette.
Pennsylvania Herald and York General Advertiser.
Philadelphia Gazette.
Porcupine's Gazette.
Richmond Examiner.
Russell's Gazette.
Rutland Herald.
Salem Gazette.
Springer's Weekly Oracle.
State Gazette and New Jersey Advertiser.
Telegraphe and Daily Advertiser.
Time Piece.
Virginia Argus.
Virginia Federalist.

PAMPHLETS

The Alarm. Philadelphia, 1798.
Bache, Benjamin. *Truth Will Out.* Philadelphia, 1798.
————. *Remarks Occasioned by the Late Conduct of Mr. Washington.* Philadelphia, 1797.
Callender, James T. *The American Annual Register.* Philadelphia, 1797.
————. *The Prospect Before Us.* Philadelphia, 1800.
————. *The History of the United States for 1796.* Philadelphia, 1797.
Cheetham, James. *Reply to* ARISTIDES. New York, 1804.

Cheetham, James. *A View of the Political Conduct of Aaron Burr.* New York, 1802.

Cobbett, William. *The Rush Light.* New York, 1800.

Emigration to America Candidly Considered. London, 1798.

The Examination of the Conduct of the Executive of the United States. Philadelphia, 1797.

Fauchet, Joseph. *A Sketch of the Present State of Our Political Relations.* Philadelphia, 1797.

Fenno, John Ward. *Desultory Reflections.* New York, 1800.

Harper, Robert G. *Observations on the Dispute Between the United States and France.* Boston, 1798.

Jay, John. *An Address to the People of the State of New York.* New York, 1787.

A Letter to George Nicholas. Philadelphia, 1799.

Morison, Samuel Eliot, editor. *The Key to Liberty.* The Manning Association, Billerica, Massachusetts, 1922.

Osgood, David. *A Sermon.* Boston, 1795.

"Philodemos." *An Enquiry whether the Act of Congress . . . Generally Called the Sedition Bill Is Unconstitutional or Not.* Richmond, 1798.

The Politicians, or A State of Things. Philadelphia, 1798.

Remarks on the Jacobiniad. Boston, 1798.

Report of the Trial of Justice Chase. Baltimore, 1805.

Taylor, John. *A Definition of Parties.* Philadelphia, 1794.

Tucker, St. George. *A Letter to a Member of Congress.* Virginia, 1799.

Webster, Noah. *A Collection of Papers.* Webster and Clark. New York, 1843.

———. *Two Letters to Dr. Priestley.* New Haven, 1800.

What Is Our Situation? By an American [Joseph Hopkinson]. Philadelphia, 1798.

Wood, John. *The Suppressed History of the Administration of John Adams.* Weber and Gillis. Philadelphia, 1846.

Volney, C. F. *A View of the Soil and Climate of the United States.* Philadelphia, 1804.

MEMOIRS AND LETTERS

Adams, Charles Francis, editor. *The Works of John Adams.* 10 vols. Little, Brown. Boston, 1853.

Adams, Henry. *The Writings of Albert Gallatin.* 3 vols. Lippincott. Philadelphia, 1879.

Ames, Seth. *The Works of Fisher Ames.* 2 vols. Little, Brown. Boston, 1854.

Broglie, Duc de, editor. *Memoirs of the Prince de Talleyrand.* 2 vols. G. P. Putnam's Sons. New York, 1891.

Cobbett, John M. and James P., editors. *Selections from Cobbett's Political Works.* A. Cobbett. London, 1835.

Cole, G. D. H., editor. *Letters from William Cobbett to Edward Thornton.* Oxford University Press. London, 1937.

Correspondence Between the Hon. John Adams and the Late William Cunningham. E. M. Cunningham. Boston, 1823.

Fitzpatrick, John C., editor. *The Writings of George Washington.* Government Printing Office, 1942.

Ford, Paul Leicester, editor. *The Writings of Thomas Jefferson.* 12 vols. G. P. Putnam's Sons. New York, 1896.

Ford, Worthington Chauncey, editor. *Writings of John Quincy Adams.* 7 vols. Macmillan. New York, 1913.

Gibbs, George. *Memoirs of the Administrations of Washington and John Adams.* Printed for the Subscribers. New York, 1846.

Hamilton, John C., editor. *The Works of Alexander Hamilton.* 7 vols. J. F. Trow. New York, 1850–51.

Higginson, Stephen, Letters of. *Annual Report of the American Historical Association* . . . 1896. Washington, 1897.

Hunt, Gaillard. *The Writings of James Madison.* 9 vols. G. P. Putnam's Sons. New York, 1901.

Johnston, Henry P., editor. *The Correspondence and Public Papers of John Jay.* 4 vols. G. P. Putnam's Sons. New York, 1893.

Kennedy, John P. *Memoirs of the Life of William Wirt.* Lea and Blanchard. Philadelphia, 1849.

King, Charles R., editor. *The Life and Correspondence of Rufus King.* G. P. Putnam's Sons. New York, 1894–1900.

Lodge, Henry Cabot, editor. *The Works of Alexander Hamilton.* G. P. Putnam's Sons. New York, 1904.

Mitchell, Stewart, editor. *New Letters of Abigail Adams.* Houghton Mifflin. Boston, 1947.

Morris, Anne Cary. *The Diary and Letters of Gouverneur Morris.* 2 vols. Charles Scribner's Sons. New York, 1888.

Warren-Adams Letters. 2 vols. Massachusetts Historical Society. Boston, 1917.

BIOGRAPHIES

Adams, Charles Francis. *The Life of John Adams.* Lippincott. Philadelphia, 1871.

Adams, Henry. *The Life of Gallatin*. Lippincott. Philadelphia, 1879.

Anderson, D. R. *William Branch Giles*. George Banta. Menasha, Wisconsin, 1914.

Austin, James T. *The Life of Elbridge Gerry*. 2 vols. Wilks and Lilly. Boston, 1827.

Beveridge, Albert J. *The Life of John Marshall*. 4 vols. Houghton Mifflin. Boston, 1916.

Brant, Irving. *James Madison: Father of the Constitution*. Bobbs-Merrill. Indianapolis, 1950.

Campbell, Charles, editor. *Some Materials to Serve for a Brief Memoir of John Daly Burk*. Joel Munsell. Albany, 1868.

Chinard, Gilbert. *Honest John Adams*. Little, Brown. Boston, 1933.

Clark, Mary Elizabeth. *Peter Porcupine in America*. Times and News Publishing Company. Philadelphia, 1939.

Clarke, A. C. *William Duane*. Privately Printed. Washington, 1905.

Cresson, W. P. *Francis Dana*. The Dial Press. New York, 1930.

Cunningham, Charles E. *Timothy Dwight*. Macmillan. New York, 1942.

Ford, Emily, and Skeel, Emily, editors. *Notes on the Life of Noah Webster*. Privately Printed. New York, 1912.

Hamilton, Allan McLane. *The Intimate Life of Alexander Hamilton*. Charles Scribner's Sons. New York, 1910.

Hamilton, John C. *Life of Alexander Hamilton*. 7 vols. Houghton, Osgood and Company. Boston, 1879.

Hilldrup, Robert Leroy. *The Life and Times of Edmund Pendleton*. University of North Carolina Press. Chapel Hill, 1939.

Koch, Adrienne. *Jefferson and Madison*. Knopf. New York, 1950.

Lodge, Henry Cabot. *Life and Letters of George Cabot*. Little, Brown. Boston, 1877.

Malone, Dumas. *The Public Life of Thomas Cooper*. Yale University Press. New Haven, 1926.

McLaughlin, J. F. *Matthew Lyon: The Hampden of Congress*. Wynkoop Hallenbeck Crawford. New York, 1900.

McRee, Griffith J. *Life and Correspondence of James Iredell*. 2 vols. D. Appleton. New York, 1857–1858.

Morison, John H. *Life of the Hon. Jeremiah Smith*. Little, Brown. Boston, 1845.

Morison, S. E. *The Life and Letters of Harrison Gray Otis*. Houghton Mifflin. Boston, 1913.

Pickering, Octavius, and Upham, C. W. *The Life of Timothy Pickering*. 4 vols. Little, Brown. Boston, 1867–1873.

Schachner, Nathan. *Alexander Hamilton*. D. Appleton-Century. New York, 1946.

Simms, Henry H. *Life of John Taylor*. William Byrd Press. Richmond, Virginia, 1932.

Spargo, John. *Anthony Haswell*. The Tuttle Company. Rutland, Vermont, 1925.

Steiner, Bernard C. *The Life and Correspondence of James McHenry*. The Burroughs Company, Cleveland, 1907.

Warfel, Harry. *Noah Webster*. Macmillan. New York, 1936.

Wyatt, Edward, IV. "John Daly Burk." *In Southern Sketches* (No. 7). Charlottesville, Virginia, 1936.

MONOGRAPHS

Adams, Brooks. *The Convention of 1800 with France.¨ Proceedings of the Massachusetts Historical Society*, Vol. 44. Boston, 1911.

Anderson, Frank M. *The Enforcement of the Alien and Sedition Acts. Annual Report of the American Historical Association* . . . 1912. Washington, 1912.

Anderson, Frank M. "Contemporary Opinion of the Virginia and Kentucky Resolutions." *American Historical Review*, Vol. V (October, 1899, and January, 1900).

Davidson, Philip G. "Virginia and the Alien and Sedition Laws," *American Historical Review*, Vol. XXXVI (January, 1931).

Koch, Adrienne, and Ammon, Harry. "The Virginia and Kentucky Resolutions." *William and Mary Quarterly* (April, 1948).

Lyon, E. Wilson. "The Directory and the United States," *American Historical Review*, Vol. XLIII (April, 1938).

Phillips, U. B. "The South Carolina Federalists," *American Historical Review*, Vol. XIV (April, July, 1909).

Walters, Raymond, Jr. "The Origins of the Jeffersonian Party in Pennsylvania," *Pennsylvania Magazine of History and Biography*, Vol. 66. Philadelphia, 1942.

HISTORICAL COLLECTIONS

Abridgment of the Debates of Congress. D. Appleton. New York, 1857.
American State Papers.
American Historical Review.
Annals of Congress.
Collections of the Massachusetts Historical Society.

Proceedings of the Massachusetts Historical Society.
T. C. Hansard, editor. *Parliamentary History of England.* London, 1812.
Proceedings of the House of Representatives. Philadelphia, 1799.

GENERAL

Allen, Gardner W. *Our Naval War with France.* Houghton Mifflin. Boston, 1922.
Ames, Herman V. *The Proposed Amendments to the Constitution: Annual Report of the American Historical Association . . . 1896.* Washington, 1897.
Bassett, John Spencer. *The Federalist System.* Harper and Brothers. New York, 1906.
Brown, Philip Anthony. *The French Revolution in English History.* Lockwood and Sons, London, 1918.
Burk, John Daly. Introduction by Brander Matthews. Publications of the Dunlop Society. New York, 1891.
Chafee, Zechariah. *Freedom of Speech.* Harcourt, Brace. New York, 1920.
Channing, Edward. *History of the United States.* 7 vols. Macmillan. New York, 1905–1925.
Dictionary of American Biography. Scribner's. New York, 1928–1936.
Duniway, C. A. *The Development of Freedom of the Press in Massachusetts.* Longmans, Green. New York, 1906.
Eyck, Erich. *Pitt Versus Fox.* G. Bell and Sons. London, 1950.
Ford, W. C. *Jefferson and the Newspaper.* Columbus Historical Society Records. Vol. VIII. Washington, 1905.
Franklin, Frank George. *The Legislative History of Naturalization, Annual Report of the American Historical Association . . . 1901.* Washington, 1901.
Hansard, T. C., editor. *Parliamentary History of England.* London, 1912.
Hofstadter, Richard. *The American Political Tradition.* Knopf. New York, 1948.
Hocking, William Ernest. *Freedom of the Press.* 1947.
Kelley, Alfred H. and Harbison, Winfred A. *The American Constitution.* Norton. New York, 1948.
Ludlum, David. *Social Ferment in Vermont, 1791–1800.* Columbia Univ. Press. New York, 1939.

Matthews, Brander. Introduction, *John Daly Burk*. See *Burk*.

McMaster, John Bach. *A History of the People of the United States*. 8 vols. D. Appleton. New York, 1885.

Morison, Samuel Eliot and Commager, Henry S. *The Growth of the American Republic*. 2 vols. Oxford Univ. Press. New York, 1942.

Morse, A. D. *The Federalist Party in Massachusetts*. Princeton Univ. Press. Princeton, 1909.

Mott, Frank Luther. *American Journalism*. Macmillan. New York, 1941.

Nevins, Allan. *American Press Opinion, Washington to Coolidge*. D. C. Heath. New York, 1928.

Penniman, Howard R., editor. *Sait's American Parties and Elections*, Appleton-Century. New York, 1948.

Robinson, William A. *Jeffersonian Democracy in New England*. Yale Univ. Press. New Haven, 1916.

Smith, J. Eugene. *One Hundred Years of Hartford's Courant*. Yale Univ. Press. New Haven, 1949.

Stauffer, Vernon. *New England and the Bavarian Illuminati*. Privately Printed. New York, 1918.

Warfield, Ethelbert Dudley. *The Kentucky Resolutions of 1798*. G. P. Putnam's Sons. New York, 1887.

Warren, Charles. *Jacobin and Junto*. Harvard Univ. Press. Cambridge, 1931.

Wharton, Francis. *State Trials of the United States during the Administrations of Washington and Adams*. 2 vols. Carey and Hart. Philadelphia, 1849.

Whipple, Leon. *The Story of Civil Liberty in the United States*. Vanguard Press. New York, 1927.

INDEX

ADAMS, ABIJAH, 121–122, 229
Adams, John, 4, 10, 23, 73, 76, 98, 107,
111n, 127, 158, 206, 207, 212, 213,
218, 223, 231; popularity of, 8–9; on
opposition to government, 25; Bache
criticizes, 29; signs Alien Enemies
Act, 50; criticizes speech by Jefferson, 55–56; description of street
fight, 62; and responsibility for Alien
and Sedition Acts, 71–72; signs
warrant for Burk's arrest, 99; and
case against Baldwin, 112–114;
burned in effigy, 144; on prospect
of war, 151; interest in Navy, 152;
and declaration of war against
France, 154–155; sends peace mission to France, 157; willing to
execute Alien Act against Collot,
189–190; refuses to use Alien Act
against French consuls, 191; on
Duane's offense, 197; letter to Coxe,
198–199; criticized by Cooper, 203,
205; and suggested use of Alien Act
against Priestley, 204; Callender's
attacks, 216–217, 219; criticized by
his own party, 224, 226; and
Hamilton, 225
Adams, Mrs. John, 57, 72
Adams, John Quincy, 97n; believes
war must be supported by public
opinion, 156; criticizes Marshall,
183; on Sedition Act, 227
Adams, Thomas, 29; indicted under
Federal and state law, 120–121;
death of, 121

Addison, Judge Alexander, 79, 141n,
164; on effect of seditious press,
32n; on public opinion, 56; favors
Sedition Act, 139–140; tries to indict Israel, 140
Albany Centinel, 30, 136; on Sedition
Act, 93; on seditious implications
of liberty poles, 114; warns against
France, 157
Albany Register, 30
Alien Act, 189; called unconstitutional, 163–164; Federalists defend,
164–165; failure to enforce, 189–
193; and Collot, 189–190; and
French consuls, 191; expires, 193;
and Dr. Priestley, 204; *see also* Alien
and Sedition Acts
Alien and Sedition Acts, 9, 21, 23, 24,
77, 78, 97, 135; purposes, 41; Hamilton's attitude, 71; Adams's attitude,
71–72; approved by Washington,
73; attitude of Federalist press, 93;
constitutionality never carried to
Supreme Court, 139; proposal in
Congress to distribute copies of,
142; Federalists defend as war
measures, 150; Virginia and Kentucky Resolves, 169–181; Republican attempts to repeal, 180; enforcement criticized, 185–187; and
overthrow of Federalists, 230; *see
also* Alien Act and Sedition Act
Alien Enemies Act, 50, 163, 188; provisions of, 51–53; aimed at press,
58–59